Church and Communion

Church and Communion

An Introduction to Ecumenical Theology

Second Edition

Philip Goyret

Edited by Joseph Thomas

Translated, revised, and expanded in collaboration between author and editor

The Catholic University of America Press
Washington, D.C.

First edition published as
Chiesa e comunione: Introduzione alla teologia ecumenica
(Verona: Fede & cultura, 2013)

The paper used in this publication meets the minimum requirements of American National Standards for Information Science—Permanence of Paper for Printed Library Materials, ANSI Z39.48-1984.

∞

Cataloging-in-Publication Data available from the Library of Congress
ISBN 978-0-8132-3463-2
eISBN 978-0-8132-3464-9

Table of Contents

Introduction

"Christ calls all his disciples to unity."[1] More than twenty-five years ago, Pope Saint John Paul II reminded us of this truth at the beginning of *Ut unum sint*, the first-ever encyclical dedicated exclusively to the theme of ecumenism. This call to unity implies an effort on the part of the whole Church, from which no Christian can be excused. In his effort to awaken the consciences of many Christians, the Holy Father would return to emphasize the same idea later in the document: "How could they refuse to do everything possible, with God's help, to break down the walls of division and distrust, to overcome obstacles and prejudices which thwart the proclamation of the Gospel of salvation in the Cross of Jesus, the one Redeemer of man, of every individual?"[2]

The cause of unity is essential to the Church. It involves all Christians and needs to be approached from a multitude of perspectives. A good sign of our times is the increasing number of Christians, of various denominations and confessions of faith, who appreciate ever more deeply that disunity cannot be accepted as the status quo.[3] Pope Francis has compared the ecumenical journey of the Church to the ship which ran aground at Malta, described in Acts of the Apostles.[4] The entire crew and passengers on the ship survived. God likewise desires the salvation of all, and in light of this truth Christians can overcome the sad divisions which have marked the Church's history. Precisely in the midst of the storms of today's world, the Church urgently needs the unity of all her children.

Christians, fully engaged in the activities of this world, are called to appreciate by faith the action of Divine Providence that works towards the fulfillment of God's design for his Church.[5] The rapid changes brought about through Christianity's spread and development in the most diverse cultures,

1 John Paul II, Encyclical Letter *Ut unum sint* (May 25, 1995), 1.

2 John Paul II, *Ut unum sint*, 2.

3 Carl E. Braaten and Robert W. Jenson, preface to *The Ecumenical Future: Background Papers for* In One Body through the Cross: The Princeton Proposal for Christian Unity (Grand Rapids, Mich.: Eerdmans, 2004), viii.

4 Pope Francis, "Homily at Celebration of 2nd Vespers for the Feast of the Conversion of St. Paul" (January 25, 2020), citing Acts 27:6–44.

5 John XXIII, "Address at the Solemn Opening of the Second Vatican Council" (October 11, 1962).

amidst accelerating globalization, offer the promise of "new language and new forms of dialogue" which can give a new impulse to the cause of ecumenism.[6]

Guided by Christian hope, ecumenism can (and must) be realized as a spiritual exercise, by means of prayer and the conversion of hearts. It should also be implemented by the joint work of Catholics and non-Catholics in favor of common Gospel values; it must result in relationships between both different denominations and among Christians at an individual level. Other dimensions are also important: one could think of the purification of memory, the effort to combat the secularization of society, and so on. In this book we will focus more specifically on ecumenism understood as a reality to study theologically. Ecumenism could be considered to be one aspect which characterizes theology as a whole, as in the case of pastoral care or spirituality. Still, I am convinced of the importance of making ecumenism a specific object of theological study, as is also done with the aforementioned fields. From this latter point of view, the most adequate place for ecumenism is within the field of ecclesiology, as we will have the opportunity to discuss later.

Ecumenical theology is a systematic reflection on the unity and mission of the Church, looked at from the perspective of the sad divisions among Christians which need to be overcome. The mission of the Church, in fact, is that of a communion which is ever called to grow. The loss of unity caused by sin has its most explicit manifestation in the scattering of peoples in the biblical account of the Tower of Babel. In the age of the Church, Pentecost marks the beginning of the reversal of Babel and the restoration of lost unity. At the end of time, unity will reach its definitive consummation, when God will be "all in all" (1 Cor 15:28). In this perspective, unity appears as an indispensable requirement for the Church; she cannot propose herself as a sign of unity among nations if she does not present herself as one and undivided.

In this introduction to the theology of ecumenism, the point of view of ecclesiology is thus a privileged one and seems to me to offer a promising path for progress in theological reflection. As the common patrimony of all Christians, the article of the creed regarding the Church constitutes a very valuable point of departure for a renewed effort to restore full ecclesial communion.[7] This focus on the Church offers the possibility of providing a healthy corrective to some of the divergent approaches towards ecumenism

6 Raimundo C. Barreto Jr., "Introduction: World Christianity as Public Religion," in *World Christianity as Public Religion*, ed. Raimundo C. Barreto Jr., Ronaldo Cavalcante, and Wanderley P. Da Rosa (Minneapolis: Fortress Press, 2017), 5.

7 Philip Goyret, "*Credo Ecclesiam* e rilancio ecumenico," *Nicolaus* 37, no. 2 (2010): 253.

over the past half century. On one hand, a certain "savage ecumenism" has raised, after Vatican II, the suspicion of relativism with regard to doctrine. On the other hand, a "healthy ecumenism" has patiently sought to apply the principles and the attitudes established by the council, but with disappointing results.[8] Perhaps this failure is due to the lack of a more decisively ecclesiological approach. Indeed, *Unitatis Redintegratio*, the council's Decree on Ecumenism, needs to be read and applied in the light of *Lumen Gentium*, the Dogmatic Constitution on the Church, which can lead us to a deeper understanding of many of the decree's affirmations.[9]

One cannot undertake a study of ecumenism and at the same time ignore theological disciplines which are outside the boundaries of ecclesiology. These other disciplines need to find their proper place in ecumenical theology. The historical dimension of the divisions of the Church has a particular importance which the student of ecumenical theology cannot ignore. In fact, the historical background is a premise to ecumenical theology and the subject of the first chapter of this work. The second chapter also has a predominantly historical character, but with reference to the history of ecumenism in general, and to the contemporary ecumenical movement in particular. The later chapters of this book—the third, fourth, and fifth—will be more directly theological, before the last chapter takes on questions of a more practical and pastoral nature.

While this book focuses on the theological and ecclesiological approach to ecumenism, we should always remember that ecumenism can never proceed as a purely intellectual study. It should move from within a living faith, seeking reason, in communion with all Christians. As Pope Francis has pointed out, ecumenism is accomplished by journeying together with our fellow Christians. This requires walking mutually along the path of prayer and the witness of the Christian life, even to the point of shedding blood together.[10] In the past half century, this itinerary has known its stops and starts. Nevertheless, under the guidance of the Holy Spirit, the Church moves forward. She follows the path of dialogue, renewal, and faithfulness to Tradition outlined by the Second Vatican Council, trusting in our Lord's petition that "they may all be one" (Jn 17:21).

8 Walter Kasper, *That They May All Be One: The Call to Unity* (New York: Burns and Oates, 2004), 1.

9 Kasper, *That They May All Be One*, 4–5.

10 Pope Francis, "Press Conference during the Return Flight from Apostolic Trip to Bulgaria," June 2, 2019.

Chapter 1

The Major Non-Catholic Denominations

We begin this study with a historical survey of the main divisions which have marked the life of the Church.[1] Such a survey is essential for offering an adequate context for understanding the conflicts which have given rise to separation among the different Christian traditions. This historical approach increasingly reveals itself as a premise for serious ecumenical dialogue. In order to comprehend the present and look correctly to the future, an objective vision of the past is necessary. If one seeks to reconstitute unity, the study of *how* the separations have come about is an obligatory step. Only then can one try to find—upon the foundation of historical experience and of the Revelation regarding the unity of the Church—a valid and realistic path towards full communion.

In this chapter we will review the historical fact of divisions among Christians, briefly presenting the most relevant details, the causes which have led towards the rupture of unity, and the participation of each of the churches in the ecumenical movement. Paradoxically, the great divisions have appeared, over the course of history, with a frequency of approximately every five centuries: in the fifth century with the Christological heresies, in the eleventh century with the Eastern Schism, and in the sixteenth century with the Reformation. Further separations have arisen in the intermediate periods, but almost always from a church already separated from Rome.

THE ANCIENT EASTERN CHURCHES

The split of these churches from communion with Rome took place during the Christological controversies of the fifth century. The separation did not

1 Some valuable sources regarding the history of division in the Church are: Konrad Algermissen, *Konfessionskunde*, 6th ed. (Hanover: Giesel, 1950); Juan Bosch, *Para comprender el ecumenismo* (Estella: Verbo Divino, 1991), ch. 2; Nicolas Lossky, ed., *Dictionary of the Ecumenical Movement* (Grand Rapids, Mich.: Eerdmans, 1991); Frank L. Cross and Elizabeth Livingstone, eds., *The Oxford Dictionary of the Christian Church*, 3rd ed. (Oxford: Oxford University Press, 1997); Johann Adam Möhler Institut, *Le Chiese cristiane nel Duemila* (Brescia: Queriniana, 1998).

arise without precedent. Well beforehand, cultural, social, ethnic, and theological traditions existed which were quite distinct from the Byzantine one and which led to rivalries among the great patriarchates.[2] Thus, when polemics came about at the Councils of Ephesus and Chalcedon, these differences would emerge with all their force. Once the boundaries of schism had been crossed, the differences would give rise to the various schismatic churches with their particular characters.[3] At the origin of these divisions we do not find an exclusively doctrinal motivation. The very geography in which these churches spread—coincident with the peripheries of the empire or beyond its frontiers—shows how much the anti-Byzantine sentiment was a factor.

From the purely doctrinal point of view, the schism that goes back to Nestorius emerged as a reaction against the position of Apollinaris of Laodicea from the fourth century. According to Apollinaris, the Word became incarnate in a body which did not have a human soul. From this perspective, the human nature of Jesus appears quite imperfect. Nestorius, patriarch of Constantinople, affirmed to the contrary that Christ possessed the union of a complete man and of the divine person of the Word, thus making the human person of Jesus a distinct person from the preexistent Word. As a consequence, the mother of Christ, the *Christotokos*—"the one who gives birth to Christ"—would not be able to receive the name *Theotokos*—"the one who gives birth to God." Cyril, patriarch of Alexandria, spoke strongly against this position, which led to Pope Celestine's convocation of a synod in Rome to condemn the Nestorian doctrine. Cyril later presided, together with a papal legate, at the Council of Ephesus in 431. This ecumenical council, held under the auspices of the Emperor Theodosius, deposed and excommunicated Nestorius, who would withdraw to a monastery in Antioch.[4] Nestorianism would receive a later and definitive blow in the Second Council of Constantinople, in the year 553, with the condemnation of the *Three Chapters*, a collection of writings dating back to or attributed to Theodore of Mopsuestia, Theodoret of Cyrus, and Ibas of Edessa; the same council also accepted the twelve anathemas formulated by Cyril against Nestorius.[5]

2 Paolo Siniscalco, ed., *Le antiche Chiese orientali* (Rome: Città Nuova, 2005), 102–8.
3 Pablo Gefaell, "Las Iglesias Orientales Antiguas Ortodoxas y Católicas," in Adolfo Montes González, ed., *Las iglesias orientales* (Madrid: Biblioteca de Autores Cristianos, 2000), 596.
4 Jean-Yves Lacoste et al., *Histoire de la théologie* (Paris: Seiul, 2009), 109.
5 *Decrees of the Ecumenical Councils*, ed. Norman P. Tanner (Washington D.C.: Georgetown University Press, 1990), vol. 1, 119–22; *Enchiridion symbolorum: Definitionum et declarationum de rebus fidei et morum*, 36th edition, ed. Heinrich Denzinger and Adolfus Schönmetzer (Barcelona: Herder, 1976), 252–63.

Among the followers of Nestorius, those who did not accept the doctrine of the Council of Ephesus with regard to the unicity of the person of the incarnate Word formed the so-called Assyrian Church of the East. This church, located in Persia, had already separated some years previously from the Syriac Church of Antioch. This schism of the Assyrian Church was due not to doctrinal reasons but to the desire for autonomy with regard to the Syriac Church of Antioch, above all to avoid persecution from civil authorities. Later, during the fifth century and still more in the sixth, Nestorian groups would have great influence in the Assyrian Church of the East, so much so that this church would take an attitude of openly defending Nestorius. In this process, the confrontation between the different theological-cultural positions—namely, between that characteristic of the East and the official Byzantine theology, which was Greek in character—would play an important role. The Church of the East extended widely throughout the East and would eventually arrive in China. Later, in the face of the spread of Islam, it would be quite reduced in size.[6] In the sixteenth century, a substantial part of this church, known today as the Chaldean Church, returned to communion with Rome. Those who remained separate from Rome would constitute the Assyrian Church, from which comes the Malabar Orthodox Church in India. Today the Assyrian Church, numbering a little more than 250,000 faithful, is smaller than the Chaldean Church and is found primarily in the United States. This church no longer holds to the errors of Nestorius in the same terms as fifteen centuries ago. In fact, they refuse the name of "Nestorians," and their position has drawn closer to that of Catholic doctrine, as evidenced in the *Common Christological Declaration between the Catholic Church and the Assyrian Church of the East* of November 11, 1994.[7]

The *Non-Chalcedonian Churches*, called the Oriental Orthodox Churches, are situated at the opposite extreme of the aforementioned views. Their doctrines originate in the positions assumed by Eutyches, who held the title of archimandrite monk of Constantinople. He, supported by Dioscorus, patriarch of Alexandria, advocated the view that the incarnate Word has only one *physis* or nature, in which the humanity of Christ would be absorbed by the divinity.[8] The Council of Chalcedon, which took place

6 P. Morelli, "Chiese non calcedoniane," in *Dizionario de ecclesiologia*, ed. Gianfranco Calabrese, Philip Goyret, Orazio F. Piazza (Rome: Città Nuova, 2010), 197–98.

7 For a more in-depth study, see Aidan Nichols, *Rome and the Eastern Churches: A Study in Schism* (New York: T and T Clark, 1992), 27–54.

8 Gerhard Müller, *Katholische Dogmatik: Für Studium und Praxis der Theologie* (Freiburg: Herder, 1995), 346.

in 451 AD and was convoked by the Emperor Marcian, would adhere to the formulations contained in the *Epistle to Flavian*. This letter was sent by Pope Leo the Great to the patriarch of Constantinople, who held a position contrary to Eutyches. The council affirmed the two natures of Christ, both human and divine. Christ is "perfect in divinity and perfect in humanity," "truly God and truly man," "consubstantial with the Father as regards his divinity, and the same consubstantial with us as regards his humanity," and is to be "acknowledged in two natures which undergo no confusion, no change, no division, no separation."[9]

One should keep in mind that the non-Chalcedonian position just mentioned is not fully endorsed by these Oriental Orthodox Churches. These churches do affirm that the person of Christ has one single divine-human nature, following the thought of Saint Cyril of Alexandria. However, they refuse to be called *Monophysites* and present themselves as *Miaphysites.*[10] Furthermore, in the schism, political factors—namely, the autonomy of Alexandria with respect to Byzantium—would have a great influence. The designation of Constantinople as ranking "next after [Rome]" was, in fact, too humiliating for the Alexandrians, whose apostolic see had held this honor up to that moment.[11]

Despite the condemnation of the Council of Chalcedon, the non-Chalcedonians would later have support from various sources—for example the empress Theodora, wife of Justinian, in the sixth century. The writings of Dionysius the Areopagite, who was erroneously held to be a disciple of Saint Paul, also have a decidedly Miaphysite bent.[12] The Monophysites were concentrated in the regions of Antioch, Armenia, and Alexandria. In Antioch, the schism gave rise to the Syro-Occidental Church (called at times, but improperly, the Jacobite Church), now present in Syria, Iraq, Lebanon, Jordan, and Turkey. Today, this church numbers a million and a half faithful.

9 Council of Chalcedon, "Definition of the Faith," in Tanner, *Decrees of the Ecumenical Councils*, https://www.papalencyclicals.net/councils/ecum04.htm.

10 Mesrob K. Krikorian, "Calcedonia: Storia, conflitti cristologici e riconciliazione," in *Il Concilio di Calcedonia 1550 anni dopo*, ed. Antonio Ducay (Vatican City: Libreria editrice Vaticana, 2003), 114–37.

11 Council of Chalcedon, "Canon 28," in *The Seven Ecumenical Councils*, trans. Henry Percival, Nicene and Post-Nicene Fathers: Second Series 14 (Edinburgh: T and T Clark, 1899), 287. Canon 28, however, was never accepted by the popes, because it based this distinction on the fact that Constantinople—"the New Rome"—was the "imperial city", and the "most holy throne." Thus, the criterion of "apostolic seats," which gave precedence to those episcopal lines which were of Petrine origin (Rome, Alexandria, and Antioch), was lost sight of.

12 Lacoste et al., *Histoire de la théologie*, 118.

From this church comes the Syro-Malankara Church in India, which left Catholic communion only in the sixteenth century.[13] The Armenian Church, another non-Chalcedonian Church, would not give rise to other churches. This church is present in Armenia, Turkey, Canada, Australia, and the United States, with seven and a half million faithful. Finally among these churches emerging in reaction to Chalcedon, in Alexandria the Coptic Church arose. This church has 8 million faithful in Egypt, Jerusalem, Sudan, and South Africa. From Alexandria, the Ethiopian Church (with 17 million faithful in Ethiopia) and the Church of Eritrea also emerged.[14] The recent history of many of these churches has been marked by ecumenical agreements: for the Coptic Orthodox Church, the *Declaration of Agreement on Christology* of February 12, 1988; for the Malankara Orthodox Syrian Church, the *Doctrinal Agreement on Christology* of June 3, 1990; for the Armenian Church, the Common Declaration of John Paul II and Armenian Patriarch Karekim I of December 13, 1996; and for the Church of Cilicia, the Common Declaration *Au terme*, of January 25, 1997.

THE ORTHODOX CHURCHES

The Orthodox call themselves "The Holy and Great Church of Christ," that which professes the "true faith," or, more literally, the "correct opinion" (in Greek: *orthòs dòxa*).[15] In the strict sense, one should really speak of Orthodox *Churches* in the plural, since among these churches there is not a common binding authority, although they coincide substantially in doctrine. The ecumenical patriarch of Constantinople possesses a primacy which is of honor only (*primus inter pares*); each Orthodox Church is autonomous, albeit in communion with each other and with the patriarch of Constantinople.

Approximately 214 million faithful belong to these churches, largely concentrated in the Near East, in the Balkans, and in the former Soviet Union. Nine patriarchates exist. The four most ancient are Constantinople, Jerusalem, Antioch, and Alexandria. In addition, there are the patriarchates of Russia, Romania, Bulgaria, Serbia, and Georgia, as well as five autocephalous churches in Greece, Cyprus, Poland, Albania, and the Czech lands

13 Johann Adam Möhler Institut, *Le chiese cristiane nel Duemila*, 109. A portion of this Church reunited with Rome in the 20th century.

14 Gefaell, "Las Iglesias Orientales," 600.

15 Nicola Bux, "Chiesa ortodossa," in Calabrese, Goyret, and Piazza, eds., *Dizionario di ecclesiologia*, 165.

and Slovakia. Three autonomous churches in China, Japan, and Finland are at times referred to as "national." Finally, one would need to add the churches of the diaspora, which were born from the migration of the faithful. These are quite large in the United States and in Canada, though in principle they depend upon their church of origin.[16]

Characteristic elements of Orthodoxy include the acceptance of the first seven ecumenical councils, the inclination towards apophatic theology, and a great development of pneumatology. Their doctrine of purgatory is quite different from the Catholic one. In the sacramental ambit, some of the characteristic features are the practice of baptism by immersion, the simultaneous conferral of the three sacraments of Christian initiation on the infant (administered ordinarily by priests), the use of leavened bread for the Eucharist, the placement of the transubstantiation in the *epiklesis,* and the nonexistence of Eucharistic cult (such as processions, adoration, and benedictions) outside of the celebration of the Divine Liturgy.[17]

The Orthodox retain the episcopate; the sacramental ordination of their ministers (bishops, priests, and deacons) is held to be valid by the Catholic Church. They accept the ordination of married men, though not for the episcopate. For this reason, a large portion of their bishops come from monasteries. The liturgical celebration of the principal Christian feasts usually does not coincide with that of the Catholic Church, given the difference between their Julian calendar (going back to Julius Caesar) and the Gregorian one in force in the West since the sixteenth century.

Orthodox spirituality is profoundly marked by the liturgical, patristic, and iconographic traditions. One of its important characteristics is the Jesus prayer, also known as the Prayer of the Heart or the Unceasing Prayer. Monasticism enjoys great prestige and its vital center is at Mount Athos in Greece, inhabited by monks since the ninth century. It was there that the Hesychast movement was born and that the *Philocalia*, an important collection of texts of the spiritual masters, was compiled. Gregory Palamas, the great Orthodox theologian of the fourteenth century, was a monk at Athos. Orthodox spirituality also includes a deep veneration for the Virgin Mary. While the Orthodox do not accept the Immaculate Conception and

16 s.v. "Orthodox Church," in Cross and Livingstone, *The Oxford Dictionary of the Christian Church*, 1198.

17 In contrast with Eastern Catholics, for the Orthodox the matrimonial bond, in some specific cases, is dissoluble by the Church.

the Assumption as dogmas, in great measure they agree with the contents of these doctrinal truths.[18]

One cannot understate the strict relationship which exists in Orthodoxy between church and state. This relationship cannot be reduced to reasons of circumstance. In Orthodoxy, in fact, there remains alive the ancient Eastern tradition regarding the *symphonia* between the two institutions. This conception of the close relationship between civil and church authority gave to the emperor a role which was also ecclesial, with points of contact with the priesthood. Historically, this vision often led to caesaropapism, in which civil and ecclesial authority are combined. Still today, among Orthodox Churches there exists a certain deference with regard to civil authority. This way of acting seems to arise out of their awareness of themselves as ethnic churches, and in this context the Orthodox notion of "canonical territory" would apply. The convergence of the centrality of the liturgy and of the "ecclesiality" of civil authority led further to a disinterest—not seen as a lack of charity—for the role of the Church in the social ambit.[19]

The schism between the Catholic Church and the Orthodox Church took place in 1054, for reasons which were more cultural and political than religious. Constantinople, the "New Rome," possessed a majesty incomparably greater than that of the "First Rome," which had already lost its imperial splendor centuries ago. The weight of this issue grows if we consider that the patriarchate of Constantinople did not base itself on a supposed character as an apostolic see (it never was one, in spite of having the relics of the apostle Saint Andrew, transferred from Ephesus), but on the political importance of the city. In the eighth century, furthermore, the Roman pontiff had left the protection of the Eastern emperor and had turned to the Franks. To all of this, one must add the separation between East and West due to the expansion of Islam and the Muslim dominion over the Mediterranean Sea. The cultural differences, and not only the linguistic one, became more acute as communication diminished. Hellenism gathered its reproaches in the celebrated treatises *Kata Latinon* (against the Latins); the Latins responded with the treatises *Contra Graecos*. In this context, one cannot be surprised to see the emergence of separatist inclinations.

18 Johann Adam Möhler Institut, *Le chiese cristiane nel Duemila*, 130–36. The Orthodox way of understanding the essence of original sin, more connected to mortality, affects their comprehension of the mystery of the Immaculate Conception, creating some difficulties from the point of view of Catholic theology.

19 Johann Adam Möhler Institut, *Le chiese cristiane nel Duemila*, 141–43.

Additionally, there existed the problem of the jurisdictions of Rome and Byzantium with regard to the different regions of missions, complicated even more by the variations of the borders of the Eastern Empire. All of this formed a complex picture which contributed to the deterioration of the relations with the pope. In light of its privileges, the Eastern Church looked with suspicion and indignation upon the interventions of Rome in the East in such matters as the deposition of bishops and judgments of appeal. The preference of Rome for the patriarchate of Alexandria as the "second see," as opposed to Constantinople, was a cause of frequent friction.

From a purely doctrinal point of view, the most important difference with the Catholic Church has been in Trinitarian theology. The Eastern side does not accept that the Holy Spirit proceeds from the Father and from the Son (*Filioque*). In this regard, it is worth recalling two historical questions that are often unspoken, each of which weighs in favor of one or the other party. The Orthodox are right when they say that the *Filioque* does not belong to the Nicene-Constantinopolitan Creed. In this creed, following to the letter John 15:26, the Greek formulation "which derives its origin from the Father" was used, which in reality is not equivalent to the Latin *a Patre procedit*. The doctrine professed in the first two ecumenical councils was solemnly reaffirmed by the Council of Chalcedon.[20] The *Filioque* was not even present in the Roman liturgy before the ninth century; indeed, its insertion into the confession of faith was explicitly rejected by Popes Adrian I and Leo III.[21]

The procession of the Holy Spirit *a Patre Filioque* appears in the fifth century, in the writings of Augustine, following upon the thought of Ambrose, as well as in Egypt with Cyril of Alexandria.[22] In the documents of the Magisterium we find it for the first time at the Third Council of Toledo in 589 AD. In this context, the phrase is a late consequence of the struggle against Arianism, so as to affirm that the Son, fully God, is not inferior to the Father.[23] The *Filioque* is also found in the Pseudo-Athanasian

20 Tanner, *Decrees of the Ecumenical Councils*, 84, 87.

21 Lacoste et al., *Histoire de la théologie*, 131.

22 "Nor, by the way, can we say that the Holy Spirit does not proceed from the Son as well." Augustine, *De Trinitate*, trans. Edmund Hill (Hyde Park, N.Y.: New City Press, 1991), 4.20.29; "The Holy Spirit proceeds from the Father and from the Son; it is evident that He is of the divine essence, proceeding essentially in it and from it." Cyril of Alexandria, *Thesaurus*, in *S. Cyrili Tomus Octavus*, edited by Jacques-Paul Migne, Patrologiae Graeca 75 (Paris: J. P. Migne, 1863), 585A. Our translation.

23 Denzinger, *Enchiridion symbolorum*, 470, and José Orlandis, *La Iglesia en la España visigótica y medieval* (Pamplona: Ediciones Universidad de Navarra, 1976), 35–60.

Creed—probably from the seventh century—through which the phrase shared in that creed's great authority.[24] From there the *Filioque* passed into the liturgy of the Franks, probably due to the influence of Alcuin of York, and was ardently defended in Carolingian theology.[25] During the Carolingian period, the Franks overcame the pope's resistance to introducing the *Filioque* into the Roman liturgy.[26] Later, in the year 1014, Benedict VIII inserted it definitively into the creed, under the pressure of Emperor Henry III, on the occasion of the emperor's coronation.[27]

On the other hand, the doctrinal question of the *Filioque* was not a cause of discord until the ninth century. Before then, there were different theological formulations in the East and the West to explain the relationship between the Son and the Holy Spirit. These included the conception of the procession of the Spirit *a Patre per Filium*, understood in the sense of proceeding principally from the Father by means of the Son—that is, as from one single principle. Similar formulas were also used in the East, by Gregory of Nyssa, Maximus the Confessor and John Damascene, without entering into conflict with the *a Patre* from the Nicene-Constantinopolitan Creed.[28] Not until later were these formulations interpreted by anyone in the exclusive sense of "only from the Father."

The different nuances between the Eastern *a Patre per Filium* and the Western *a Patre Filioque* "[do] not ultimately have a basis and motivation which is dogmatic (in the strict sense), but [are] the result of the fact that Eastern Trinitarian theology had to take a position against modalism, while Western theology had to take a stand against late forms of Arianism and Priscillianism."[29] The patriarch Photius, in his struggles against the pope, saw

24 "The Athanasian Creed," in *Creeds and Confessions of Faith in the Christian Tradition*, ed. Jaroslav Pelikan and Valerie Hotchkiss (New Haven, Conn.: Yale University Press, 2003), 1:673–78.

25 Bernard Capelle, "Alcuin et l'histoire du symbolo de la Messe," in *Travaux liturgiques de doctrine et d'histoire*, ed. Bernard Capelle (Louvain: Volz, 1962), 211–21.

26 The epistolary discussions can be found in "Acta Collationis Romanae" in Smaragdus of Saint-Mihiel et al., *Opera omnia ex variis editionibus nunc primum in unum collecta*, ed. Jacques-Paul Migne, Patrologiae Latina 102 (Paris: J. P. Migne, 1851), 971–73.

27 Walter Kasper, *That They May All Be One*, 111. The oldest profession of faith promulgated by a pope which contains the insertion of the *Filioque* is, according to Denzinger, that of Leo IX, contained in the Letter *Congratulamur vehementer* of April 13, 1053, addressed to the patriarch of Antioch. Denzinger, *Enchiridion symbolorum*, 682: "*Credo etiam Spiritum Sanctum, plenum et perfectum verumque Deum, a Patre et Filio procedentem*."

28 Gregory of Nyssa, *Against Eunomius*, Patrologiae Graeca 45:369A; Maximus the Confessor, *Epistula ad Marinum*, Patrologiae Graeca 91:136; John of Damascus, *An Exposition of the Orthodox Faith*, trans. Edward W. Watson and Leighton Pullan (Buffalo, N.Y.: Christian Literature Publishing, 1899), 1.8, https://www.newadvent.org/fathers/33041.htm.

29 Müller, *Katholische Dogmatik*, 458–59. Our translation.

the *Filioque* as a reason to accuse Rome of heresy and to proclaim the Eastern Church as the true guardian of orthodoxy. According to him, the proposal of Latin theology was equivalent to confusing the first two divine persons, renewing the Sabellian heresy, and putting at risk the monarchy of the Father described by Eastern Trinitarian theology. From then on, even after the short schismatic period of the ninth century, the *Filioque* would be the banner of opposition against Rome. These developments in the East triggered a reaction in the West, in the form of polemical treatises such as the *Contra Graecorum opposita Romanam Ecclesiam infamantium* of Ratramnus of Corbie and the *Liber adversus Graecos* of Aeneas of Paris.

The final outcome of the schism would be the mutual excommunications proclaimed in July 1054. Cardinal Humbert of Silva Candida, a man who was not very diplomatic, had been sent to Constantinople to clarify the umpteenth jurisdictional problem between the Roman see and that of Constantinople. The issue at hand was the longstanding controversy regarding the use of unleavened bread in the Eucharist.[30] Not coming to an agreement, the cardinal deposited the decree of excommunication of Patriarch Michael Cerularius on the altar of the Hagia Sophia. A few days later the Patriarch Michael convoked a synod which in turn excommunicated the bishop of Rome, Leo IX, who had actually died three months earlier.

The schism of the eleventh century arose, therefore, predominantly from an ecclesiastical polemic. For a long time, among the general population, there was no awareness of a separation. Only after the taking of Constantinople at the hands of the Crusaders in 1204, with the subsequent looting of the city and the erection of the Latin patriarchate, did the schism assume all of its anti-Latin virulence at the popular level. Eastern theology—both Trinitarian as well as that relative to other matters—also took on a decidedly anti-Roman character.

In light of this atmosphere, it is surprising that only seventy years later an agreement of union was reached at the Second Council of Lyon in 1274. Various interests of the Eastern emperor, Michael Palaeologus, came together at this event. The emperor had recently regained power in Constantinople, although in an unstable manner, and therefore needed to be on good terms with the West. There was also a certain lessening of the importance given to the question of the *Filioque*, even though this Trinitarian doctrine was included in the profession of faith made by the

30 Nichols, *Rome and the Eastern Churches*, 235–37.

Greek emperor and received at the council. At Lyon, the focal points instead included the question of the primacy of the bishop of Rome, which the Byzantine Patriarch John Bekkos was willing to accept. Another key point of interest was the doctrine on purgatory, which from then on became a perennial theme in theological discussions between the Greeks and Latins. Regarding the material used for the Eucharist—unleavened bread in the Latin context—the Orthodox recognized the validity of the Latin practice. However, the irenic atmosphere prevalent in Lyon was completely absent in Byzantium. After the return of the emperor and the Orthodox delegates to that city, a synod held only three years later completely repudiated the terms of union.[31]

In the fifteenth century, another ephemeral union took place, sanctioned by the Bull *Laetentur Caeli* of the Council of Florence in the year 1439. This union showed the convergence of the unionist passion of Pope Eugene IV, which was also present among others in the East, and the political needs of the Emperor John VIII Palaeologus. This emperor, threatened by the Ottoman Turkish troops, desired help from the armies of the Christian West. These extra-ecclesial factors were certainly significant. Still, it should be noted that in the discussions of the council and in the elaboration of the documents there were a significant number of Eastern theologians and bishops, supported by the presence both of the emperor and the patriarch of Constantinople, Joseph II. With regard to the Trinitarian question, the council established that "the explanation of those words 'and from the Son' [*filioque*] was licitly and reasonably added to the creed for the sake of declaring the truth and from imminent need."[32] The bull, however, left space open for the two explanations of the procession of the Holy Spirit; it specifically says: "We declare that when holy doctors and fathers say that the holy Spirit proceeds from the Father through the Son, this bears the sense that thereby also the Son should be signified, according to the Greeks indeed as cause, and according to the Latins as principle of the subsistence of the holy Spirit, just like the Father."

According to historians, the failure of the union can be attributed to three causes. First, there was the failure of the crusade which was sent to the aid of Constantinople, whose army was annihilated at the Battle of Varna in 1444. Second, the overwhelming majority of the population of the Eastern Empire

31 Nichols, *Rome and the Eastern Churches*, 247–61.
32 Council of Florence, Bull *Laetentur Caeli* (July 6, 1439).

was decidedly against the union. Finally, with the fall of Constantinople in 1453, not only did the hopes of receiving help from the West cease, but many saw the fall as being sent by God as a punishment for the "betrayal" perpetrated in Florence. In the year 1484, a synod in Byzantium formally renounced the union of Florence and even decreed that Latins converted to Orthodoxy were obliged to negate the doctrine of the *Filioque*.[33]

In addition to these historical events, the styles and methods of Eastern and Western theology grew ever more distinct. While in the West the scholastic method stood out, in the East *Hesychasm*—from the Greek *hesychia*, rest—held sway. This system of thought, associated with Gregory Palamas, was dominant in the fourteenth and fifteenth centuries, flowered again in the twentieth century and today characterizes Orthodox theology to a great extent. Hesychasm teaches that in contemplation and in mystical union one sees not God himself, but the divine energies, which are mediating forces between created humanity and the persons of the divine Trinity. In this way, Orthodox theology sought to maintain the divine transcendence, with significant consequences for the study of the Trinity and soteriology.[34]

In recent years, the positions with regard to the Trinitarian question have come closer, at least on the Catholic side. There is in fact a recognition of a Trinitarian approach that can be shared, although it remains different in form. In 1995, the Pontifical Council for Promoting Christian Unity published the document *The Greek and Latin Traditions about the Procession of the Holy Spirit* which specified that "the Catholic Church acknowledges the conciliar, ecumenical, normative and irrevocable value, as expression of the one common faith of the Church and of all Christians, of the Symbol professed in Greek at Constantinople in 381 by the Second Ecumenical Council."[35] At the same time, the document states: "The Catholic Church interprets the *Filioque* with reference to the conciliar and ecumenical, normative and irrevocable value of the confession of faith in the eternal origin of the Holy Spirit, as defined in 381 by the Ecumenical

33 Nichols, *Rome and the Eastern Churches*, 263–80.

34 Johann Adam Möhler Institut, *Le chiese cristiane nel Duemila*, 120.

35 Pontifical Council for Promoting Christian Unity, "Greek and Latin Traditions Regarding the Procession of the Holy Spirit," *L'Osservatore Romano: Weekly Edition in English*, September 20, 1995, 3. Regarding this topic, one may consult Alfred Stirnemann and Gerhard Wilfinger, eds., *Von heilegen Geist: Der gemeinsame trinitarische Glaube und das Problem des Filioque* (Innsbruck: Tyrolia, 1998); and Elena Álvarez, *Procede del Padre y del Hijo: Estudio de la "Clarificación Romana" de 1995 y de sus fuentes patrísticas* (Bern: Lang, 2011).

Council of Constantinople in its Symbol." According to Walter Kasper, the Orthodox would not need to adopt the *Filioque*, but they should admit that it is not heretical and that it can be an interpretation made in light of the common creed.[36]

The Orthodox understanding of the unity of the Church is still quite distant from the Catholic view.[37] The Orthodox conceive each local church as being complete in itself. The unifying factor among these local churches would be only the mutual recognition of being in communion with one another. This way of understanding the unity of the Church received a new impetus with the concept of *sobornost,* or conciliarity, in the nineteenth century. Aleksey Khomyakov developed this idea without specific reference to the councils but rather in regard to an understanding of the Church as a unity in diversity. In this ecclesiological vision, the primacy of the bishop of Rome does not find an adequate place, and therefore this doctrine is rejected. At present, this issue of the Roman pontiff's role is the main obstacle on the path towards unity.

The Russian theologians of the diaspora (caused by the communist persecution of the twentieth century and the consequent emigration to the West) have come to exercise a great influence on ecumenism. In this context, a number of Orthodox theologians were present at the Saint Sergius Theological Institute in Paris, creating a lively forum for dialogue between the East and the West. Some of them, like Sergei Bulgakov, had known Vladimir Soloviev, a nineteenth-century Russian theologian. Soloviev distinguished himself for his studies on *sophiology* and had understood well the difference between Latinity and Romanness. In this way, he drew near to Catholic positions. For Soloviev, such ideas fused with the thought of Pavel Florensky regarding the "metaphysics of charity" and generated a religious philosophy with interesting ecclesiological possibilities. Soloviev's thinking was criticized by the so-called neopatristic part of the same school, in the work of Vladimir Lossky and Georges Florovsky, and later by John Meyendorf and neo-Palamism. Still, in this atmosphere, conditions suitable for a profound Catholic-Orthodox intellectual dialogue developed. This dialogue took on a particular intensity at the other pole of Russian theology in the West, Saint Vladimir's Theological Seminary in New York. In the area of Greek Orthodox theology, J. D. Zizioulas's speculations on the connection

36 Kasper, *That They May All Be One*, 113–14.

37 An important work on this subject is Yannis Spiteris, *Ecclesiologia ortodossa: Temi a confronto tra Oriente e Occidente* (Bologna: Dehoniane, 2003).

between ecclesiology and Trinitarian ontology offer an interesting reference point for ecumenical dialogue.[38]

These developments have opened up the possibility of conceiving unity as an essential aspect of the Church's mystery, in contrast to the polemics of the past and in parallel with the Catholic renewal in ecclesiology. As the Greek Orthodox theologian Nikos Nissiotis noted in an important address at the Third Assembly of the World Council of Churches, at New Delhi in 1961:

> In Orthodox thinking Church Union is an absolute reality pre-established by God. . . . Unity among Christians is to be identified with the union of the Father and the Son—"that they may be one, even as we are one" (Jn 17:22–23). Unity among men in the Church is the result, the reflection, of the event of the Father's union with Christ by his Spirit realized in the historical Church on the day of Pentecost. . . . Unity is not an *attribute* of the Church, but its very *life*.[39]

In order to deepen this unity, ecclesial communities would need to return to the reality of the primitive Church, which the Orthodox Church sees herself as preserving. Nonetheless, the reality of ethnic, national, and political factors, even within the churches in the United States, has made it difficult for the Orthodox Churches to realize this profound conception of unity.[40]

The involvement of the Orthodox Churches in ecumenical dialogue was not very enthusiastic at first.[41] Only gradually did the churches enter into the World Council of Churches (WCC). This delay was due to the predominantly Protestant origin of the ecumenical movement. Nonetheless, the Orthodox Churches have made an important contribution to ecumenism in affirming the indivisibility of the One Church and in their continuity with the apostolic tradition.[42] With regard to the Catholic Church, the reciprocal repeal of the excommunications of 1054 on December 7, 1965, has had great significance. This repeal sought to eliminate the resentments caused by the regrettable events of 1054 and to inaugurate a

38 Ioannis Asimakis, "Alcune considerazioni sull'ecclesiologia ecumenica," *Studi ecumenici* 29, no. 2 (2011): 224–26.

39 Quoted in Vigen Guroian, "The Crisis of Orthodox Ecclesiology," in Braaten, *Ecumenical Future*, 162–63.

40 Guroian, "The Crisis of Orthodox Ecclesiology," 162–75.

41 Gustave Thils, *Histoire doctrinale du movement œcuménique* (Louvain: E. Warny, 1962), 313–19.

42 Carl E. Braaten and Robert W. Jenson, eds., *In One Body through the Cross: The Princeton Proposal for Christian Unity: A Call to the Churches from an Ecumenical Study Group* (Grand Rapids, Mich.: Eerdmans, 2003), no. 69.

dialogue of mutual charity between the two churches. Other gestures along these same lines have been made, such as the exchange of visits on the occasions of the feasts of Saints Peter and Paul and of Saint Andrew.

A more recent milestone was the historic meeting between Pope Francis and the Russian Patriarch Kirill in February 2016 on the island of Cuba, the first-ever meeting between the bishop of Rome and the Moscow patriarch. In the face of the varied challenges confronted by Christians, both from threats to religious freedom as well as from "an often very aggressive secularist ideology," the Roman pontiff and the Russian patriarch expressed their desire "to combine our efforts to give witness to the Gospel of Christ and to the shared heritage of the Church of the first millennium, responding together to the challenges of the contemporary world."[43]

The mutual repeal of excommunications opened the way for the start of an official theological dialogue between Catholics and Orthodox. These exchanges took place first at the local level, and then, since 1980, at the international level by means of a special mixed commission.[44] A review of the documents from this dialogue shows that the topics dealt with have been rather narrow.[45] At the same time, they have been indispensable prerequisites for taking on the key points which separate the two traditions at a broader level. With the document signed by the mixed commission in Ravenna in 2007, entitled *Ecclesiological and Canonical Consequences of the Sacramental Nature of the Church: Ecclesial Communion, Conciliarity and Authority*, it appears that this preliminary period has finally been concluded and that the issue of the Roman primacy can be taken up at the level of international dialogue.[46]

43 Pope Francis and Patriarch Kirill, *Joint Declaration* (February 12, 2016).

44 Giovanni Cereti, *Ecumenismo: Corso di metodologia ecumenica* (Rome: Istituto di Teología a Distanza, 1991), 108–11.

45 The principal documents published until now are: *The Mystery of the Church and of the Eucharist in the Light of the Mystery of the Holy Trinity* (Munich, July 6, 1982); *Faith, Sacraments and the Unity of the Church* (Bari, June 16, 1987); *The Sacrament of Order in the Sacramental Structure of the Church, with Particular Reference to the Importance of the Apostolic Succession for the Sanctification and Unity of the People of God* (Valmo, June 26, 1988); *Uniatism: Method of Union of the Past, and Present Search for Full Communion* (Balamand, June 23, 1993); *Ecclesiological and Canonical Consequences of the Sacramental Nature of the Church: Ecclesial Communion, Conciliarity and Authority* (Ravenna, October 13, 2007); *Synodality and Primacy during the First Millennium: Towards a Common Understanding in Service to the Unity of the Church* (Chieti, September 21, 2016).

46 At the local level, rather, there is the joint statement of the Orthodox/Roman Catholic Commission of the United States, *An Agreed Statement on Conciliarity and Primacy in the Church* (Brighton, 1989).

The Ravenna Document examines the relationship between conciliarity and primacy at the local, regional, and universal levels and concludes by expressing the desire for a "greater depth" of study with regard to "the question of the role of the bishop of Rome in the communion of all the Churches."[47] This desire was partially accomplished some years later with the document *Synodality and Primacy during the First Millennium: Towards a Common Understanding in Service to The Unity of the Church.*[48] The conclusions of this document state: "Throughout the first millennium, the Church in the East and the West was united in preserving the apostolic faith, maintaining the apostolic succession of bishops, developing structures of synodality inseparably linked with primacy, and in an understanding of authority as a service (*diakonia*) of love."[49]

In the last years of the twentieth century, the relations of Orthodox Churches with the World Council of Churches suffered because of the increasingly liberal Protestant orientation of the latter organization. Relations of the Orthodox with the Catholic Church have cooled due to the revival of the Catholic Churches of Eastern Rite in ex-Soviet territory, an issue which has come about with the fall of the Soviet Union. These circumstances have led the Orthodox to accuse the Catholic Church of undue proselytism. The panorama of current conditions highlights ever more the importance, so far not sufficiently appreciated, of the differences in understanding the catholicity of the Church. "Catholic" must be grasped not simply as signifying a denomination but rather in its genuine theological sense. Catholicity, in fact, not only involves the idea that the Gospel must reach all persons but is intrinsically linked to religious freedom. Where such freedom does not exist, catholicity cannot easily be actualized. The link between the autocephalous church and the nation, rooted in the orthodox notion of "canonical territory," makes it difficult to assert the value of religious freedom, and with it a genuine sense of catholicity.[50]

47 Joint International Commission for the Theological Dialogue between the Roman Catholic Church and the Orthodox Church, *Ecclesiological and Canonical Consequences*, no. 45.

48 Chieti, September 21, 2016.

49 Joint International Commission for the Theological Dialogue between the Roman Catholic Church and the Orthodox Church, *Synodality and Primacy during the First Millennium*, no. 20.

50 Walter Kasper, "Le radici teologiche del conflitto tra Mosca e Roma," *La Civiltà Cattolica* 3642 no. 1 (2002): 531–41.

THE LUTHERANS

The most immediate predecessors to the Lutheran reform were John Wycliffe (1324–1384) and Jan Hus (1369–1415). Wycliffe, a Franciscan priest, studied and taught theology at Balliol College at Oxford. He founded the reform movement of the Lollards and was a prolific writer; among his works is a *Summa Theologiae* in 14 volumes. His proposals of reform, combined with theological positions contrary to the freedom of God, sacramental causality, Eucharistic transubstantiation, and the role of the Church in salvation, encountered fierce opposition from the English bishops and the condemnation of the Council of Constance.[51]

The ideas of Wycliffe arrived in Bohemia by means of its royal family, related to the English royal family. Hus, a priest born of a peasant family in southern Bohemia and an untiring preacher, became the great promoter of Wycliffe's vision. Within an apocalyptic perspective, Hus criticized the Church of his time and the pope with ever greater intensity, openly challenging the authorities of Prague and Rome. In 1413, he wrote his best-known work, *The Church*, which was widely read both then and later among the Waldensians and Lutherans. Hus was also condemned in the Council of Constance, where he was executed.[52]

At the beginnings of the modern period in Renaissance Europe, the sixteenth century was the time of the great divisions of the Church in the West. The undisputed protagonist of the Reform was the German Augustinian religious Martin Luther (1483–1546). Born in Eisleben in lower Saxony, he studied philosophy and theology at Erfurt before becoming an able teacher of exegesis at the University of Wittenberg. His positions on the nature of man, radically corrupted by sin, germinated on the terrain of studies on the Psalms and the Pauline corpus, in particular the Letter to the Romans. According to Luther, man, after original sin, can only find justification in the act of faith without the mediation of works. The German reformer understood the "justice of God" spoken of in Romans 1:16–17 not as a divine intervention which rewards the just and punishes sinners, but as an act by which the merciful Lord covers over the sins of those who abandon themselves to him in faith. This interpretation found confirmation

51 Orazio Piazza, "Wycliff, John," in *Lexikon: Dizionario dei teologi*, ed. Luciano Pacomio and Giuseppe Occhipinti (Casale Monferrato: Piemme, 1998), 1325.

52 Franco Buzzi, *Breve storia del pensiero protestante: Da Lutero a Pannenberg* (Milan: Ancora, 2007), 7–12.

in the so-called Tower (*turmerlebnis*) Experience, an episode which forever marked Luther's life. As he said, "that place in Paul was truly for me the gate to paradise."[53]

The symbolic date of the beginning of the Reform is October 31, 1517. On this date, after sending his celebrated Ninety-Five Theses to Bishop Albert of Brandenburg, he attached the theses to the door of the church of the Castle of Wittenberg. Nearby, the Dominican Johann Tetzel continued ever more widely to preach on indulgences. Pope Julius II encouraged Tetzel in this task, in order to raise funds for the construction of Saint Peter's Basilica. After being tried in Rome and after intense discussions with theologians of such caliber as Thomas Cajetan and Johann Eck, Luther was declared a heretic by Leo X in the Bull *Exsurge Domine* of 1520. The pope subsequently excommunicated the reformer in the Bull *Decet Romanum Pontificem* of 1521. In that year, Luther published three of his most popular works: *To the Christian Nobility of the German Nation*, *On the Babylonian Captivity of the Church*, and *On the Freedom of a Christian*.

Philip Schwarzerd, better known by the Greek name Melanchthon, a great humanist and colleague of Luther's in Wittenberg, enthusiastically espoused the cause of the Reform. He consolidated the intellectual foundations of the movement begun by Luther, often moderating its extremes.[54] Melanchthon wrote the *Apology of the Augsburg Confession* (1531) in response to the *Pontifical Confutation* of the Augsburg Confession.[55] Article four of this work, on the topic of justification, is one of the most wide-ranging Lutheran expositions on the subject. Melanchthon also wrote the *Treatise on the Power and Primacy of the Pope* (1537).

The scholastic theology of the period was decayed, out of date, and under the grip of a nominalism going back to William of Ockham. This theology could not muster sufficiently strong resources to stop the proposals of reform. The convergence of a series of historical events—above all the favor of the princes, the use of printed paper and, last but not least, the moral decadence of the ecclesiastical hierarchy of the time—greatly favored the spread of Lutheranism. This growth took place especially in Germany

53 Martin Luther, "Preface to the First Volume of Latin Writings," trans. Lewis W. Spitz, in *Luther's Works*, ed. Helmut T. Lehmann (Philadelphia: Muhlenberg Press, 1960), 34:337.

54 Michele De Rosa, *Teologia protestante: Momenti e figure* (Salerno: Elea Press, 1990), 34–36.

55 Text in *The Augsburg Confession and the Apology of the Augsburg Confession with Key Historical Documents: The Concordia Reader's Edition*, ed. Paul T. McCain (St. Louis, Mo.: Concordia, 2020), 55–240.

and in the Nordic countries, where Lutheranism became the state religion. Later, the movement spread rapidly in the United States through German immigration. Currently, the total number of Lutherans worldwide is around 90 million, grouped together in the Lutheran World Federation.[56]

Although all of the aforementioned factors have their importance in Lutheranism, the basic question of this ecclesial community—the basic question upon which the Church stands—is the theological notion of justification by faith alone and not by works. Luther believed himself to have discovered that the monastic penances, the preaching of indulgences, and the veneration of the saints manifested a world which favored the merit of man to the detriment of the gratuitous justification obtained by Christ. As already mentioned, on this question the discrediting of the broadly nominalist scholastic theology of the time had a large impact.

On the basis of Romans 1:17, Luther understood the justice of God no longer as a judgment but as justice given to the sinner and received by means of faith. This justification would not make a man just but would only make him aware of being considered by God as such. The principle of "Scripture alone"—*sola Scriptura*—only appeared later. This latter principle developed when Luther was faced with the need to propose a highest doctrinal authority, as he had lost the possibility of settling the controversy within the Church to which he belonged. The German translation of the New Testament, masterfully prepared by Luther while in refuge in the Wartburg fortress and under the protection of Frederick of Saxony, was very well received. The most complete statement of Lutheran doctrine is found in the Augsburg Confession (1530), though this statement has no normative value.[57]

The concept of justification by faith alone implies an emphasis on God's total initiative in favor of justification, and involves the principles "Christ alone," "faith alone," and "grace alone." Lutheranism does not accept justification as implying an inner regeneration of man. Therefore, the Christian

56 The Christians emerging from the Reformation were called "Protestants" because in the Diet of Speyer (1529) they protested against the pope and the emperor, demanding the reform of the Church according to the principles of Luther. There is a tendency to avoid this terminology today, even if it is still very widespread among some. In fact, today there exists the journal "Protestantism," published by the Waldensians. Some Christians traditionally known as Protestant prefer the term "Evangelical"; Giorgio Bouchard, *Chiese e movimenti evangelici del nostro tempo*, 3rd ed. (Turin: Claudiana, 2006), 27.

57 "Augsburg Confession," in *The Augsburg Confession and the Apology of the Augsburg Confession with Key Historical Documents: The Concordia Reader's Edition*, ed. Paul T. McCain (St. Louis, Mo.: Concordia, 2020), 7–54; for a more in-depth analysis, see Giorgio Tourn, ed., *La confessione augustana del 1530* (Turin: Claudiana, 1980).

is at once declared just by God yet remains a sinner (*simul justus et peccator*). The authority of the Bible is singular. Tradition is not accepted as a hermeneutical criterion but rather only as the first expression of what was later written in the sacred books. "Scripture alone" always remains the guiding and ultimate norm of faith.

The Church is not, in the Lutheran system, a salvific community or an instrument of salvation, but exclusively the "community of the saved." It follows that the doctrine with regard to the sacraments does not include any kind of instrumental causality. Baptism is of central importance in Lutheran theology. This sacrament is an absolutely gratuitous event in which the person is justified; the baptism of children is therefore a regular practice. Lutherans recognize in the Eucharist the real presence of the Lord in the "Holy Supper," in, with, and under the species of bread and wine. Since the Eucharist—always distributed under the two species—is understood only as a meal, this sacrament is stripped of any sacrificial value. The honor given to the Eucharist is limited to the moment of celebration. Baptism and the Eucharist are considered to be the only sacraments contained in Revelation. Lutheran rites exist which are parallel to some of the other sacraments of the Catholic Church. Still, Lutherans do not accept the sacramental nature of these rites.

Pastoral life for Lutherans is centered on preaching. This is in keeping with a conception of the Word of God that does not have need of sacramental mediation for the work of salvation. The ordained ministry is devoid of sacramental value.[58] Lutherans consider this ministry as necessary for the Church's well-being but not something which belongs to her essence. Ministry arises from the common priesthood of all the faithful but is nevertheless conferred by ordination made with the laying on of hands. The Lutherans conceive of the ordained ministry as a public service to the community and as an identity that can be revoked. Among the Scandinavian Lutherans and some communities in northern Germany, the episcopate exists and is understood to serve a function of vigilance over local churches. Luther possessed a deep sense of the unity of all who believe in Christ. Still,

58 Luther's position on this theme is clear: "Of this sacrament the Church of Christ knows nothing; it is an invention of the church of the pope. Not only is there nowhere any promise of grace attached to it, but there is not the least mention of it in the whole New Testament. Now it is ridiculous to put forth as a sacrament of God that which cannot be proved to have been instituted by God." Luther, *The Babylonian Captivity of the Church*, in *Works of Martin Luther*, trans. Albert T. W. Steinhaeuser (Philadelphia: Castle Press, 1915), 2:273.

he could not prevent the Protestant reformers from quickly dividing into separate groups.[59] We will return to this issue in the following pages. As for mainstream Lutheranism, in the seventeenth century this community developed towards a so-called Lutheran orthodoxy, in the context of a theological and systematic formulation of the thought of Luther. This systemization was accompanied by a great institutionalization of religious life and by strict control on the part of civil authority. Paradoxically, Lutheran orthodoxy was not always faithful to Luther, precisely because of its systematic character which was foreign to the mind of its founder.[60]

Pietist spirituality arose as a reaction to the aridity of this approach and lasted until the eighteenth century. This movement sought to cultivate religious sentiment in a less intellectualist way. The publication of *Pia Desideria* in 1675 by the Lutheran theologian Philipp Spener had great importance in the beginnings of Pietism. [61] The keystone of this work was the concept of rebirth, which shifted the focus of Lutheran spirituality from faith to piety. In privileging the personal experience of God through the Bible alone, without catechisms or manuals, and outside the sphere of an organized collectivity, Pietism revealed itself to be extremely critical of the institutional Church.[62] With August Hermann Francke (1663–1727), the Pietist movement opened itself to social works in the form of schools and orphanages, as well as to missionary concerns. Nicolaus von Zinzerdorf (1700–1760) was a prominent proponent of the "logic of the heart" in Pietism, especially with the publication in London of *Twenty-One Discourses or Dissertations upon the Augsburg-Confession*. In this work, the text of the *Confession* was expressed according to the criterion of what one might feel, rather than what one believes.[63]

From the end of the eighteenth century, Pietist circles came under the influence of Enlightenment thought. In this period, Friedrich Schleiermacher was a key figure. In his works *On Religion: Speeches to its Cultured Despisers* (1799) and *The Christian Faith* (1821), sentiment takes on a central role. Of note as well is Søren Kierkegard, a deeply Christian thinker who nonetheless had a critical attitude towards institutionalized religion.

59 Luder G. Whitlock Jr., *Divided We Fall: Overcoming a History of Christian Disunity* (Philipsburg, N.J.: P and R Publishing, 2017), 44–48.
60 Lacoste et al., *Histoire de la théologie*, 297.
61 The complete title is *Pia desideria oder Herzliches Verlangen nach gottgefälliger Besserung der wahren evangelischen Kirche*.
62 Johann Adam Möhler Institut, *Le chiese cristiane nel Duemila*, 276–79.
63 Lacoste et al., *Histoire de la théologie*, 348.

He held that one is not a Christian but rather becomes one, in the sense that what matters is not be called a Christian but to act as a Christian.[64] Among the rationalists, one might mention the religious positions of Georg Wilhelm Friedrich Hegel (1770–1831), who, in the last academic course held at the end of his life, professed himself an evangelical Lutheran.[65]

From the second half of the nineteenth century, liberal Protestantism made its rise, especially with Adolf von Harnack (1851–1930). Harnack, in his lectures on "The Essence of Christianity," held in the University of Berlin in 1900 and subsequently published, distinguishes between the Gospel in which Christ is the object, and the Gospel truly proclaimed by Christ, which would be of a Semitic mold not distorted by Hellenic mediation. A little later, Ernst Troeltsch (1865–1923), with his work *The Absoluteness of Christianity and the History of Religions* (1912), of relativist character, came to conceive of Christianity as a culture. In the twentieth century, liberal theology took a new shape with Rudolf Bultmann (1884–1976) and his distinction between the Jesus of history and the Christ of faith. For Bultmann, this distinction would come to encompass the whole Christian message, thus attempting to "demythify" the New Testament. On the other hand, the work of Wolfhart Pannenberg (1928–2014) aligns itself with Hegelian rationalism. In the attempt to reconcile faith and reason, Pannenberg conceives history as a continuous revelation of God, as shown in his work *Revelation as History* of 1963.

Along with these developments, the twentieth century was also characterized by a return to Lutheran authenticity. A prime example is Dietrich Bonhoeffer (1906–1945), a German pastor and theologian, who was executed in a concentration camp by the Nazis. An active protagonist of the "Confessing Church," he had, since the beginning of his theological work, a great interest in ecclesiology. In his work *The Cost of Discipleship*, from 1937, he strongly criticizes a Lutheranism too focused on justification by faith alone and thus dispensed from a life in conformity with the Gospel. In a later work, *Ethics* (1940), he proposes the conceptual formula of "existence for others" as the central nucleus of Christian life. One should also mention the desire, expressed by more than one Lutheran theologian of the last century, to "rediscover the first Luther" and "go back to the original

64 Lacoste et al., *Histoire de la théologie*, 372.
65 On the incidence of Hegelian thought in Lutheranism, see Fortunato M. Cacciatore, *Protestantesimo e filosofia in Hegel* (Soveria Mannelli: Rubettino, 2003).

spirit of the reform," which for many of these theologians does not coincide with contemporary Protestantism.[66]

The Lutheran Church has always had an intense involvement in ecumenical dialogue. With regard to the Catholic Church, this effort has been carried out by the Lutheran-Roman Catholic Commission on Unity. This commission initiated its work in 1967 and issued its first document, entitled *The Gospel and the Church*, in 1972. In a second stage of dialogue (1973–1984), diverse topics were dealt with, such as the Eucharist, ministry in the Church, and issues more directly connected with ecumenism, such as those addressed in the documents *Ways to Community* and *Facing Unity*. In 1986, a third phase of dialogue began, which focused on ecclesiology and justification and continued until 1993. As a fruit of this third phase, at a time and place filled with significance, on October 31, 1999, a joint declaration was signed at Augsburg which affirmed some doctrinal points regarding justification. This document constitutes a landmark for Catholic-Lutheran dialogue and an important step forward at the theological level.[67] In 1995, a fourth phase of dialogue began, on the topic of the apostolicity of the Church. In 2006, the Lutheran-Roman Catholic Commission published a study document on this issue, which appears to be ever more at the center of the ecumenical debate regarding ministry.[68] In 2013, in view of the five hundredth anniversary of the Reform and fiftieth anniversary of the start of official dialogue, the commission published the document *From Conflict to Communion: Lutheran—Catholic Common Commemoration of the Reformation in 2017.*

Even if the *Joint Declaration* of 1999 did not reestablish full ecclesial communion, the document officially seals the reciprocal reception of the positions expounded within it, and therefore merits special consideration. The statement "is inspired by a model of ecumenical consensus which applies the principle according to which unity in the faith, fundamental for ecclesial communion, does not necessarily require that the common faith be said with the same concepts, but allows for different doctrinal expres-

66 Harding Meyer, "La Chiesa Popolo di Dio, Corpo di Cristo, Tempio dello Spirito Santo, nel dialogo tra la Chiesa cattolica romana e le confessioni protestanti: Una prospettiva luterana," in *L'ecclesiologia trent'anni dopo la "Lumen gentium,"* ed. Pedro Rodríguez (Armando: Rome 1995), 225–28.

67 Walter Kasper, "Una pietra miliare nel cammino dell'ecumene," in *Dossier sulla giustificazione*, ed. Angelo Maffeis (Brescia: Queriniana, 2000), 305–9; José R. Villar, "La declaración común luterano-católica sobre la doctrina de la justificación," *Scripta Theologica* 32, no. 1 (2000): 101–29.

68 Lutheran-Roman Catholic Commission for Unity, Study "The Apostolicity of the Church," *Service d'Information* 128, no. 2 (2008): 59–133.

sions."[69] The declaration affirms a "consensus on basic truths of the doctrine of justification," and in fact, in the third part of the text, describes a "Common Understanding of Justification."[70] In the fourth part, the statement describes the different ways in which each of the traditions understands the powerlessness of man with regard to justification, the forgiveness of sins and sanctification, the role of faith and of grace, the sinful nature of the justified person, the law and the Gospel, the question of the certainty of salvation, and the good works of the justified person.[71]

The official response of the Catholic Church, while on one hand affirming that "it is rightly stated that there is a consensus in fundamental truths of the doctrine of justification," on the other hand adds that "we cannot yet speak of a consensus such as to eliminate every difference between Catholics and Lutherans in the understanding of justification."[72] There remain divergences on issues which are not insignificant. Such issues include, among others, the Lutheran affirmation of man as at once sinful yet just (*simul iustus et peccator*), which is not shared by Catholics; the position of the doctrine on justification within the whole perspective of the truths of faith; and the character of human cooperation in justification.[73] These points should not take away value from the agreement which has been reached. As has been justly said, at Augsburg "not all of the knots of the controversy between Catholics and Lutherans have been untied—not even with respect to justification—but a path has been found to bring about new convergences."[74]

The year of common commemoration of the Reformation, from October 31, 2016, to October 31, 2017, provided a special opportunity to "move beyond the controversies and disagreements that have often prevented us from understanding one another," continuing the path of conversion, reconciliation, and theological dialogue.[75] On this occasion, Pope

69 Maffeis, "La riconciliazione possible," In *Dossier sulla giustificazione*, ed. Maffeis, 15–16. Our translation.

70 Lutheran World Federation and Roman Catholic Church, *Joint Declaration on the Doctrine of Justification* (October 31, 1999), 5; 14–18.

71 Lutheran World Federation and Roman Catholic Church, *Joint Declaration*, 19–21; 22–24; 25–27; 28–30; 31–33; 34–36; 37–39.

72 Congregation for the Doctrine of the Faith and Pontifical Council for Promoting Christian Unity, "Presentation to the Vatican *Sala Stampa* of His Eminence Edward Idris Cardinal Cassidy" (June 25, 1998), 8.

73 Congregation for the Doctrine of the Faith and Pontifical Council for Promoting Christian Unity, "Presentation *Sala Stampa*."

74 Carlo Porro, "Dichiarazione congiunta sulla giustificazione: Orientamenti per la lettura," *Rassegna di Teologia* 41, no. 6 (2000): 897. Our translation.

75 Pope Francis, "Common Ecumenical Prayer at the Lutheran Cathedral of Lund" (October 31, 2016).

Francis affirmed that the past divisions between Lutherans and Catholics were not simply due to issues of faith, but also to cultural misunderstanding: "Certainly, there was a sincere will on the part of both sides to profess and uphold the true faith, but at the same time we realize that we closed in on ourselves out of fear or bias with regard to the faith which others profess with a different accent and language."[76] The Catholic Church, in the present context, is in a better position to appreciate the authentic contributions of the Reform. As the Holy Father noted at the beginning of the commemoration of the Reform, the "Reformation helped give greater centrality to sacred Scripture in the Church's life" and Luther's doctrine of justification by grace alone "expresses the essence of human existence before God."[77]

With the passing of the years, the *Joint Declaration on the Doctrine of Justification* has become an important sign of Christian unity which has reached beyond the sphere of Catholics and Lutherans. Various other denominational bodies have associated themselves with the joint declaration: the World Methodist Council in 2006, the Anglican Consultative Council in 2016, and the World Communion of Reformed Churches in 2017. Twenty years after the signing of the original declaration, representatives of the five global Christian communities subscribing to the document met in Indiana at the University of Notre Dame, reaffirming the basic truths of justification and expressing the desire to work together from the perspective of unity.[78]

THE REFORMED CHURCHES

Contemporaneous with the Lutheran reform, in present-day Switzerland two other reform movements developed: one at Zurich, commenced by Ulrich Zwingli (1484–1531), and the other in Geneva, led by John Calvin (1509–1564). Zwingli was born in Wildhas in a very religious family, in which three brothers were priests and two sisters were religious. He served as a parish priest at Glarus and later became a tireless preacher in Zurich. He was a friend of Erasmus of Rotterdam, who was a strong influence on him. Zwingli counted on the strong support of the bourgeois class of Zurich to struggle against the rampant corruption present in a good portion of the city's clergy. Characteristics of Zwingli's thought include the denial of the

76 Pope Francis, "Ecumenical Prayer at Lund."

77 Pope Francis, "Ecumenical Prayer at Lund."

78 *Statement from Notre Dame Consultation: Visible Unity and Common Witness*, 2019, https://www.lutheranworld.org/news/statement-notre-dame-consultation-visible-unity-and-common-witness.

validity of exterior forms of worship and an emphasis on the ethical life. He did not recognize the authority of the pope and the ecumenical councils. His ideas took form in three of his works, published in the early years of the reform he initiated: The *Sixty-Seven Conclusions* (1523), the compendium *Short Christian Introduction* (1523), and the essay *Commentary on True and False Religion* (1525). Zwingli had personal contacts with Luther, although this relationship did not lead to a shared vision of doctrine, especially with reference to the Eucharist.

Several historical events, above all military defeat and the death of Zwingli in the battle of Kappel, led Zwingli's followers to become part of Calvin's reform movement. John Calvin, in 1536, began to implement his political-religious ideas in the city of Geneva but was expelled from it after two years. Returning to full activity in 1541, he devoted all his energies to the construction of a kind of "city-church," based on the famous ordinances he promoted.

Calvin established a theocratic society that was highly intransigent on ethical issues, both in the private and public sphere. He set up a form of government based on pastors elected by each congregation. These pastors were flanked by doctors and elders and assisted by deacons. Calvin gave great importance to both civil and religious education.[79] The Reformers, or "Calvinists," spread to the Netherlands (with the decisive support of William of Orange), as well as France, Hungary, Romania, and Scotland. In the latter country, the Reform was implemented in 1560 by the work of John Knox, whose followers took the name of "Presbyterians." From Scotland, this community migrated to North America, which today has one of the largest populations of Presbyterians. As a whole, the Reformed tradition has more than 87 million adherents, gathered in the World Communion of Reformed Churches.[80]

Calvin's thought, which was the fruit of his extensive preaching in the cathedral of Geneva, is explained in his work *Institutes of the Christian Religion*. This book was first published in 1536 and successively expanded until the definitive edition of 1560. The *Institutes* is a true theological *summa* of Reformed Protestantism. In it, Calvin resolutely distances himself from medieval tradition, and particularly from scholasticism, in an attempt to restore the primitive purity of Christianity. Calvin had a high appreciation

79 De Rosa, *Teologia protestante: Momenti e figure*, 36–39.
80 Bouchard, *Chiese e movimenti evangelici*, 45.

for the Church's unity and longed for unity with the Roman Catholic Church, though he insisted that Catholics recognize the ecclesiality of the Protestant communities.[81]

The *Institutes* and the *Heidelberg Catechism* (1563) constitute the most significant writings of the Reformed Church, though they are not considered binding for these churches. The Calvinist doctrine substantially takes up Lutheran doctrine, but in a more radical way. The Church is the "community of the predestined"; there is a strong emphasis on the transcendence and the majesty of God; and the moral life tends towards rigorism, as a consequence of the total corruption of man. In the "Lord's Supper," as Calvinists describe the Eucharist, only a spiritual presence of Christ is affirmed. In general, Calvinism is quite similar to Lutheranism, though it has the particular characteristic of rejecting the episcopate, as a result of which Calvinists are called Presbyterians in some countries. Another specific characteristic is the common dignity which Calvinism assigns to both the Old and the New Testament, which has helped to exclude the anti-Jewish positions present in the writings of Luther.

With regard to worship, Reformed churches possess a great sobriety and simplicity, so as to avoid any kind of mediation in the direct access of the believer to the word of God. Hence, their liturgies lack flowers, incense, liturgical vestments, and the like, although music has great importance. Preachers wear a black pulpit gown, an austere symbol of authority. Calvinist spirituality is centered on the reading of the Bible and greatly fosters a drive for action and progress. Calvinists in England took on the name of "Puritans" as a result of their initial desire to "purify" the Church of papalist remnants. Calvinist Puritanism is, however, more known today as an ethical outlook which had great influence in the American democratic project and in the education of many generations of the Western world, above all through renowned universities such as Yale, Princeton, and Harvard.

In the twentieth century, Calvinism in its original form was taken up and reshaped by prominent thinkers such as Karl Barth (1884–1968) and Oscar Cullmann (1902–1999). Barth taught at Göttingen and Bonn in Germany before returning to his hometown of Basel due to his opposition to Nazism. In the second edition of his commentary on the Letter to the Romans (1922), Barth departs from the liberal Protestant tradition, to which he had adhered to up to then, and lays the foundations of his greatest

81 Whitlock, *Divided We Fall*, 49–52.

contribution to contemporary theology: dialectical theology. In this theology, the Word of God is placed at the center of theological thought and serves as a link between the infinite transcendence of God and the egocentric finitude of man. This line of thought deepens further in 1927 with *Prolegomena to Church Dogmatics*.

The most ecclesiologically relevant work of Barth is, without doubt, *Church Dogmatics*, which began with the publication of the first of thirteen volumes in 1932 and remained unfinished at the time of his death. In this work, Barth rejects outright the "preambles of faith" (*preambula fidei*) traditional in fundamental theology, since the only access to the totally transcendent God is that of supernatural Revelation. Another traditional concept, the *analogia entis*, or analogy by which one can come to know God through created reality, is completely rejected. The Church is understood from the dogmatic point of view as having a strongly Trinitarian and Christological imprint, in which the emphasis shifts from the "community of the predestined" to those who are chosen by God in Christ.[82]

Cullmann was a professor of early church history in his hometown of Strasbourg as well as in Paris. He was also a great scholar of the New Testament and a passionate participant in ecumenism, serving as an observer at the Second Vatican Council. He is known above all for his book *Christ and Time* (1946), in which history is considered as a dimension of salvation and, still further, as the place where salvation is realized. In the work, the Kingdom of God appears as a truly historical reality as well as an eschatological one. Thus, Cullmann distances himself from the "demythologization" of Christianity initiated by Rudolf Bultmann. Cullmann's work *Peter: Disciple, Apostle, Martyr* (1952) has a more immediate relevance to ecumenism. In this work, contrary to the opinion then prevailing in Protestant exegesis, Cullmann affirms that the words of Matthew 16:13–19, addressed by Jesus to Peter, give him a genuine primacy. This precedence of Peter, however, did not involve succession, though it could serve as a model for the exercise of ecclesial authority. Another work with a strong ecumenical dimension is *Unity through Diversity* (1986). The ideas in this essay have found traction in ecumenical dialogue, although the work as a whole has been judged minimalist by both Catholics and Protestants.[83]

82 Aldo Moda, *Strutture della fede: Un dialogo con Karl Barth* (Padua: Edizioni Messaggero, 1990).

83 Giovanni Iammarrone, "Cullmann, Oscar," in Pacomio and Occhipinti, *Dizionario dei teologi*, 341–44.

Calvinists participate in the ecumenical movement less enthusiastically than the other groups born from the sixteenth-century Reformation. This is mainly due to their specific ecclesiology, which leaves little room for the visible dimension of the Church. The relationship of Calvinism with Lutheranism crystallized in the form of communion called "reconciled diversity," the basis of the 1973 Leuenberg Agreement.[84] An official dialogue between the World Communion of the Reformed Churches and the Catholic Church has already concluded its fourth phase. The first phase (1970–1977) ended with the publication of *The Presence of Christ in Church and World*; the second (1984–1989) with the report *Towards a Common Understanding of the Church*; the third (1998–2005) with the document *The Church as Community of Common Witness to the Kingdom of God*. The fourth and most recent phase lasted from 2011–2015 and produced *Justification and Sacramentality: The Christian Community as an Agent for Justice*.

THE ANGLICAN COMMUNION

Even though the origin of the Church of England had its immediate motivation in the issue of heredity and the consequent desire of King Henry VIII to obtain the nullification of his marriage, one should keep in mind the background of the centuries preceding this event. In this period, the seeds of the Anglican Communion were already present among broad sections of English society. In fact, in the fourteenth century, the reformist movement of John Wycliffe (1320–1384) took root, and the popular Lollardy movement kept his evangelical theology alive. In the sixteenth century, Luther's influence was felt, along with that of the humanism of Erasmus of Rotterdam. John Tyndale (1494–1536) successfully made an English translation of the Bible, which would serve as the basis for the future King James Version of 1611.

When King Henry VIII proclaimed himself head of the Church of England by means of the Act of Supremacy (1534), the schism took place. The later Act of Uniformity, during the long reign of Elizabeth I (1568–1603), definitively confirmed the break with Rome. In the Elizabethan Religious Settlement, Archbishop Thomas Cranmer (in office 1533–1555), the cleric Richard Hooker (1544–1600), and Bishop John Jewel (1522–1571) played important roles. Cranmer helped consolidate the ecclesial positions

84 Text available in Hotchkiss and Pelikan, *Creeds and Confessions*, 3:744–52.

of government. Hooker—especially with his work *Ecclesiastical Polity*, in eight volumes—gave Anglicanism a theological framework.[85] Through Jewel—by means of his essay *The Apology of the Church of England* (1562)—the English reform acquired credibility outside the bounds of the Church of England.

Later, in the seventeenth century, "Carolingian" theology, more devoted to a compromise position, flourished. This school of thought was the work of the Caroline Divines, so called because they were protected first by King Charles I and then by Charles II. The Authorized Version of the Bible, also known as the King James Version, was published in 1611 and had a major impact on English culture and language. At the same time, however, the Puritan movement, with similarities to Calvinism, emerged within the English Church. The movement was particularly hostile to Catholicism and hierarchical structures of an episcopal nature. Puritanism became particularly strong under the leadership of Oliver Cromwell (1599–1658), Lord Protector from 1653 until his death.

Born from a schism which was largely motivated by issues unrelated to the Church, Anglicanism initially emerged without a specific set of doctrines, but within the great catholic tradition. The desire for a specific identity led this church to take its theological ideas first from Lutheranism and then from Calvinism. Thus, the broad spectrum that characterizes Anglicanism came to be configured: the High Church, closer to Catholicism (Anglican-Catholics); the Low Church, more inclined to Lutheranism (Anglican-Evangelicals); and the Broad Church, of a more liberal character. All of these groups identify with the contents of the *Book of Common Prayer* of 1549 and 1552. On the other hand, the famous Thirty-nine Articles, first published in 1553, later re-elaborated in 1563 and again definitively in 1571, do not enjoy general acceptance today.

The Anglican Communion spread especially in the British colonies, although it extended to other regions from the nineteenth century onwards due to emigration and missionary efforts. After independence, the church in the United States separated from the Church of England and took the name of the Episcopalian Church in 1789. At the global level, the Anglican Church is a communion of autonomous churches. These recognize the seat of the Church of England, held by the archbishop of Canterbury, as having

85 Aidan Nichols, *The Panther and the Hind: A Theological History of Anglicanism* (Edinburgh: T and T Clark, 1994), 37–53.

a primacy of honor over the whole Anglican communion. Nonetheless, the archbishop of Canterbury does not have authority over the other churches. All the churches participate in the Lambeth Conference, which since 1867 has been held every 10 or 12 years. The conference has no legislative power and its decisions are not binding. Currently, the Anglican Communion numbers about 82 million faithful distributed in 39 different provinces.[86]

The Lambeth Conference of 1888 has a particular doctrinal relevance for its famous document known as the *Chicago-Lambeth Quadrilateral*, which elaborated four pillars upon which the Anglican Communion rests. The first of these is Scripture, considered "as containing all things necessary to salvation" and therefore the norm and rule of faith. The second pillar involves the creeds, especially the Apostles' and Nicene Creeds, which are considered to be the baptismal symbols *par excellence* and authentic summaries of faith. Third are baptism and the Eucharist, held to be the only two sacraments willed by Christ himself. The fourth and final pillar is the *historic episcopate*, affirmed to be an essential element of the Church.[87] The question of the historic episcopate has become crucial in ecumenical dialogue, especially since the end of the nineteenth century, following the refusal by the Catholic Church to recognize the validity of Anglican ordinations.[88]

Perhaps the most distinguishing characteristic of Anglicanism can be expressed by the word *comprehensiveness*. This relatively recent term refers to the capacity to reunite within this Church diverse doctrinal, pastoral, and liturgical tendencies. The three orders of ordained ministry exist in all the churches. Women have been admitted to the ordained ministry since the last decade of the twentieth century and can now be ordained as bishops. The two sacraments accepted by all the Anglican churches are baptism and the Eucharist. The others are practiced to varying degrees in the different

86 Bouchard, *Chiese e movimenti evangelici*, 57–58.

87 W. R. Curtis, *The Lambeth Conferences: The Solution for Pan-Anglican Organization* (New York: Columbia University Press, 1942), 297.

88 Leo XIII, Bull *Apostolicae curae* (September 13, 1896), on Anglican ordinations; Giuseppe Rambaldi, *Ordinazioni anglicane e sacramento dell'ordine nella Chiesa: Aspetti storici e teologici a cento anni della bolla Apostolicae curae di Leone XIII* (Rome: Editrice Pontificia Università Gregoriana, 1995); Christopher Hill and Edward Yarnold, eds., *Anglican Orders: The Documents in the Debate* (Norwich: Canterbury Press, 1997); R. William Franklin, ed., *Anglican Orders: Essays on the Centenary of Apostolicae Curae 1896–1996* (London: Mowbray, 1996). A new factor is currently affecting these ordinations—namely, the fact that from the first half of the twentieth century, when Anglicans and Old Catholics acknowledged the validity of each other's ordinations, several Old Catholic bishops have participated in many Anglican episcopal ordinations as consecrating ministers. The Catholic Church does not doubt the validity of the ordinations of Old Catholic bishops. This is a very complicated matter, which we cannot delve into here.

churches, but without the sacramental sense professed in the Catholic Church. The Eucharist is always distributed under the two species, and only in some churches are the species reserved for adoration.

In the nineteenth century, religious life, which had been abolished in the days of Edward VI, was restored. With Catholic emancipation in 1829, those faithful to Rome were given back some of their civil rights and allowed to worship in private. From an ethical point of view, the Anglican-driven efforts to abolish slavery—obtained thanks to William Wilberforce in 1833—and to regulate working hours—fruit of the tenacity of Anthony Shaftesbury, in 1847—are particularly noteworthy. During this period, the poet Samuel Taylor Coleridge (1772–1834) emerged as a defender—rare at the time—of the noncontradiction between science and faith, and also as an advocate of Christianity as an exclusively moral phenomenon. In this latter conception, the unity of the Church would be built upon ethical foundations.[89]

Although the non-British Anglican churches maintain the principle of separation between church and state, the Church of England is still the official church within England. The head of the Church of England is the king or queen. The civil government takes a role in the appointment of bishops, although this task has now become a formality. Many of the bishops occupy a seat in the House of Lords.

Anglicanism has been a pioneer in the ecumenical movement. Due to its history and structure, it is considered a "bridge Church," especially between Catholics and Lutherans. The Anglicans maintain complete intercommunion with the so-called Old Catholics and with the Nordic and Baltic Lutheran Churches.[90]

With regard to the relationship of the Anglican Church to the Catholic Church, the Oxford Movement of the nineteenth century is a key point of reference. Through a return to the writings of the Fathers of the Church, this movement rediscovered the Catholic past of the Church of England and revealed a nostalgia for the unity of the Church. The great figures of this movement include John Keble, a pastor and professor of poetry at Oxford. He became well-known with his 1833 sermon "National Apostasy," in which

89 Lacoste et al., *Histoire de la théologie*, 406–7.

90 Joint Commission of the Anglican Communion and the Old Catholic Churches, *Joint Declaration* (Bonn, July 2, 1931); Lutheran World Federation, Anglican Consultative Council, et al., "The Porvoo Common Statement, Järvenpää 1992," in *Anglican-Lutheran Agreements: Regional and International Agreements 1972–2002* (Geneva: Lutheran World Federation, 2004), 145–76. The whole Anglican Communion was not involved in the agreement, but only the Churches of England, Ireland, Scotland, and Wales.

he criticized the civil authority's growing dominance over the Church and advocated for a return to the original sources of the Christian faith.

Together with John Henry Newman and Edward Bouverie Pusey, Keble began an intellectual project which developed a series of works known as *Tracts for the Times*, published between 1833 and 1841. The "Tractarians" were the principal promotors of the idea of Anglicanism as a "middle way" between Catholicism and Protestantism. They saw Christian orthodoxy as the consensus of the first five centuries. Newman first achieved renown for his work *Arians of the 4th Century* (1833), which became a classic. In 1841, he published the celebrated *Tract 90*, in which he proposed an interpretation of the Thirty-nine Articles of the Anglican Church in light of the Council of Trent. The work caused a great controversy among Newman's colleagues. Shortly after publishing *An Essay on the Development of Christian Doctrine* (1845), Newman became Catholic. His later works include *The Idea of a University* (1852), *Grammar of Assent* (1870), and *Apologia pro Vita Sua* (1864). The *Grammar* is of great importance for understanding the harmony of the act of faith with natural human reason. In *Apologia*, Newman recounts the process of his conversion.

The influence of Newman on the England of his time has been not yet been adequately appreciated, and many of his ideas remain highly relevant today. As Benedict XVI said in the homily for Newman's beatification, "his insights into the relationship between faith and reason, into the vital place of revealed religion in civilized society, and into the need for a broadly-based and wide-ranging approach to education were not only of profound importance for Victorian England, but continue today to inspire and enlighten many all over the world."[91] Newman's canonization in 2019 provided another occasion to appreciate the Oxford churchman as a figure capable of uniting Christians, in particular Anglicans and Catholics, around the apostolic faith to which he was so dedicated. As the Prince of Wales commented on this occasion, Newman's life and teaching offers a model for harmony within diversity, rooted in the mystery of the Trinity: "As such, difference is not to be feared. . . . As an Anglican, he guided that church back to its Catholic roots, and as a Catholic he was ready to learn from the Anglican tradition, such as in his promoting the role of the laity."[92]

91 Benedict XVI, "Homily at the Mass with the Beatification of Venerable Cardinal John Henry Newman," (Birmingham, September 19, 2010).

92 Charles, Prince of Wales, "John Henry Newman: The Harmony of Difference," *L'Osservatore Romano*, October 12, 2019.

A legacy of the Oxford Movement was the Anglican-Catholic contact begun by Lord Halifax and Fernand Portal in the late nineteenth century, and resumed later, under the guidance of Cardinal Mercier, in the Malines Conversations from 1921 to 1927. Over the course of these discussions, the most substantial divergences between Catholics and Anglicans were studied. Also significant from an ecumenical perspective was the Lambeth Conference of 1920. This conference addressed the entirety of the people of God and reformulated the Quadrilateral of Lambeth in a way more acceptable to the non-episcopal Christian communities.

After the Second Vatican Council, dialogue with the Catholic Church—dormant since the time of the Malines Conversations—resumed with the creation of the Anglican-Roman Catholic International Commission (ARCIC).[93] In 1981, the commission published a final report on the agreements reached during the first phase of dialogue with regard to the themes of the Eucharist, ministry, and authority in the Church.[94] However, the results did not find the same agreement with the respective ecclesiastical authorities.[95] Dialogue later continued within ARCIC II, this time more focused on ecclesiology, and in 1986 the commission issued the joint declaration *Salvation and the Church*.[96] In 1990, the Joint Declaration *The Church as Communion* was published. During this period, the admission of women to the ordained ministry created a new problem at the doctrinal level and made agreement between Anglicans and Catholics more difficult.[97] However, dialogue has continued. In 1998, ARCIC II issued another important bilateral document on authority in the Church, *The Gift of Authority*, and in 2004, the joint statement on Mariology, *Mary: Grace and Hope in Christ*, was brought to completion in Seattle. In 2011, ARCIC III was inaugurated, focusing on more specific ecclesiological questions—namely, the relationship

93 Anglican-Roman Catholic International Commission I, *The Malta Report* (February 2, 1968).

94 ARCIC I, *The Final Report* (September 3, 1981).

95 Pontifical County for Promoting Christian Unity, *The Catholic Church's Response to the Final Report of ARCIC I*, 1991.

96 The Congregation for the Doctrine of the Faith expressed its reservations with its *Observations on ARCIC II's "Salvation and the Church"* (November 18, 1988).

97 Joseph Ratzinger, "Problems and Prospects of the Anglican—Catholic Dialogue," in *Church, Ecumenism and Politics: New Endeavors in Ecclesiology*, trans. Michael J. Miller et al. (San Francisco: Ignatius Press, 2008), 69–99. The "Porvoo Common Statement" mentioned above also raises problems in Catholic-Anglican dialogue, because it takes positions regarding apostolic succession which are not compatible with Catholic doctrine. On this and other difficulties, see Charles Morerod, "Réflexions sur l'Accord de Porvoo entre Anglicans et Luthériens," *Nova et Vetera* 72, no. 3 (1997): 71–103.

between the universal Church and local churches, and the Church's discernment of ethical teaching.[98] Since the year 2000, the International Anglican-Roman Catholic Commission for Unity and Mission (IARCCUM) has existed, charged with tasks complementary to the work of ARCIC.

In recent times, the issue of homosexuality, including at the presbyterial and episcopal level, has led to division within the Anglican Communion, with inevitable consequences in the ecumenical sphere. The election of some women to the episcopate and the establishment of the Global Anglican Future Conference (2008) have also complicated the picture. This conference, which seems opposed to the Lambeth Conference, tends to blur the unique identity of the Anglican Church as an interlocutor for the Catholic Church.[99] Some Anglican faithful considered the recent developments within the Anglican Communion to be the last straw and sought admission to full Catholic communion. In light of this pastoral reality, Benedict XVI established the personal ordinariates with the Apostolic Constitution *Anglicanorum coetibus* of 2009. This constitution made it possible to receive groups of Anglicans into the Catholic Church as communities, while allowing them to preserve their Anglican liturgical and spiritual patrimony within Catholicism. So far, three personal ordinariates have been erected, covering England, the United States, and Australia, as well as some neighboring countries. We will return to this subject later on.

CONGREGATIONALISTS

Congregationalism carries the Calvinist ecclesiological premises to their logical conclusions and favors the local assembly of believers. This assembly is called together by the word, a word which is welcomed with personal and free decision on the part of each individual. From these principles, one can understand why only adults are baptized, and why this group rejects any institutional structure and dependence, especially on the civil government. The community of the faithful, even if small and limited, is considered to be the Church in the true and proper sense. Congregationalism lacks any centralist tendency. Similarly, all the faithful are equal; pastors are considered as such exclusively for practical reasons. Congregational churches—they do not always use this name—arose in the seventeenth century as an

98 *Service d'Information* 136 (2011): 19.

99 Giuseppe Dal Ferro, "L'anglicanesimo, presenza cristiana di comunione," *Studi Ecumenici* 39, no. 2 (2011): 62–264.

anticonformist movement in opposition to the structures of the Church of England. The same can be said of Baptists, Pentecostals and more generally the Free Churches, in addition to Congregationalists in the strict sense.[100]

The latter group has its origin in Robert Browne. Towards the end of the sixteenth century, he coined the first definition of the Congregational Church: a "company or number of Christians or believers, which, by a willing covenant made with their God, are under the government of God and Christ, and keep his laws in one holy communion."[101] Calling, congregation, and alliance are key themes of Congregational ecclesiology. Many elements of the Westminster Confession of 1643, a document from the Presbyterian ecclesiastical sphere, are also significant in the Congregational vision of the Church. The community has experienced developments and divisions. During the nineteenth century in the United States, a particular divergence took root between liberal tendencies, known as the Unitarians, and other more traditionalist tendencies, known as Trinitarians.

From a historical point of view, Congregationalism is linked to John Robinson (1576–1625). He and other Anglicans emigrated to Holland and founded a community there. They then embarked on the famous voyage of the *Mayflower*. In 1621, they arrived on the coast of Massachusetts. The Pilgrims who survived the harsh initial winter felt the need to offer gratitude to God and started the tradition of Thanksgiving Day. The original thirteen colonies tended towards a typically theocratic form of society, sometimes known as the New England style. This style became in some ways an interdenominational ecclesial model, shared in great part by the Mennonite, Baptist, Presbyterian, and Methodist traditions, and was also very influential among the "Free Churches" of England and Scotland.

The Congregational phenomenon was very prominent in the work of interdenominational cooperation. Some such enterprises, such as the American Education Society (1815) and the American Bible Society (1816), were geared towards special goals. At other times, the cooperative efforts were directed towards greater ecclesial impact, as seen in the Congregational Union of England and Wales (1832) and the United Church of Christ (1957) in the United States. Congregationalism has also fostered international

100 s.v. "Congregationalism," in Cross and Livingstone, *The Oxford Dictionary of the Christian Church*, 399–400; Johann Adam Möhler Institut, *Le chiese cristiane nel Duemila*, 255–62.
101 Robert Browne, *Life and Manners of all Christians* (Middleburgh: Painter, 1582), quoted in John Browne, *History of Congregationalism and Memorials of the Churches in Norfolk and Suffolk* (London: Jarrold and Sons, 1877), 34.

coordination through such organisms as the International Congregational Council (1891) and the International Federation of Free Evangelical Churches (1948).[102]

The Congregationalist movement, quite widespread by the eighteenth century, has had a considerable influence on the independence movement of the United States and on American culture. Some examples are the foundations of Harvard University (1636), Yale (1701) and Princeton (1746); the Abolitionist movement (among other ways, through the work of Harriet Beecher Stowe, author *of Uncle Tom's Cabin*), and the Social Gospel movement, which became widespread in the later part of the nineteenth century. Doctrinally the Congregationalists are very close to Calvinism. An accentuated parochialism has been the cause of frequent controversies among themselves and with other Christian denominations.[103]

BAPTIST COMMUNITIES

Baptists have their historical roots in Anabaptism. This latter movement was contemporary to Zwingli but more radical, with a very firm position on the rejection of the baptism of children and the necessity of adult baptism. Because of their pacifism and their total refusal to cooperate with the state, the Anabaptists were harshly persecuted and almost disappeared completely. At the beginning of the seventeenth century, the movement took shape again in the Christian community founded in Holland by the Anglican cleric John Smyth. This group was intended to be a counterpoint to the institutionalism prevailing in the Anglican churches of that time. The same phenomenon occurred in London through the work of Thomas Helwys. In Holland, meanwhile, a parallel movement was led by Menno Simons. His followers were known as "Mennonites," and this community was an anti-conformist reaction to the official churches of Protestantism. These movements converged in the Baptist phenomenon. Due to persecution in the Old World, the Baptists spread more widely among the British colonies in America. The first American Baptist church was founded by Roger Williams in Providence, Rhode Island in 1631.

The Baptist churches increased greatly during the eighteenth and nineteenth centuries. This growth led to a strong presence in the African Amer-

102 T. F. Rossi, "Ecclesiologia congregazionalista," in Calabrese, Goyret, and Piazza, *Dizionario di ecclesiologia*, 479–85.
103 Bosch, *Para comprender el ecumenismo*, 73–74.

ican community. In the United States, Baptists are divided, for doctrinal reasons along with historical issues regarding the question of slavery, between the churches of the North, the South, and the African American community. In the second half of the nineteenth century, through the work of the German businessman Johann Gerhard Oncken, Baptist churches spread widely in the German-speaking European countries. The twentieth century was a period of further expansion in the United States, due in part to the well-known pastor Martin Luther King Jr., as well as such politically and economically important figures as President Harry Truman and billionaire John Rockefeller. The last century was also the period of the development of Gospel music and African American spirituals. According to the Baptist World Alliance Website, in 2016 there were forty-eight million Baptists belonging to 238 member bodies.[104]

For Baptists, the Bible is the only rule of faith and life. There is no official doctrine or binding tradition, though the doctrine which has been developed by Baptists coincides, in its essential points, with Calvinism. Baptist ecclesiology is of a Congregationalist type, which views the Church as consisting exclusively of convinced believers. Each local community is completely autonomous, and separation from the state is held to be essential. Elders, who are nominated from among the members, preside over each community. This structure does not, however, eliminate the radical equality among all the baptized. The fundamental part of Baptist worship is preaching, which is intensely biblical and has a strong emotional component. Baptism is administered by immersion and only to adults, and the Eucharist is celebrated as simply a remembrance of the Lord's Supper. The other sacraments are not accepted.[105]

The World Baptist Alliance has begun conversations with the Catholic Church and, at the end of the meetings held between 1984 and 1988, a report was published on the convergences and divergences between the two communities.[106] The issues dealt with included the person and the work of Christ, discipleship and proselytism, and witness. A second round of dialogue, from 2006–2010, produced the report *The Word of God in the Life of the Church.*

104 Bouchard, *Chiese e movimenti evangelici*, 71. More information is in the entry "Baptists," in Cross and Livingstone, *The Oxford Dictionary of the Christian Church*, 154; and in Johann Adam Möhler Institut, *Le chiese cristiane nel Duemila*, 269–71.

105 Bosch, *Para comprender el ecumenismo*, 72–73.

106 Report *Summons to Witness to Christ in Today's World* (Falls Church, Va.: Baptist World Alliance, 1988); see also Gideon Goosen, *Bringing Churches Together: A Popular Introduction to Ecumenism* (Geneva: World Council of Churches, 1993), 89.

THE QUAKER COMMUNITY

The Quakers originated from dissent within Anglicanism in the seventeenth century. Although the official name of the denomination is the "Religious Society of Friends," they are more commonly known as Quakers. The term comes from the verb "to quake," due to the strong and stern words of the founder of this denomination, George Fox (1624–1691). In the face of accusation, he warned his judges to "tremble at the word of the Lord."[107] Persecuted in England as well as in Massachusetts, where they had immigrated, through the efforts of William Penn they became concentrated in the state which was named for him. The state of Pennsylvania was at first an attempt to politically realize Quaker religiosity. The refusal of any kind of proselytism or missionary activity has made them numerically few; today their population numbers around 250,000. Still, the Quakers have exerted an influence considerably larger than their numbers.[108]

Fox took a deeply anticonformist stance with regard to the Church of England. An enemy of any structure, he promoted the absolutely direct relationship of every person to God, without the need for any sacramental, liturgical, or priestly mediation. For the Quakers, therefore, it is necessary to experience the "light of Christ" in the soul and to lead a moral life cohering with that light. Quakers do not possess their own body of doctrine: they are explicitly nondogmatic. The life of their communities has little in the way of worship, and their spirituality is centered on the inner light of the Spirit of God. Their meetings, presided over by any man or woman, give ample space to silence and an attitude of meditation and adoration. Short biblical readings and some songs are allowed, though austerity prevails.

The Quakers are great defenders of religious freedom, of equality (shown in their longtime opposition to slavery), and especially of pacifism. Enemies of any war, they have often refused to perform military service and they participate in various movements in favor of peace. Quakers oppose the death penalty and the taking of oaths.

Their nature as a Christian entity has a certain ambiguity, given their diminished conception of baptism—often not practiced—and their uncertainties with regard to the Bible. Some Quakers view the Scriptures with

107 According to others, the name is connected to the "tremors" that Fox and his followers experienced in conjunction with the perception of an "inner light"; see Johann Adam Möhler Institut, *Le chiese cristiane nel Duemila*, 314.
108 Bouchard, *Chiese e movimenti evangelici*, 131.

skepticism and see them as an intervention incompatible with the vision of an absolutely direct relationship between man and God. For these reasons, Quakers do not participate in the ecumenical movement.[109]

METHODIST COMMUNITIES

The Anglican cleric John Wesley (1703–1791) emerged in the context of the English anticonformism of the eighteenth century, when the first signs of the Industrial Revolution and scientific and philosophical Enlightenment appeared on the horizon. Although he never had the intention of founding a church separate from the Church of England, he is the father of the Methodist Churches which arose after his death. Wesley was a university lecturer, a devout Anglican, and a great admirer of Thomas à Kempis's *Imitation of Christ*.

On May 24, 1738, he had an intense spiritual experience after a reading of Luther's *Preface to the Letter of St. Paul to the Romans* in community. Wesley experienced within himself the forgiveness of his sins. From that moment on, he devoted his entire life to spreading a religious experience centered on the love of God, the forgiveness of sins, and the gratuitousness of justification by faith. He immediately promoted, at Oxford University, a religious system of life which included Bible study, almsgiving, and participation in the Holy Supper. The name of the movement he started came from the extremely "methodical" nature of this system. Wesley was a tireless preacher for the working class, in streets and in public squares, and advocated numerous social reforms in favor of workers. Thus, he gave Methodism its characteristic feature of union between preaching and social action. Wesley was also a great composer of sacred hymns, which continue to be sung today.

While it encountered opposition in England, Methodism spread widely in the United States due to its strong missionary dynamism and had a vital role in the Great Awakening. The latter movement had a significant impact on the life of immigrants to the United States during the eighteenth century. Central to this movement were the Calvinist Jonathan Edwards (1703–1758) and his widely read work *Religious Affections* (1746).

The theological structure of Methodism contains many elements taken from the sixteenth-century Reformation and from the subsequent Pietism. Still, since the movement came about in an anticonformist context and

109 Bosch, *Para comprender el ecumenismo*, 78–80.

without fundamental doctrinal motivations at its root, Methodists do not possess a clear and defined body of doctrine. Wesley's preaching is of great importance, along with the "General Rules," which were given by Wesley to his communities in 1743 and are substantially ethical in content. Also crucial to the doctrine of Methodism are the twenty-five articles prepared by Wesley for the American Methodist movement in 1784.[110]

The Methodists have suffered numerous divisions over the course of their history, including a difference of positions with regard to slavery. In 1881 they were able to join together in the World Methodist Conference, based in Lake Junaluska, North Carolina. The Methodist community has a general resemblance to the churches of the Protestant tradition as well as some aspects specific to the Congregationalists. From Calvinism, the Methodists have taken a rather pessimistic view of human nature. However, their spirituality emphasizes the cooperation of the believer and an intense life of meditation and contemplation. This asceticism finds expression in small group meetings for mutual encouragement and for the confession of faults. There are more than 50 million Methodists worldwide.[111]

The dialogue with the Catholic Church has the particularity that there was no immediate dispute between the two communities since Methodism arose from a division within Anglicanism. In the first published reports of Methodist-Catholic dialogue—Denver 1971, Dublin 1975, Honolulu 1981—topics such as ecclesial praxis, spirituality, moral life, and practical collaboration are dealt with.[112] In the second phase of the dialogue, the documents deal more closely with the most substantial areas of difference.[113] Since then, the Joint International Commission has focused on the Church and the sacraments, reaching significant convergence in two reports: *The Grace Given You in Christ: Catholics and Methodists Reflect Further on the Church* (Seoul, 2006); and *Encountering Christ the Saviour: Church and Sacraments* (Durban, 2011). Their 2016 report, from a meeting in Houston, is entitled *The Call to Holiness: from Glory to Glory* and considers how the two

110 John Wesley, "Methodist Articles of Religion," in *The Creeds of Christendom*, 4th ed., ed. Philip Schaff (Grand Rapids, Mich.: Baker Book House, 1977), 3:807–13.

111 Bouchard, *Chiese e movimenti evangelici*, 81.

112 Pontifical Council for Promoting Christian Unity, *The Denver Report* (1971), *The Dublin Report* (1976), and *The Honolulu Report* (January 31, 1981).

113 Pontifical Council for Promoting Christian Unity, Report *Towards a Statement on the Church* (Nairobi, 1986); and Report *The Apostolic Tradition* (Singapore, 1991). Dialogue has continued quite regularly and has produced other documents: *The Word of Life* (Rio, 1996), *Speaking the Truth in Love* (Brighton, 2001), *The Grace Given You in Christ* (Seoul, 2006). More information is found in Goosen, *Bringing Churches Together*, 89.

communities "understand the nature and effect of divine grace upon the human person and the implications for the Christian life."[114] Most recently, in 2021, representatives of the United Methodist Church and the United States Conference of Catholic Bishops issued the first book of a two-part publication entitled *Catholics and United Methodists Together*. The work represents a continued attempt to deepen communion through an emphasis on shared belief and prayer.

ADVENTIST COMMUNITIES

Adventism was born in the nineteenth century in the United States, on the wave of the Second Great Awakening in the Anglo-Saxon Protestant world. The initial spark came from a particular eschatological revelation said to have been received by the Baptist William Miller (d. 1849). Miller is universally recognized as the initiator of contemporary Adventism, even though the movement had other precursors. After erroneous predictions of the second coming of Christ, the Adventist movement received the decisive support of Ellen Gould Harmon (1827–1915). Harmon, initially Methodist, wrote numerous books on eschatological issues and was better known as "Mrs. White."

Often divided because of eschatological issues, the most important Adventist Church is known as the Seventh-day Adventist Church, which began in 1860, followed by other minor denominations. This movement's numerous radio stations and publishing houses have facilitated its spread, along with the boost of a massive distribution of Bibles, books, newspapers, and similar publications. The revival of the Jewish principle of tithing, by which every Adventist gives the church 10 percent of his or her earnings, greatly facilitates the financing of missionary structures.

Seventh-day Adventists are conservative Evangelicals, faithful to the traditional doctrines of the Reformation and defenders of a morality with a clearly Puritan bent. Without a doubt, their particular doctrines on eschatological subjects—with regard to the second coming of Christ, the mortality of the souls of the condemned, millenarianism, and so on—make them appear to many as a sect. They celebrate the biblical Sabbath on Saturday instead of Sunday. The human body, as a temple of the Holy Spirit, is held in high esteem. Hence, they have a strong interest in health institutions

114 Joint International Commission for Dialogue between the World Methodist Council and the Roman Catholic Church, *The Call to Holiness: From Glory to Glory* (2016), 4.

(they operate numerous medical centers), are inclined to a vegetarian diet, and generally disapprove of coffee, tea, pork, alcohol, and tobacco.[115]

The cooperation of the Adventists in the reunification of the Church is basically nonexistent; they do not belong to any ecumenical body. Their number is currently around 20 million.[116]

THE OLD CATHOLIC CHURCH

This Church is also known as the Christian Catholic Church or Union of Utrecht. It arose when some Christian communities of Central Europe rejected the dogma of papal infallibility, proclaimed by the First Vatican Council in 1870. These groups joined a small church that already existed in the Netherlands, and which had separated from Rome because it rejected the Bull *Unigenitus* of 1713 against Jansenism. The Old Catholic Church is episcopal in nature and has just over 500,000 faithful.

The doctrinal foundation for the Old Catholic Church is contained in the Utrecht Declaration of 1889. The most notable feature of this declaration is the veneration for the most ancient tradition of the Church, which is the basis for the rejection of the supposed innovations of the First Vatican Council. Consonant with this attitude, the Old Catholics also reject the Marian dogmas of the Immaculate Conception and of the Assumption. The Old Catholics have the triple ministry of the episcopate, the presbyterate, and the diaconate; celibacy of clerics was abolished in the early twentieth century. They believe in the seven sacraments, even though they have stopped practicing individual confession.

A founding member of the World Council of Churches, the Old Catholic Church maintains a total internal communion with the Anglican Churches and recognizes the validity of Anglican ordinations. In ecumenical dialogue, the Old Catholics maintain relations above all with Catholics and Orthodox.[117]

EVANGELICAL CHURCHES

The Evangelicals have great relevance for the Church today as well as for ecumenism, though they do not fall strictly within the bounds of a specific denomination. Evangelicalism refers to a transdenominational movement

115 Bosch, *Para comprender el ecumenismo*, 75–77.
116 Bouchard, *Chiese e movimenti evangelici*, 95.
117 Johann Adam Möhler Institut, *Le chiese cristiane nel Duemila*, 324–31.

which emphasizes conversion by being "born again" though faith in Jesus Christ. Through this experience, the Christian is justified by faith, enabled to live a holy life through the Spirit, and by the Spirit united with all other believers in the Body of Christ.[118] Evangelicals accept the Bible as the supreme authority in matters of faith and conduct and are marked by their willingness to spread their faith to others. In spite of many distinctions, they share the key theological convictions of the sixteenth-century Protestant Reformers.[119]

The word *evangelical* comes from the Greek noun *euangelion*, which has the original sense of "good news." The New Testament regularly uses this word to describe the "glad tidings" of Christ's coming to earth for the salvation of man.[120] In the sixteenth century, the word began to take on a more specific meaning to describe the Protestant Reformation. In this context, *evangelical* described Martin Luther and his followers and their desire for a Christ-centered and Bible-centered reform of the Church.[121] In the sixteenth century, the Lutherans, who stressed faith in Christ and adherence to Scripture, were known as Evangelicals. The term served to distinguish the followers of Luther from Calvinists, who were known as the Reformed.

Over the centuries, the word "Evangelical'" has come to take on a significance beyond the Lutheran community. The eighteenth-century religious revivals in Europe, Great Britain, and North America were generally referred to as the Evangelical revival.[122] In this time period, the word took on the specific sense it has today and alluded to Protestants who place "a heightened emphasis on experiencing the redeeming work of Christ personally and on spreading the good news of that message."[123] The growing strength of the movement led to the formation of the World Evangelical Alliance in London in 1846.

118 "Statement of Faith," Who We Are, World Evangelical Alliance, https://worldea.org/en/who-we-are/statement-of-faith/.

119 Basil Meeking and John Stott, eds., Introduction to *The Evangelical-Roman Catholic Dialogue on Mission, 1977–1984: A Report* (Grand Rapids, Mich.: Eerdmans, 1986), http://www.vatican.va/roman_curia/pontifical_councils/chrstuni/evangelicals-docs/rc_pc_chrstuni_doc_20141007_report-1977–1984_en.html.

120 Mark A. Noll, "Defining Evangelicalism," in *Global Evangelicalism: Theology, History and Culture in Regional Perspective*, ed. Donald M. Lewis and Richard V. Pierard (Downers Grove, Ill.: InterVarsity Press, 2014), 19.

121 Noll, "Defining Evangelicalism," 20.

122 *Encyclopedia Britannica Online*, s.v. "Evangelical Church," last modified July 19, 2016, https://www.britannica.com/topic/Evangelical-church-Protestantism.

123 Noll, "Defining Evangelicalism," 20.

In the face of the pressures towards liberalism and fundamentalism faced by the main Protestant denominations in the mid-twentieth century, the Evangelical movement emerged as a significant cultural force, strengthened by charismatic preachers such as Billy Graham. In this context, the term "Evangelical" came to designate a group of Christians who, across denominational boundaries, sought to remain faithful to core Christian belief and at the same time remain in dialogue with the modern world.[124] This group also experienced a rapid worldwide expansion during the last century, such that today Evangelicals have a large presence in Africa, Latin America, and Asia.[125]

Currently, the World Evangelical Alliance serves as an institutional voice for the more than six hundred million evangelical Christians.[126] The National Association of Evangelicals, founded in 1942, offers a network which represents Evangelical Christians in the United States.[127] The Evangelical movement is not a monolithic entity, and the Catholic Church was not able to begin a dialogue with Evangelicals in an official manner until 1977. The dialogue began not so much as a search for unity, but as "a search for such common ground as might be discovered between Evangelicals and Roman Catholics as they each try to be more faithful in their obedience to mission."[128] The dialogue has served to highlight the authentic points of unity between Catholics and Evangelicals, particularly regarding Jesus Christ, the Scriptures, and evangelization, as well as to elaborate more precisely the points of disagreement. Most recently, the International Consultation between the Catholic Church and the World Evangelical Alliance, which took place from 2009–2016, published its report *'Scripture and Tradition' and 'the Church in Salvation': Catholics and Evangelicals Explore Challenges and Opportunities*. The document expresses the desire to work together on the common challenges faced by Christians today, grounded in a common faith in the Trinity and appreciation for the Scriptures.

The emergence of Evangelicals as a dominant force in Christianity has brought with it a new and more complex dynamic for ecumenism. In large

124 *Encyclopedia Britannica Online*, s.v. "Evangelical Church," last modified July 29, 2016, https://www.britannica.com/topic/Evangelical-church-Protestantism.
125 Noll, "Defining Evangelicalism," 17.
126 "Our History," Who We Are, World Evangelical Alliance, https://worldea.org/en/who-we-are/our-history/.
127 National Association of Evangelicals homepage, https://www.nae.net/
128 Meeking and Stott, Introduction to *The Evangelical-Roman Catholic Dialogue on Mission, 1977–1984, A Report*, paragraph 3.

part, the growth of Evangelicals has coincided with a decline in membership with the traditional Protestant denominations.[129] Evangelicals tend to prefer small, independent churches which often maintain a loose association with one another. While this identity makes official theological dialogue difficult, the Evangelicals nonetheless remain a very significant Christian force. Their faithfulness to fundamental Christian teachings offers a valuable basis for unity with other Christian denominations and the Catholic Church. The effort to bear common witness to Gospel values in the face of the contemporary challenges has given rise to such initiatives as the 1994 statement *Evangelicals and Catholics Together: The Christian Mission in the Third Millennium*, signed by various leaders within the respective communities. The document expresses the "necessary connection between the visible unity of Christians and the mission of the one Christ" and the resolve "to explore patterns of working and witnessing together in order to advance the one mission of Christ."[130] The authentic Christian values found among Evangelicals have led many of them to appreciate the need for a deeper sense of ecclesial unity, especially in the face of social fragmentation.[131] Perhaps this recognition offers a point of dialogue with the Catholic Church and other ecclesial communities so as to arrive to a more complete vision of the Church. At the same time, the spiritual vibrancy of Evangelicals offers a pressing call for Catholics and other ecclesial communities to appreciate the central Gospel truths which are the foundation of the Church as a visible institution.

PENTECOSTALISM

This phenomenon originated in American Protestant circles at the beginning of the twentieth century. Some itinerant preachers of different denominations agreed on the need to help faithful who seemed dormant have a living experience of holiness by means of a new Pentecost. This new outpouring of the Spirit would begin with "baptism in the Spirit" and develop through the gifts and power of the Spirit, mentioned in 1 Corinthians and Romans 12.

The first strong experience of this kind, with the speaking of tongues, took place on April 9, 1906, in Los Angeles, in response to William Sey-

129 Whitlock, *Divided We Fall*, 125.
130 "Evangelicals and Catholics Together: The Christian Mission in the Third Millennium," *First Things*, May 1994, https://www.firstthings.com/article/1994/05/evangelicals-catholics-together-the-christian-mission-in-the-third-millennium.
131 Whitlock, *Divided We Fall*, 76–80, 161.

mour's preaching. This date is considered to be the starting point of the Pentecostal movement. Rejected by their denominations of origin, the Pentecostal preachers went on to found the first autonomous communities, not always with their current name. Today, the Assemblies of God, which arose in Hot Springs, Arkansas in 1914, make up the largest group within Pentecostalism. The ecclesiastical structure of the Pentecostal communities is quite varied, from a Congregationalist- or Methodist-type model to more specific forms established by the founders of the respective communities.

Pentecostals accept the basic doctrinal framework of Protestantism and strongly tend towards liberality in interpreting the Bible; in general, they are opposed to exegetical studies. They place great emphasis on sanctification and the manifestation of the works of the Spirit by means of the gifts of tongues, healing power, and prophecy. The church model described in Acts of the Apostles is normative for them. Baptism is practiced by immersion, and the Eucharist is considered only as a commemoration of the Lord's Supper. On the moral level, Pentecostals promote a decidedly Puritan ethos with very practical consequences: alcohol, tobacco, and drugs are forbidden. Pentecostal spirituality is strongly based on the emotions.

As an interdenominational phenomenon, the number of Pentecostals is thought to perhaps reach six hundred million members (equivalent to 25 percent of all Christianity), although it is difficult to establish precise statistics.[132] Purified of its non-Catholic elements, its influence on the Catholic Church has given rise to several movements of renewal in the Spirit.[133]

The dialogue between the Catholic Church and non-Catholic Pentecostalism, initiated in 1969, has a peculiar character, given the ambiguous institutional status of the movement. Rather than reestablishing unity, the first years of conversation sought to develop a climate of mutual understanding and to find common aims for collaboration.[134] The second phase of the dialogue, from 1977 to 1982, was summarized in a *Final Report* regarding the differences in theological understanding and spiritual experience.[135] The third phase of dialogue, from 1985 to 1989, produced the document *Perspectives on Koinonia*, and manifested a growing interest on the

132 Bouchard, *Chiese e movimenti evangelici*, 108.

133 Bosch, *Para comprender el ecumenismo*, 77–78.

134 *Final Report of the Dialogue between the Secretariat for Promoting Christian Unity of the Roman Catholic Church and Leaders of Some Pentecostal Churches and Participants in the Charismatic Movement within Protestant and Anglican Churches 1972–1976* (1976).

135 *Final Report of the Dialogue between the Secretariat for Promoting Christian Unity of the Roman Catholic Church and Some Classical Pentecostals 1977–1982* (May 9, 1984).

part of the Pentecostal community.[136] The fourth phase of conversations, which lasted from 1990 to 1997, ended with the publication of the report *Evangelization, Proselytism and Common Witness.* Subsequent dialogues have focused on Christian initiation, baptism in the Spirit, and charisms in the life of the Church.[137]

Although the lack of a strong institutional element can make for difficulties in ecumenical dialogue with the Pentecostals, the intense growth of this phenomenon in recent years has been a renewed cause for reflection. As Pope Francis commented in 2018 with regard to Pentecostals, as well charismatics and Evangelicals, "the constant growth of these new expressions of Christian life is a very significant phenomenon, which cannot be overlooked."[138] A greater spirit of dialogue and cooperation with these groups, Francis continued, can help Catholics to recognize the elements in these communities which are "by no means devoid of meaning and value in the mystery of salvation (cf. *Unitatis Redintegratio*, no. 3)," and even the departure of Catholic faithful to these communities can become a motive for "examination and pastoral renewal."

Pentecostalism recalls to Catholics those essential elements of the Church which go beyond the institutional aspect. The Roman pontiff expressed his hope that, through a growth in fraternal relations, these separated Christians "will be helped to overcome prejudices about the Catholic Church and to recognize that in the priceless treasure of tradition, received from the Apostles and kept in the course of history, the Holy Spirit is not at all extinguished or suffocated, but continues to operate effectively."[139] Although both Pentecostals and Evangelicals lack the conception of visible, institutional unity essential for ecumenism, Christian communities should not neglect their significant role in Christianity today: "All churches may benefit from their vitality, their zeal for evangelism and their commitment to Scripture."[140]

FINAL CONSIDERATIONS

Though the presentation of this historical framework has been deliberately concise, one should not forget that at the origin of the great separations

136 *Perspectives on* Koinonia (1989).
137 Goosen, *Bringing Churches Together*, 90.
138 Pope Francis, "Address to Participants at the Plenary of the Pontifical Council for Promoting Christian Unity" (Vatican City, September 28, 2018).
139 Pope Francis, "Address at the Plenary" (September 28, 2018).
140 Braaten and Jenson, *Princeton Proposal*, no. 67.

there have often been authentic spiritual convictions, true theological insights, and reasons of conscience which led to division. Those who separated themselves from the Catholic Church felt that the "essence" of the Gospel had been distorted. Also, at times, sincere religious attitudes led to the banishment from the Church of those who were considered "corrupters" of the Gospel. Many divisions begin with a profound desire for interior renewal in the Church. Separation then arises in the face of the difficulty or impossibility of fulfilling this desire. We can thus appreciate the importance of a continual process of renewal in the Church—and, when necessary, purification—so as not to be faced with the need for radical reforms, which would easily turn into divisions.[141]

Furthermore, the importance of cultural considerations cannot be underestimated. In the controversies among Christian communities, not only theological factors are at play. Often, we are dealing with clashes between different cultures. Each of the great historical churches has its own cultural context: Orthodoxy is in the Eastern ambit, while Lutheranism is a characteristically German phenomenon. The British mentality leaves a strong mark on Anglicanism. This reality constitutes a call for a renewed attention to the catholicity of the Catholic Church, who cannot allow herself to be exclusively a Western or Latin entity.

The Catholic Church is "Catholic" not only as a title to distinguish her from non-Catholic Christian Churches, but also as a specific property. In the theological sense, in fact, we believe the Church to be one, holy, catholic, and apostolic. Because of her catholicity, the Church, in an *extensive* manner, is called to spread the Gospel to all men, without distinctions such as race, sex, and language. In an *intensive* way, she is called to be the bearer of the entirety of salvific goods, announcing the Gospel in a way which is accessible to all, as at Pentecost. Making herself "all things to all men," the Church fosters and takes to herself "insofar as they are good, the ability, riches and customs in which the genius of each people expresses itself," and in so doing she "purifies, strengthens, elevates and ennobles them."[142]

While taking note of all of these factors, one cannot fail to also note the great harm caused by division. The fact that many different Christian communions present themselves as the true followers of Christ, the Second Vat-

141 "*[Ecclesia] sancta simul et semper purificanda.*" Vatican Council II, *Lumen Gentium* (November 21, 1964), 8.
142 *Lumen Gentium*, 13.

ican Council noted, makes it seem "as if Christ Himself were divided."[143] The council's Decree on Ecumenism goes on to enumerate the deleterious effects of these separations: "Such division openly contradicts the will of Christ, scandalizes the world, and damages the holy cause of preaching the Gospel to every creature."[144] The presence of the aforementioned divisions can lead, as some ecumenical theologians have noted, echoing Saint Paul, to a decisive weakening of the Church's message: "Much current preaching, catechesis, and discipline are emptied of the power of the cross of Christ."[145]

Such a failing becomes all the more painful in light of the growth of secular ideologies which seek to marginalize Christianity. As distinct denominational identities take shape, Christian communities are faced with the temptation "to relish the special marks that distinguish our communities from others, and not to glory in the confession of the crucified Lord we share in common."[146] With the passage of time, the search for each community's specific identity has unfortunately, at times, taken precedence over the desire to be faithful to the truth of Divine Revelation.[147] We should thus not be surprised that Christians belonging to these various groups, in the midst of their divisions, have felt urgently the need to restore the unity desired by Christ. The history of these efforts will form the subject of the next chapter.

143 Vatican Council II, *Unitatis Redintegratio* (November 21, 1964), 1.
144 *Unitatis Redintegratio*, 1.
145 Braaten and Jenson, *Princeton Proposal*, no. 31.
146 Braaten and Jenson, *Princeton Proposal*, no. 32.
147 Braaten and Jenson, *Princeton Proposal*, no. 41.

Chapter 2

A Historical Perspective on Ecumenism

THE TERM "ECUMENISM"

The word *oikoumene*, from classical Greek, belongs to a family of words which refer to the house, home, and to permanence. *Oikos* means "house"; *oikeiotês* makes reference to relationship of kinship; and *oikoumene* means "inhabited and civilized earth" or "universe." In secular Greek literature, *oikoumene* indicated the realm of Hellenic civilization; beyond this was the world of barbarians. Following the *Pax Romana*, the *oikoumene* began to indicate the geographic-cultural area under the empire's rule.[1]

The New Testament uses this term in the same profane sense but also uses the word in a specifically religious way. In this latter sense, *oikoumene* indicates the world, understood as the cosmos in its transitory nature, which awaits its transformation in Christ. In this eschatological perspective, the term is also sometimes applied to human beings: "The future 'oikoumene,' of which Hebrews 2:5 speaks, represents the universal totality of humanity as it will be absolutely subject to his Lordship [that of Jesus Christ]."[2]

The term was introduced into official ecclesiastical language when the Council of Constantinople (381 AD) referred to that of Nicaea (325 AD), naming it an "Ecumenical Council." Since then, the term has been utilized with regard to those doctrines, usages, and events which are accepted as valid, authoritative, and universal norms in the Catholic Church. Thus, the ecumenical councils are distinguished from the provincial ones.[3]

The current technical and theological meaning of "ecumenical" has only come about from the twentieth century onwards, although the nineteenth

1 Willem A. Visser 't Hooft, "The Word 'Ecumenical': Its History and Use," in *A History of the Ecumenical Movement (1517–1948)*, 2nd ed., ed. Ruth Rouse and Stephen Neill (Philadelphia: Westminster, 1967), 735–40; Aloys Klein, "Ökumene," in *Lexikon für Theologie und Kirche*, ed. Walter Kasper (Freiburg: Herder, 1993–2001), 1017.

2 Gustave Thils, *Histoire doctrinale*, 158. Our translation. The 1962 version of the book contains some further developments from the original 1955 edition that are helpful for this work.

3 Thils, *Histoire doctrinale*, 220–27.

century manifests some occasional traces of this signification. The current usage developed particularly during the time of the First World War, within the Faith and Order movement and its counterpart, the Life and Work movement. During this period, the sense of unity and universality, present in the profane and biblical usage of the term "ecumenical," was judged to be especially apt for describing the mystery of the Church, within the context of the effort to restore communion.[4] At the Oxford Conference of 1937, the term already clearly indicated the efforts of different communities towards strengthening the unity of the Church. This sense of "ecumenism" occurred in spite of a certain linguistic resistance from the Anglo-Saxon ambit, within which "ecumenical" is strongly associated with the ecumenical councils. Hence, in this sphere one uses the title "World Council of Churches" rather than "Ecumenical Council of Churches."[5]

WAYS FOR RESTORING THE UNITY OF THE CHURCH

Since its beginnings, the Church has had to face divisions of various kinds which arose from within. The New Testament attests in several moments to the reaction of the Church to the presence of the "Judaizers" and of Gnostic elements which imperceptibly penetrated the community of the faithful. Later, the Church had to face the Novatians, the Donatists, the Arians, the Pelagians, and others. While in some cases these divisions were a question of doctrinal deformations within the Church herself, at other times autonomous "parallel churches" developed with their own hierarchy. Some divisions have been overcome because the separated groups have died out due to extra-ecclesial reasons. Such was the case with the Donatists. In other instances, as in the case of the Arians, there was a conversion on the part of the separated party. In some cases, as in the Western Schism, unity was reconstituted.

Over the course of her two-thousand-year history, the Church has become increasingly aware that she cannot remain indifferent to the lack of unity among Christians and has sought to promote unity in various ways. For this reason, one can say that ecumenism, understood as the concern to preserve and extend the unity of the Church, is as old as the Church herself, even

4 Thils, *Histoire doctrinale*, 155–57.

5 However, as early as 1950 the executive committee of the World Council of Churches examined this issue and recommended the elimination of this expression from ecumenical circles, because "World Church" evokes the idea of a "Superchurch with a centralised administrative machinery." "World Council Diary," *The Ecumenical Review* 2 (Spring 1950): 298–99.

though the term "ecumenism"—in its contemporary sense—was only coined in the twentieth century. Studies of ecumenical theology distinguish three different ways along which the Church has directed her ecumenical efforts: the so-called Constantinian way, the Unionist way, and the Missionary way.[6]

The *Constantinian way* corresponds to the historical period between the Constantinian peace and the eighth century. In this period, political and religious dimensions were fused, and therefore ecclesial unity had a great importance in the political realm. In this context, one can understand the interest of the emperors in promoting religious unity, an interest which was so great that it led them to convene the great councils of the first millennium.

More than a path to unity expressly sought by the Church, in which she would make use of imperial power to restore unity, the Constantinian way corresponds to the peculiar historical ordering of society at the time. In fact, the Church had to struggle tenaciously to free herself from the entanglement of civil and ecclesiastical power. From the theological point of view, this type of "ecumenism" does not offer valid points of reference for contemporary ecumenism. Due to the vanishing of the circumstances that motivated it, this path to unity fell out of use. In any case, one might speak of a resurgence of the Constantinian way during the period of the Catholic Counter-Reformation.

It is not easy to make an exact judgment regarding the legitimacy of this "ecumenical" modality, since we are dealing with a vision of society very different from our current one. One should keep in mind that this is a way also practiced by non-Catholics, who, in more than one case, still retain at least some intermingling of ecclesiastical and civil authority. In any case, the current inadequacy of the Constantinian way is clear from various perspectives, including a theological one. Authentic unity of the Church, both in the visible and invisible dimensions, is always born from within and is independent of extra-ecclesial factors.

The *Unionist way*—also called, imprecisely, the "way of return"—corresponds more particularly to the relationship of the Catholic Church with the Eastern schismatic communities. This way involved the effort to promote the return of the schismatic groups as a community. Examples of this method were the ephemeral unions obtained in the Councils of Lyon in the thirteenth century and Florence in fifteenth century, the one carried out successfully in

6 Giovanni Cereti, *Molte Chiese cristiane, un'unica Chiesa di Cristo: Corso di ecumenismo* (Brescia: Queriniana, 1992), 30–41. Our translation.

the Union of Brest in 1596 with the Ukrainian Church, and some other later agreements which involved smaller communities.[7] The first two cases involve the union of entire churches with the Catholic Church; in the others, the union was extended only to a part of the Church involved in the process. The members of this part were called, in a rather derogatory way, "Uniates."

The Uniats were welcomed into the Catholic Church as a community, and not one by one. Still, the theological context underlying this incorporation did not discern a true ecclesiality in the separated communities, although they were called "churches" even in official Catholic documents.[8] It is true that the baptism conferred by these communities was considered valid and in fact was not repeated. Nonetheless, the fact that one was a Christian did not imply that one was seen as part of the Church.[9] For this reason, this path to unity was a one-way union which involved a "return to the Catholic Church," outside of which there would simply be an ecclesial emptiness.

Ecumenical historiography often refers to unionism in negative terms. This way is seen as an unfair attitude of the Catholic Church, which "takes away pieces" of other Churches. The one-way orientation of the union, without internal changes on the part of the Catholic Church, is also an object of criticism. To this is added the accusation that Eastern Churches would be Latinized as a consequence of union with Rome. The terminology of "return" is also disputed. The phrase implies a previous exit from the Catholic Church, which in many cases is not exactly correct.[10] However, one

7 Oscar Halecki, *From Florence to Brest (1439–1596)* (Rome: Sacrum Poloniae Millennium, 1958). The following ecclesial communities, among others, returned to communion with Rome: in 1181, the Maronite Church, whose patriarchate has its seat in Bkerké (Lebanon) today; in 1553, with the creation of the Catholic Patriarchate of the Chaldean rite, a part of the Syrian Church of the East; in 1742, with the creation of the Armenian Catholic Patriarchate of Cilicia, a part of the Armenian Church; in 1774, a part of the Syriac Church of Antioch; also in the eighteenth century, a part of the Coptic Orthodox Church, which in 1895 became the Coptic Catholic Patriarchate of Alexandria (although based in Cairo); in the nineteenth century the Ethiopian Catholic Church arose as a partial union with the Ethiopian Orthodox Church, based in Addis Ababa; in 1930, part of the Syro-Malankara Church, in southern India. See Johann Adam Möhler Institut, *Le chiese cristiane nel Duemila*, 24–26.

8 Yves Congar, "Appendix IV: Sur les termes employés dans les documents catholiques officiels récents pour désigner les dissidents," in *Chrétiens désunis: Principes d'un "oecuménisme" catholique* (Paris: Cerf, 1937), 381–82.

9 Bernardo Schultze, "Riflessione teologica sul significato di 'Chiesa Orientale' and 'Ortodossia,'" *Gregorianum* 42, no. 3 (1961): 444–62; Georgius Hofmann, "Notae historicae de terminologia theologica Concilii Florentini," *Gregorianum* 20, no. 2 (1939): 257–63.

10 Moreover, those churches or ecclesial communities whose origins go back to an exit from the Catholic Church would not want to return to their previous situation, but to an improved Church. On this topic, see Thils, *Histoire doctrinale*, 293–94.

needs to adequately distinguish unionism from uniatism.[11] The first concept consists in the reestablishment of full communion between different churches, taken in their entirety. According to the second concept, only a part of a church reenters into full communion with another. Unionism as such could be considered as a legitimate mode of ecumenism, insofar as it seeks full communion among the churches.[12]

Uniatism, even if it does not correspond to the criteria of the current ecumenical movement, should not be immediately branded as an illegitimate practice.[13] A closer historical look reveals that, in reality, "there is not just one uniatism as a single uniform phenomenon," and, further, "it is not only found on the side of the Catholic Church."[14] In fact, in many cases the union with Rome came from the initiative of the other party, while the Catholic side simply facilitated the process. In other cases, the Catholic Church took the initiative, turning to the competent authorities of the other church; while the reception of the whole community was proposed, often only a part of it accepted union.[15]

With respect to the "one-way" direction of unionism, the history of the life of the relevant churches shows some cases of Latinization after being fully received into the Catholic Church. Still, this Latinization was not a permanent praxis and, especially after Leo XIII, was abandoned.[16] The Catholic Church

11 Gefaell, "Las Iglesias Orientales," 601–2; and Adriano Garuti, *Saggi di ecumenismo* (Rome: Pontificium Athenaeum Antonianum, 2003), 91–97.

12 Despite a terminology that does not distinguish uniatism from unionism, the following affirmations of Gerardo Cioffari seem quite apt: uniatism should be "rejected as it has come to be understood in the centuries of the struggle with Orthodoxy, with the negative consequence of a hybrid assimilation to Latinism," but "original uniatism would be accepted (referring to that of the Council of Florence in the fifteenth century)." Such uniatism is "of a pure and simple communion with Rome, authentically respectful of the Orthodox tradition." "Il vero uniatismo in un sincero dialogo ecumenico," *Studi Ecumenici* 11, no. 2 (1993): 180. Our translation.

13 Joint International Commission for the Theological Dialogue between the Roman Catholic Church and the Orthodox Church, *Uniatism: Method of Union of the Past* (Balamand, June 23, 1993). On this complicated question, see Eleuterio Fortino, "El diálogo teológico entre la Iglesia Católica y la Iglesia Ortodoxa: III. La cuestión del 'uniatismo' y su solución," in González Montes, *Las iglesias orientales*, 565–92.

14 Kasper, *That They May All Be One*, 87.

15 According to Taras Khomych, "the establishment of these partial unions may not be explained exclusively by the aggression of the Roman Catholic Church. In the majority of cases it came about as the result of a complex interaction of various motives." "Eastern Catholic Churches and the Question of 'Uniatism': Problems of the Past, Challenges of the Present and Hopes for the Future," *Louvain Studies* 31, no. 3–4 (2006): 219. We also need to keep in mind that uniatism was also practiced by the Orthodox, as attested by specific historical cases by the same author. "Eastern Catholic Churches," 229–30.

16 Vittorio Peri, "Considerazioni sull'uniatismo," in *Lo scambio fraterno tra le Chiese* (Vatican City: Libreria editrice Vaticana, 1993), 384.

fundamentally asked for the acceptance of the Roman pontiff's primacy. It would not be correct to say that the Catholic Church asked for an overall and unilateral renunciation of the traditions of the separated churches.[17]

One should keep in mind that the Church is Catholic not only as a denomination, but above all as a theological *property*; in the words of Benedict XV, "the Church of Jesus Christ . . . should not be Latin, nor Greek, nor Slavic, but Catholic."[18] With regard to respect for the traditions of Eastern Catholics, the Second Vatican Council "accords to this ecclesiastical and spiritual heritage the high regard which is its due and rightful praise" and affirms that they "have a full right and are in duty bound to rule themselves, each in accordance with its own established disciplines."[19]

There is an "equal dignity" between the particular churches of the West and the East, "so that none of them is superior to the others as regards rite and they enjoy the same rights and are under the same obligations, also in respect of preaching the Gospel to the whole world."[20] In the case of Christians received into the fullness of Catholic communion, each of these is exhorted to "retain his own rite wherever he is," to "cherish it and observe it to the best of his ability."[21] These conciliar indications did not remain a dead letter. In order to facilitate their implementation and conservation, the Eastern Churches have gradually been removed from the jurisdiction of the Congregation for the Evangelization of Peoples and placed within the specific Congregation for the Eastern Churches. The establishment of colleges and seminaries for the formation of Eastern clergy has been promoted, and institutes for the study of the Christian East have been created. The passage of Latin ecclesiastics to the Eastern rites has also been allowed.[22]

At the beginning of the twenty-first century, the migration of communities of Anglican faithful, along with their pastors, to the Catholic

17 It is, however, necessary to point out that the general directives of the Holy See about the due respect to the Eastern traditions did not always resonate with the local Latin authorities. Thus, for example, we have a strong defense of these traditions in Leo XIII's Encyclical Letter *Orientalium dignitas* (November 30, 1894). Still, in spite of this, "a good number of Latin priests and institutions have persevered in their policy of Latinization. They have always succeeded in getting around the law and have always avoided the sanctions provided." Pierre K. Medawar, "On Safeguarding the Rights of the Oriental Church," in *The Unity of the Churches of God*, trans. Polycarp Sherwood (Baltimore, Md.: Helicon, 1963), 27.

18 Motu proprio *Dei providentis* (May 1, 1917), in *Acta Apostolicae Sedis* 9 (1917), 530. Our translation.

19 Vatican Council II, *Orientalium Ecclesiarum* (November 21, 1964), 5.

20 *Orientalium Ecclesiarum*, 3.

21 *Orientalium Ecclesiarum*, 4.

22 Cereti, *Ecumenismo*, 29.

Church has given rise to a phenomenon in the West which, according to some, would be analogous to the Eastern uniatism of the previous centuries. In fact, these Anglican faithful are received together into full Catholic communion, within a pastoral structure created specifically for them. This structure is that of personal ordinariates, in which these faithful can live as Catholics while conserving the heritage of the Anglican liturgical and spiritual tradition.[23] Thus, it does not seem legitimate to put this more contemporary phenomenon and previous Eastern uniatism on the same level. In the case of the groups of Anglican faithful, the entire process has occurred within the context of a great harmony between the authorities of the Anglican Communion and the Catholic Church. Furthermore, one should not lose sight of the fact that Eastern uniatism has always been in reference to two churches structured in an episcopal manner, while this is not the case with the Anglican Communion. According to the Catholic viewpoint, the latter communion does not preserve a sacramentally valid episcopate.

However, it is also true that unionism is frequently understood in a one-way sense and therefore differs ecclesiologically from the current ecumenical movement. Today unionism is considered a politically incorrect theme, because it is conceived of as an absorption into the Catholic Church, which—naturally—the other ecumenical partners are not willing to accept. The Second Vatican Council itself does not speak of a return (*redditus*), but rather of a of restoration (*redintegratio*) of unity. Beyond the terminological aspect, from a theological point of view it is difficult to conceive of a separation between one's identity as a Christian and one's identity within the Church because salvific grace is itself unifying grace. The Church is not a reality that is superimposed upon our Christian condition; we belong to the Church through baptism, and by this same sacrament we become Christians.

The *Missionary way*—also called "apologetic" or "controvertistic"—corresponds, in ecumenical studies, to the attitude that the Catholic Church assumes with respect to the divisions that arose from the Reformation.[24] The Catholic Counter-Reformation had a political-military component, but two other elements were significant for ecumenical questions. The first was the sending of missionaries to the areas which had been taken over by the reformers. The second was the development of polemical-apologetic litera-

23 Benedict XVI, Apostolic Constitution *Anglicanorum coetibus* (November 4, 2009).

24 Erwin Iserloh, Joseph Glazik, and Hubert Jedin, *Handbook of Church History*, ed. Hubert Jedin and John Patrick Dolan, vol. 5, *Reformation and Counter-Reformation* (New York: Crossroad, 1967), 431–610.

ture. This type of writing was often not free from defamation on both sides and had among its objectives the goal of exposing the other party's errors.[25] This period of polemic continued in the following centuries without success on the part of any of the parties involved. To the contrary, the interactions between Catholics and Protestants slipped into a sterile methodology, and these conditions contributed to a stiffening of mutual opposition.[26]

Here, one should distinguish between that which belongs to sociology and that which refers more directly to theology. The problems concerning the first aspect have been overcome to a great degree. Today there is an air of cordiality which prevails in the sincere quest to know better the reality of the other party and to find points of agreement. The polemical tones of past centuries must be understood in light of the historical circumstances and the particular style of writing at the time.

With respect to the second aspect, the theological aspect, we must bear in mind that the Catholic Church's attempt to win conversions—always at the individual level—sometimes took place in a framework that did not accurately distinguish the separated Christian or heretic from the non-Christian. Converts were not rebaptized. Still, baptism received while in heresy, though valid, was held to be inoperative. For not a few authors, the traditional affirmation that salvation does not exist outside the Church—*extra Ecclesiam nulla salus*—excluded any salvation outside of the Catholic Church. If one-way unionism did not perceive the ecclesiality of the schismatics, in this case the Christian identity of heretics was not appreciated.

In any case, one cannot ignore the reality that this presentation of the ways for restoring unity belongs to a historiography of ecumenism which—more or less consciously—seeks to distance itself from these same ways, in favor of the contemporary ecumenical movement. In doing so, there is a tendency to exaggerate what is seen as a pretentious or prideful attitude on

25 Marie-Joseph Le Guillou, "Des controverses au dialogue oecuménique," *Istina* 5, no. 1 (1958): 65–112, especially the section on *Les rapports entre protestants et catholiques* (81–90). The works of the following have become famous: Johann Eck (*Enchiridion locorum communium adversus Lutherum et alios hostes Ecclesiae*, 1525); Robert Bellarmine (*De controversiis christianae fidei adversus huius temporis haereticos*, Naples: J. Giuliano, 1857); and François Feuardent (*Theomachia calvinistica sedecim libris profligata, quibus mille et quadringenti huius sectae novissimae errores refelluntur*, 1604), on the Catholic end; in the Lutheran sphere, with the same polemical style, we can cite Flacio Illyrico, *Antilogiae Papae, hoc est de corrupto Ecclesaie statu et totius cleri papistici perversitate scripta aliquot veterum authorum*, 1555; Calov, *Päpstliche Torheitslehre*, 1650.

26 Yves Congar, *Dialogue between Christians: Catholic Contributions to Ecumenism*, trans. Philip Loretz (Westminster, Md.: Newman Press, 1966), 136–39.

the part of the Catholic Church. The history of the three ways therefore offers valid points for reflection but should not be dogmatized. The various positions of the Church of Rome with respect to non-Catholics do not come so much from elaborate theological positions but are rather the result, as has already been noted, of the circumstances of the moment.

The contemporary ecumenical movement is conceived of according to a vision much different from the aforementioned ways. This movement seeks union not as the result of a *return* to a flock, but rather as the result of a *mutual journey of conversion and of reform*, towards a reintegration of all authentically Christian values and all churches in the catholicity of the one Church of Christ.[27] Saint John Paul II exhorted the churches of the East and West to strive towards "the rediscovery through prayer and dialogue of visible Unity in perfect and total communion, 'the unity which [. . .] is neither absorption nor fusion'. Unity is a meeting in truth and love, granted to us by the Spirit."[28]

HISTORICAL OVERVIEW OF THE ECUMENICAL MOVEMENT

The expression *Ecumenical Movement* indicates the particular form which ecumenism has taken since the twentieth century, as an effort towards unity inspired by the Holy Spirit within the Church. We will now examine, briefly, the key points of a historical perspective regarding this movement.[29] A theological analysis will be presented in later chapters.

Historians usually indicate the World Missionary Conference in Edinburgh in 1910 as the point of departure for the contemporary Ecumenical Movement. However, the ideas of some authors of the nineteenth century, later developed in the ecclesiological renewal of the early twentieth century, prepared the way for ecumenism. A key figure of the school of Tübingen is Johann Adam Möhler (1796–1838), whose two fundamental ecclesiological works are *Unity in the Church or the Principle of Catholicism: Presented in the Spirit of the Church Fathers of the First Three Centuries* (1825), and *Symbolism: Or, Exposition of the Doctrinal Differences Between Catholics and Protestants as Evidenced by Their Symbolical Writings* (1832). In these works, Möhler

27 Congar, *Chrétiens désunis*, 333–44.

28 John Paul II, Encyclical Letter *Slavorum Apostoli* (June 2, 1985), 27.

29 See also the contributions of Ruth Rouse, "Voluntary Movements in the Second Half-Century"; "The World Christian Lay Movements"; "World Denominational Fellowships," in *A History of the Ecumenical Movement (1517–1948)*, 2nd ed., ed. Ruth Rouse and Stephen Neill (Philadelphia: Westminster, 1967) 1:324–32; 1:599–612; 1:613–20. See also Thils, *Histoire doctrinale*; and the work of Pedro Rodríguez, *Iglesia y ecumenismo* (Madrid: Rialp, 1979).

departs from an ecclesiology focused on the juridical and societal aspects, predominant at that time, to give more attention to the Church as mystery.

In the first work, Möhler emphasizes that the principle of unity in the Church is the Holy Spirit, thus reaching a greater clarity with respect to the organic continuity existing between Christ and the Church. In *Symbolism*, Möhler focuses instead on Christological aspects, and the Church is understood as a continuation or prolongation of the incarnate Word. Although these ideas did not find wide acceptance at the time, Möhler's thought is at the basis of the theology to be found later in the Encyclical *Mystici Corporis* of Pius XII, and even more so in Vatican II's ecclesiology of communion.[30]

Another precursor of contemporary ecumenism, just after Möhler, was Matthias Joseph Scheeben (1835–1888). In his celebrated book, *The Mysteries of Christianity*, from 1865, the Church is contemplated in the context of the Trinitarian and Christological mystery and of God's will to take on human flesh for man's salvation.[31] John Henry Newman (1801–1890), with his *Essay on the Development of Christian Doctrine* (1845) and other works, delineated the fundamental characteristics of the "hierarchy of truths." This idea would find wide acceptance at the Second Vatican Council and would come to be an important instrument in ecumenical dialogue.[32]

In the nineteenth century, various interdenominational institutions arose as a reaction to the Church's general loss of influence on society. The Young Men's Christian Association, or YMCA, was founded in England in 1844, and later spread widely in the United States. This organization had the principal concern of evangelizing youth. Other examples include the Youth Women's Christian Association (YWCA, founded in England in 1854), parallel to the YMCA, and the World Student Christian Association, founded in England in 1895. Finally, the World Alliance for International Friendship through the Churches was founded at the beginning of the twentieth century to foster world peace. Although these associations worked across denominational lines, they did not aim directly at the unity of churches.[33]

30 Carlo Pioppi, "Scuola di Tubinga," in Calabrese, Goyret, and Piazza, *Dizionario di ecclesiologia*, 1297–98.

31 Carlo Pioppi, "Scuola romana," in Calabrese, Goyret, and Piazza, *Dizionario di ecclesiologia*, 1300–1301.

32 Harold E. Ernst, "The 'Hierarchy of Truths' in the Thought of John Henry Newman," *Irish Theological Quarterly* 70, no. 4 (2005): 330.

33 In this section, which is of a historical nature, the word "church" is used in a more sociological sense, also so as to respect the names of the various Christian communities, without prejudice to the theological evaluation of this term, which will be discussed later.

Another phenomenon that might be considered a predecessor to ecumenism was the creation, during the nineteenth century and the beginning of the twentieth century, of alliances or federations of churches belonging to the same confessional tradition. These groupings took place among the denominations born of the Reformation, or started from these, as well as between Anglicans and Old Catholics. The main ones, with the year of foundation, are:[34]

1. Lambeth Conference (1867), of the Anglican Communion
2. Alliance of Reformed Churches (1875), then World Alliance of Reformed Churches, now World Communion of Reformed Churches
3. Ecumenical Methodist Conference (1881); since 1951, called the World Methodist Council
4. Union of Utrecht of the Old Catholic Churches (1889)
5. International Congregational Council (1891)
6. World Baptist Alliance (1905)
7. World Lutheran Convention (1923); since 1947, called the Lutheran World Federation

The aforementioned phenomena have prepared the way for ecumenism insofar as, for the first time, they brought about interdenominational realities or institutionalized alliances of unification. Still, interdenominationality and unification have taken separate and parallel paths. Only in Edinburgh, in 1910, did these paths converge. In fact, by the initiative of the Methodist John Mott (1865–1955), representatives of various churches met in this city—Catholics and Orthodox did not participate—to analyze the issues created by the coincidence of different denominations within the same mission territory. Here there emerged, for the first time, an awareness of the scandal created by the existing divisions, and the difficulties which these divisions posed to evangelization. The conference participants became convinced of the necessity of bringing about the visible unity of churches. To this end, the International Missionary Council was established as a permanent body and would be integrated in 1961 into the World Council of Churches.

At the same time, the foundations of the Life and Action movement were being put into place by the Swedish Lutheran bishop Nathan Söderbom (1866–1931). Söderbom, with the motto "doctrine separates, action

34 Goosen, *Bringing Churches Together*, 14–15.

unites," sought to bring about collaborative action of the various churches on social, moral, and other types of issues. The Faith and Order movement was also born in Edinburgh, founded by the Canadian Episcopalian bishop Charles Brent (1862–1929) and set up as a basis for interdenominational doctrinal dialogue. Both movements were incorporated into the World Council of Churches from the origins of the council in 1948. Faith and Order is still active, with this name, as a permanent commission within the same council.

The World Council of Churches, or WCC, was established at its first general assembly in Amsterdam, in 1948. This body is neither a church, nor a super-church, nor the church of the future, nor a council or synod. The World Council does not make decisions on behalf of the churches represented, nor does it have authority over them; the churches that are part of the council continue to keep their respective identities. Although incorporation into the council does not imply the recognition of a particular conception of the unity of the Church, there does exist a minimum ecclesiology of its members, explicitly mentioned in the council's constitution: "The World Council of Churches is a fellowship of churches which confess the Lord Jesus as God and Saviour according to the scriptures and therefore seek to fulfil their common calling to the glory of the one God, Father, Son and Holy Spirit."[35]

To be accepted as a member, a church must be authentically Christian in nature. Each member church must therefore adhere to a common doctrinal foundation: faith in the One and Triune God, Jesus Christ, the Bible, the desire to come to visible unity. The aim of the WCC is to offer a common forum for dialogue, both in the area of doctrine and with regard to collaborative action.[36] Currently, 348 churches are members of the WCC.[37]

The World Council of Churches holds meetings of the supreme legislative body, or "Assembly," every eight years, which have served as important loci for ecumenical dialogue. The Statement on Unity from the Third Assembly, held in New Delhi in 1961, remains a classic formulation of the visible unity which ecumenism necessarily strives for. The document speaks of God's will for a visible unity of all those baptized in Jesus Christ, "brought by the Holy Spirit into one fully committed fellowship, holding the one apostolic faith preaching the one Gospel, breaking the one bread,

35 English translation in Goosen, *Bringing Churches* Together, 14–15.

36 Thils, *Histoire doctrinale*, 159–66.

37 Bouchard, *Chiese e movimenti evangelici*, 152.

joining in common prayer, and having a corporate life reaching out in witness and service."[38] William Rusch sees the Delhi Statement as a landmark formulation of unity within the biblical and patristic notion of communion, a topic which we will discuss later.[39] Other assemblies have offered important insights into the mystery of the Church and her unity. At the same time, in recent decades some have criticized the World Council for favoring political and social agendas at the expense of a concern for unity in the faith and sacraments.[40]

Even though relations with the WCC have always been cordial, the Catholic Church has never asked for admission as a member, despite having been invited. The Catholic Church nevertheless has permanent observers at the council and participates fully, through officially delegated theologians, in the doctrinal dialogues of the Faith and Order commission. Since 1965 there has also been a joint working group, made up of members of the WCC and the Catholic Church. At the beginning, the refusal of the Catholic Church to be part of the World Council was a consequence of its lack of participation in ecumenical dialogue. The current reasons for not entering the World Council are only partly due to pastoral reasons, which include the risk of possible confusion among the faithful. In reality, the current organization of the council would give to the Catholic Church a weight that is not desired by any of the parties involved.[41]

Within this council, official bilateral and multilateral dialogues have developed between the various Christian communities. This collaboration has produced an abundance of documents, which, though official, do not automatically imply acceptance from the participating churches. Rather, these documents are theological agreements on specific issues that might later pass through the process of reception in each of the churches.

In the early stages, the ecumenical movement did not find acceptance in the Catholic Church and, indeed, it was explicitly rejected by Pius XI in

38 World Council of Churches, *New Delhi Statement on Unity* (December 31, 1961), 2, https://www.oikoumene.org/en/resources/documents/assembly/1961-new-delhi/new-delhi-statement-on-unity.

39 William G. Rusch, "A Survey of Ecumenical Reflection about Unity," in Braaten and Jenson, *Ecumenical Future*, 5.

40 Braaten and Jenson, *Princeton Proposal*, no. 61.

41 The number of representatives of each church at the World Council of Churches is proportional to the number of faithful in that respective church. According to 2010 statistics, there are nearly 1.1 billion Catholics worldwide, about half the number of Christians worldwide. "The Global Catholic Population," Religion and Public Life, Pew Research Center, https://www.pewforum.org/2013/02/13/the-global-catholic-population/.

the Encyclical *Mortalium animos* of January 6, 1928. Later, when the World Council of Churches began activities in the 1948 Amsterdam assembly, the Holy Office published a *monitum* on June 5, 1948, which absolutely forbade Catholic participation in this meeting.[42] Only with the pontificate of John XXIII would the Church begin to make a determined commitment to ecumenism.

Still, there are some earlier indications of such a commitment, which in fact are prior to the ecumenical movement itself. Pope Leo XIII was deeply concerned with the issue of Christian unity, and during his pontificate the week of prayer for Christian unity officially began. Originally, this period of prayer was structured as a novena preceding the solemnity of Pentecost. With Leo's initiative, the "Pontifical Commission for Promoting the Reconciliation of Dissidents with the Church" was created, although this commission did not survive beyond his pontificate.[43]

In the first decade of the twentieth century, the Octave of Prayer for Christian Unity, ending with the feast of the Conversion of Saint Paul on January 25, took precedence over the Pentecost novena. The octave was born through the initiative of Paul Watson (1863–1940), the founder of the Franciscans of the Atonement, and was later spread widely, including among other Christian churches, by Paul Couturier (1881–1954). This octave corresponds to today's Week of Prayer for Christian Unity.

Besides the aforementioned Malines Conversations, the Benedictine abbey of Chevetogne, founded in Belgium in 1939, also had a significant influence on the ecumenical movement. This abbey originated from the Priory of Amay-sus-Meuse, founded by Dom Lambert Beauduin in 1925. Chevetogne is dedicated to the study of monasticism and the spirituality of the East and publishes the well-known magazine *Irénikon*. The Istina Center was also created in 1925 by the Dominican C. J. Dumont; the center has published another ecumenical journal of note, *Istina*, since 1954. Other significant ecumenical institutions include the *Unitas* association, begun in Rome in 1947,[44] and the Johann Adam Möhler Institute, which started in Paderborn, Germany in 1957. Finally, another important step of the Catholic Church in the ecumenical direction was the Instruction *Ecclesia Cathol-*

42 There were other previous indications from the Holy See in the same direction: see Thils, *Histoire doctrinale*, 296–98.

43 Thils, *Histoire doctrinale*, 302.

44 Maurice Villain, *Introducción al ecumenismo* (Bilbao: Desclée de Brouwer, 1962), 303–21.

ica, issued by the Holy Office on December 20, 1949.[45] The instruction greatly reframed the prohibitions then in force, allowing for a discreet Catholic participation in interdenominational theological dialogue.

Although the Catholic Church permitted the creation of the aforementioned institutions, during the first half of the twentieth century the Church refused to officially participate in the ecumenical movement. Still, during this period a more and more widespread theological trend developed which was favorable towards ecumenism and the official entry of the Catholic Church into the ecumenical movement. Among the different theologians who worked in this area was Yves Congar, whose work *Divided Christendom: A Catholic Study of the Problem of Reunion* was first published in French in 1937.

In this context, the fundamental conditions arose for the emergence of official Catholic participation in ecumenism during the pontificate of John XXIII. The biblical, patristic, and liturgical movements contributed to this important step, but the greatest factor was the renewal of ecclesiology. This latter field had developed from the consideration of the Church as a "perfect society"—with little room for ecumenism—to the contemplation of the Church as the Mystical Body of Christ and, later, as mystery of communion. In view of the Second Vatican Council, John XXIII created the Secretariat for Promoting Christian Unity. The first president was Cardinal Augustin Bea, who was succeeded by Cardinal Johannes Willebrands (1969), Cardinal Edward Cassidy (1989), Cardinal Walter Kasper (2001), and, since 2010, Cardinal Kurt Koch. The secretariat was originally a preparatory commission to the council and would remain as a stable organism during and after the council. In 1989, by the Apostolic Constitution *Pastor Bonus* on the Roman Curia, the secretariat became the current Pontifical Council for Promoting Christian Unity.[46]

The Second Vatican Council represented a true Copernican revolution for the attitude of the Catholic Church with respect to ecumenism. From a doctrinal point of view, the Dogmatic Constitution *Lumen Gentium* marked a decisive change of direction for ecclesiology. The document's exposition of the

45 The document is also called *On the "Ecumenical Movement."* The text is available in *Acta Apostolicae Sedis* 42 (1950): 142–47.

46 On the occasion of the fiftieth anniversary of the creation of the secretariat in 2010, the Vatican Publishing House released the brochure *Unità dei cristiani: Dovere e speranza*, edited by the Pontifical Council for Promoting Christian Unity, with abundant information on the life of the Secretariat/Pontifical Council, especially on its role over the course of the Second Vatican Council.

mystery of the Church, contemplated as a communion, definitively opened the doors to the ecumenical movement. In this dogmatic constitution, the subsistence (*subsistit in*) of the Church of Christ in the current Catholic Church is understood as a nonexclusive relationship of identity, as we will examine later on.[47] This affirmation allowed for the recognition that "many elements of sanctification and of truth are found outside" the visible structure of the Church.[48] Therefore, "in some real way" non-Catholic Churches and ecclesial communities "are joined" with the Catholic Church.[49] The document affirms without hesitation that "to them too [the Holy Spirit] gives His gifts and graces whereby He is operative among them with His sanctifying power."[50]

This new attitude of openness on the part of the Catholic Church made possible the publication, during the same council, of the Decree *Unitatis Redintegratio*. This document can be considered, for Catholics, a milestone in the area of ecumenism. The decree is, in fact, the first-ever document of an ecumenical council entirely dedicated to this subject. Significantly, the decree has the same date of promulgation as *Lumen Gentium*: November 21, 1964. As Pope Paul VI noted on this day, the doctrine regarding the Church is more fully explained in the Decree on Ecumenism.[51]

As a document belonging to the solemn Magisterium, the teaching of *Unitatis Redintegratio* is theologically binding, though in a differentiated manner as in other conciliar documents.[52] In other words, the document has doctrinal value, and is not just pastoral and disciplinary in nature.[53] After a brief exposition on the Catholic conception of the unity of the Church, the decree affirms, in continuity with *Lumen Gentium*, that "men who believe in Christ and have been truly baptized are in communion with the Catholic Church even though this communion is imperfect."[54] Starting from this "imperfect communion," quite different from the situation of non-

47 *Lumen Gentium*, 8
48 *Lumen Gentium*, 8.
49 *Lumen Gentium*, 15.
50 *Lumen Gentium*, 15.
51 Paul VI, "Speech at the Conclusion of the Third Session of the Second Vatican Council" (November 21, 1964).
52 Kasper, *That They May All Be One*, 8.
53 See the considerations of Fernando Ocáriz in regard to a specific doctrinal point of *Unitatis Redintegratio*: the attribution of the title "Churches" to the Christian communities that are separated from the Catholic Church, which preserve apostolic succession and therefore also the valid Eucharist; Presentation to Francisco Gil Hellín, *Decretum de oecumenismo* Unitatis redintegratio (Vatican City: Libreria editrice Vaticana, 2005), vii–ix.
54 *Unitatis Redintegratio*, 3.

Christians, the council expresses the Catholic Church's desire to work towards full communion.

The need to see *Unitatis Redintegratio* in relation with *Lumen Gentium*, as mentioned by Paul VI, should also be extended to *Orientalium Ecclesiarum*, the Decree on the Eastern Catholic Churches. The council approved this decree on the same date as the other two documents. The Secretariat for Christian Unity promoted two other conciliar declarations, which have had significant repercussions in the ecumenical sphere: *Dignitatis Humanae*, on religious freedom, and *Nostra Aetate*, on non-Christian religions. Both of these documents were approved during the last period of the council, in the year 1965.[55]

Shortly after Vatican II, the *Ecumenical Directory* was published in two parts, in 1967 and 1970. The Pontifical Council for Christian Unity issued in a new version, entitled the *Directory for the Application of Principles and Norms on Ecumenism*, on March 25, 1993. The publication of John Paul II's Encyclical *Ut unum sint* on May 5, 1995, was another milestone. The encyclical is the first papal document dedicated entirely to ecumenism. In 1997, the Pontifical Council for Christian Unity published another significant work, *The Ecumenical Dimension in the Formation of Those Engaged in Pastoral Work*. There are some other documents, issued by the Congregation for the Doctrine of the Faith, which deal with some specific aspects of ecumenism: the Declaration *Mysterium Ecclesiae* (June 24, 1973), the Letter *Communionis notio* on some aspects of the Church understood as communion (May 28, 1992), the *Note on the Expression "Sister Churches"* (June 30, 2000), the Declaration *Dominus Iesus* regarding the unicity and salvific universality of Jesus Christ and of the Church (August 6, 2000), and the *Responses to Some Questions Regarding Certain Aspects of the Doctrine on the Church* (June 29, 2007). In 2020, the Pontifical Council for Promoting Christian Unity published *The Bishop and Christian Unity: An Ecumenical Vademecum*, a practical guide aimed at helping bishops live their responsibility in the Church's ecumenical mission.

The aforementioned magisterial texts, official guides, and directories are addressed most immediately to Catholics, though they also are written with non-Catholics in mind. In addition to these works, the Catholic Church is also involved in ecumenism through interdenominational doc-

55 For a detailed view of the involvement of the secretariat in the elaboration of these documents during the council, see Pontifical Council for Promoting Christian Unity, *Unità dei cristiani: Dovere e speranza*, 31–67.

uments of dialogue. Some of these documents have been discussed in regard to the specific Christian communities and will be discussed later on as well. Suffice it for the present to say that, from the time of the last ecumenical council to the present day, the Catholic Church has committed herself to this doctrinal dialogue, and the various exchanges have produced an abundance of bilateral documents.

At the same time, however, after some years of naive optimism in the immediate postconciliar period, there is the feeling among many that ecumenism is now going through a phase of hibernation. The achievement of certain agreements in dialogue has at the same time led to the sudden appearance of intense disagreements on other issues. Some have criticized the World Council of Churches for losing its biblical grounding and focusing too much on interreligious dialogue.[56] Over the course of the last fifty years, faced with intense internal and external difficulties, there has been a "loss of passion about ecumenism within mainline Protestantism."[57] The Catholic Church has not been immune from similar challenges.

In some circles, "there is a widespread conviction that traditional differences are irrelevant for the majority of people today and could be simply overlooked." From this attitude and as a reaction to it, which Cardinal Kasper calls "wild ecumenism," there has come about a new denominationalism. "The ecumenical movement has been held responsible for the development of relativism and indifference in questions of faith. In reality, a sound ecumenism as defined by Vatican Council II is the victim, rather than the origin, of this widespread apathy."[58] A number of contemporary American theologians have felt that the ecumenical movement, as of the turn of the twenty-first century, has allowed social and political agendas to take precedence over matters of faith. As a result, the original spiritual and missionary sense of ecumenism has been lost.[59]

Despite these challenges, the recent years have not failed to bring progress and signs of hope also, to which the following pages will also seek to call attention. Recent theology has continued the council's desire to present the truths of faith in a manner which is more understandable to separated

56 Geoffrey Wainwright, "The Global Structures of Ecumenism," in Braaten and Jenson, *Ecumenical Future*, 19.

57 William J. Abraham, "Ecumenism and the Rocky Road to Renewal," in Braaten and Jenson, *Ecumenical Future*, 178.

58 Kasper, *That They May All Be One*, 1.

59 Carl Braaten and Robert W. Jenson, Preface to *Ecumenical Future*, viii.

Christians. Furthermore, the passage of time has allowed for a clearer understanding and appreciation of the teaching of separated Christians, and the possibility of a greater integration of these teachings into the one deposit of faith. This theological progress has been accompanied by an awareness that true progress in Christian unity will never simply be the result of advances in theological or historical understanding but requires a deeper change of heart on the part of each of the Christian communities.

This deeper spiritual attitude has been described by such terms as "spiritual ecumenism" and "receptive ecumenism."[60] Such an attitude leads Christian communities to see their existing differences not as a threat but as an opportunity for a deeper maturation in ecclesial identity. The consolidation of such a disposition in the past decades, in contrast to the polemical tendencies of the past, offers a solid foundation by which the Holy Spirit might help to remove the remaining obstacles to full visible union.

Just as at the dawn of the ecumenical movement, the awareness of a renewed need for proclaiming the Gospel in a time of growing secularism continues to lead Christian communities to feel more urgently the need to be united with one another. Leaving behind the illusory enthusiasm at times present in past years, the passage of time has allowed for a more authentic understanding of the conciliar teaching, in line with the hermeneutic of continuity outlined by Pope Benedict XVI forty years after the close of the council.[61] Such a conciliar understanding keeps in mind the wider orientation of the Church to be a sign and instrument of union with God and "the unity of the whole human race," and in which ecumenical work offers a stimulus to a broader fraternal unity among religions and peoples.[62] As Pope Francis and the Russian patriarch affirmed in their historic joint statement in 2016, "this world, in which the spiritual pillars of human existence are progressively disappearing, awaits from us a compelling Christian witness in all spheres of personal and social life. Much of the future of humanity will depend on our capacity to give shared witness to the Spirit of truth in these difficult times."[63]

In light of both the challenges and the promises of the current moment, a return to the authentic ecumenical vision of the Second Vatican Council,

60 Paul Murray, "Receptive Ecumenism and Catholic Learning—Establishing the Agenda 1," in *Receptive Ecumenism and the Call to Catholic Learning: Exploring a Way for Contemporary Ecumenism*, ed. Paul Murray (Oxford: Oxford University Press, 2008), 15, http://dx.doi.org/10.1093/acprof:oso/9780199216451.003.0002

61 Pope Benedict XVI, "Address to the Roman Curia" (December 22, 2005).

62 *Lumen Gentium*, 1.

63 Pope Francis and Patriarch Kirill, "Joint Declaration" (February 12, 2016), n. 28.

with an in-depth study of the relevant documents, is all the more relevant. Therefore, in the following chapters, without ignoring the later Magisterium and postconciliar theology, the original conciliar doctrine will be given special attention. From this conciliar perspective, we shall attempt to clarify the basic theological principles that should guide ecumenism in the Catholic Church.

Chapter 3

A Theological Framework for Ecumenism

Contemporary theology understands ecumenism to be that aspect of the Church's mission which seeks to lead all Christians to full communion within the one Church of Christ. Throughout history, efforts towards unity have taken on the various forms which have just been examined. The current form of these efforts is that of the *Ecumenical Movement*—that is, "the initiatives and activities planned and undertaken, according to the various needs of the Church and as opportunities offer, to promote Christian unity."[1]

The activities contemplated within this movement are "first, every effort to avoid expressions, judgments and actions which do not represent the condition of our separated brethren with truth and fairness." Second comes "'dialogue' between competent experts from different Churches and Communities" in which each of these experts "explains the teaching of his Communion in greater depth and brings out clearly its distinctive features." Third is "cooperation between them in the duties for the common good of humanity which are demanded by every Christian conscience," which may include "prayer in common." Finally, in these activities, "all are led to examine their own faithfulness to Christ's will for the Church and accordingly to undertake with vigor the task of renewal and reform." In this way, the participants in ecumenism try to work in such a manner that, "when the obstacles to perfect ecclesiastical communion have been gradually overcome, all Christians will at last, in a common celebration of the Eucharist, be gathered into the one and only Church in that unity which Christ bestowed on His Church from the beginning."[2] *Unitatis Redintegratio* affirms that "this unity subsists in the Catholic Church as something she can never lose."[3]

1 *Unitatis Redintegratio*, 4.
2 *Unitatis Redintegratio*, 4.
3 *Unitatis Redintegratio*, 4.

Before studying ecumenical theology as an ecclesiological reflection on the unity to be reestablished in the Church, it is first necessary to offer a theological framework for ecumenism, elucidating its subject, its nature, its scope, and its specific quality with respect to other ecclesial activities. The present chapter is dedicated to this task.

A CHRISTIAN REALITY

Ecumenism is an activity carried out among Christians—that is, among all those who have validly received the sacrament of baptism (including Catholics, Orthodox, Lutherans, and Anglicans) and "who invoke the Triune God and confess Jesus as Lord and Savior."[4] Hence, ecumenism is distinct from interreligious dialogue, which refers to dialogue with non-Christian religions (Muslims, Buddhists, Hindus, etc.) and from dialogue with non-believers (atheists and agnostics).[5] Ecumenical activity consists in searching for unity grounded in faith in Christ and in the Holy Spirit. In this context one should keep in mind that "ecumenism is not a concern for secular ideals of community, perhaps to be achieved at the expense of fidelity to normative tradition."[6] This specifically theological and Christian vision of unity must be kept in mind; otherwise, ecumenical activity can run the risk of being focused on "strategic tasks and goals" rather than the specific supernatural unity willed by Christ for his Church."[7]

Therefore, it is important to not speak of non-Catholic communions and non-Christian religions within the same context. This is a difference that is easy to grasp as a matter of fact, but more difficult to understand at the terminological and conceptual level. From a merely factual point of view, belonging to Christianity, within Catholic and non-Catholic "communions" as we might call them, depends on baptism and on the Trinitarian-Christological faith, as just mentioned. The words "communion" and "communions," however, are used here in a more nominal than theological sense. This usage risks impoverishing a concept that is at the center of ecumenical theology, as will be studied in the next chapter.

The term "communion," in fact, has the merit of having overcome the previous terminology—in truth never accepted by everyone—focused on

4 *Unitatis Redintegratio*, 1.
5 Kasper, *That They May All Be One*, 41.
6 Braaten and Jenson, *Princeton Proposal*, no. 6.
7 Lois Malcolm, "'It Has Seemed Good to the Holy Spirit and to Us': Mission and Ecumenism in the Power of the Holy Spirit," in Braaten and Jenson, *Ecumenical Future*, 220.

the expression "Christian confession(s)." According to this previous view, the different confessions of faith—the ancient symbols or creeds—would have given rise to the different Christian confessions. The Catholic Church, however, has habitually shown herself to be hesitant to use this terminology, as it implies a certain relativism with respect to the concept of the symbol of faith.[8] In the current ecumenical environment, the expression is furthermore associated with the idea of "confessionalism," in the sense of an undue attachment to formulas at the expense of content, and thus something to be avoided. Ecumenism should avoid this extreme, but it should also not lead to confusion with regard to the content of one's own faith. Such confusion has been, unfortunately, recurrent among the different partners in ecumenical dialogue, to the point where some authors have advocated a return to the symbolic theology of Johann Adam Möhler.[9]

The attempt to establish the content of the concept of religion, both Christian and non-Christian, presents even greater complexities.[10] One reason for this is that concepts such as the sacred, divinity, and transcendence are substantially different within each form of religion. Furthermore, the study of religion requires a fundamentally holistic approach, one which does not confine itself to an exclusively philosophical, anthropological, sociological, or even theological context.[11] We might say, in trying to identify the essential elements, that the concept of religion indicates the ambit of man's relationship with a reality which is considered transcendent and superior to human nature, within the context of a consolidated and socially relevant structure. Religion is thus not a mere question of religiosity, even if it presupposes such an attitude.[12]

Returning now to the distinction between religion and communion, an essential concept for ecumenism is that a non-Catholic communion is not simply a religious system of thought or a group of persons characterized by the fact of being baptized and having some form of organization. Instead,

8 Yves Congar, "Note sur les mots confession, Église et communion," *Irénikon* 23 (1950): 14–20.

9 Walter Kasper, *Harvesting the Fruits: Aspects of Christian Faith in Ecumenical Dialogue* (London: Continuum, 2009), 201–2.

10 Regarding this topic, too great to be covered here, there are some valuable reflections contained in Giulio Maspero and Giuseppe Tanzella-Nitti, eds., *La verità della religione: La specificità cristiana in contesto* (Siena: Cantagalli, 2007).

11 Maspero and Tanzella-Nitti, *La verità della religione*, 6.

12 Mariasusai Dhavamony, "Religion: Definition," in *Dictionary of Fundamental Theology*, ed. René Latourelle and Rino Fisichella (New York: Crossroad, 1994), 819–27.

such communion implies an authentic participation in the divine life through Christ, by means of genuine ecclesial bonds. This reality of belonging is not realized according to all the obligations and possibilities existing within the Catholic Church. Still, non-Catholic communion absolutely exceeds the realm of non-Christian religions. The latter do not have a participation in the divine life through Christ, which objectively proceeds from the specific elements of their religious forms. As a consequence, an adequate theological appreciation of the nature of non-Catholic communions is an indispensable premise for ecumenical dialogue.

Ecumenical theology also needs to bear in mind the particular identity of the Jewish people, who, though not Christians, are the "sons of the promises," the "chosen people," and "our older brothers in the faith," and with whom we share the Old Testament. They therefore deserve special consideration among non-Christians. The Church establishes an institutional relationship with the Jewish people by means of a special section of the Pontifical Council for the Promotion of Christian Unity.

On the other hand, the relation of the Catholic Church with the so-called sects or, as some suggest calling them, "the new religious movements," does not belong to the realm of ecumenism. These groups do not possess a valid baptism nor do they reconcile their beliefs with the Revelation contained in Sacred Scripture, even if at times they make use of some elements from Christianity. Examples of such organizations include New Age, Scientology, and the Children of God. For the same reasons, ecumenism does not include relatively older religious phenomena, such as the Mormons or Jehovah's Witnesses. We shall return to this subject later on, with regard to sins against communion.

The "certificate of citizenship" as a partner within the ecumenical movement is not an automatic consequence of being a Christian. In addition, there is a need for a genuine willingness for dialogue on a level of equality, without the pretension of imposing one's own position. Ecumenism also requires a desire for mutual enrichment and a desire to learn from the experience of the other in the tireless search for a common language.

Furthermore, partners in ecumenical dialogue must have the firm conviction that the current situation of division is anomalous and contradicts both the will of the Lord and the ecclesial nature of the churches. Therefore, those who, despite being Christians, explicitly reject dialogue are not valid interlocutors within ecumenism. Within this category of non-participation are various Christian sects born from the churches of Protestantism, many fundamentalist communities of the Reformed tradition, and others. From the beginning, the ecumenical movement met with opposition from a certain part of Calvinism due to the way ecumenism places its goal in the visible unity of the Church. Such external unity was considered to be contrary to the principle that the Church is exclusively a spiritual community, a principle considered essential during the Reformation. To counteract the World Council of Churches, the International Council of Christian Churches—founded by Carl McIntire in 1948—arose, though it has had a rather limited relevance.[13]

AN INSTITUTIONAL APPROACH

In ecumenical dialogue, other Christians are not considered individually, but inasmuch as they form parts of communities. This is to say that, properly speaking, ecumenism seeks to foster unity among churches and ecclesial communities, rather than simply the unity of individual Christians.[14] This principle implies that ecumenism seeks to establish dialogue between institutions but also includes the fact that "the other side" is contemplated as an ecclesial reality. Each institution should appreciate that each of the other institutions in dialogue is a community constituted by truly ecclesial bonds and not simply an association of individual Christians. One should not, however, isolate these dimensions in an absolute way, because faith is a reality both personal and ecclesial. When a Christian community is welcomed into full communion, the personal assent of individual members to the Catholic faith is also necessary.

Ecumenism, therefore, is to be distinguished from individual acceptance into the fullness of Catholic communion.[15] These are two distinct activities, though they are certainly not opposed to one another. Indeed, the Second Vatican Council, in expressly declaring that "when individuals wish for full Catholic communion, their preparation and reconciliation is an undertaking which of its nature is distinct from ecumenical action," goes on to say that "there is no opposition between the two, since both proceed from the marvelous ways of God."[16]

Having said this, the experience of recent years also demonstrates that one must be aware that each party to ecumenical dialogue can have a different

13 Rodríguez, *Iglesia y ecumenismo*, 59–60.
14 Thils, *Histoire doctrinale*, 288–89.
15 Thils, *Histoire doctrinale*, 292–93.
16 *Unitatis Redintegratio*, 4.

type of institutional identity. Often, the parties lack centralized institutional and doctrinal unity. In some of these communities, the local pastors can be the ones vested with authority. At times, the denominational bodies which participate in official dialogue have not received acceptance of the agreements from dialogue within their own denomination. In light of this reality, some have questioned whether these denominational bodies should serve as proper representatives for their respective communities.[17] David Yeago goes so far as to suggest that ecumenical decisions should be made at other local levels, such as that of synod, diocese, or even congregation.[18] In any case, the greater the sense of institutional and doctrinal unity present in each party to ecumenical dialogue, the more fruitful such dialogue will be. Recent years have shown that the most promising advances towards unity have taken place where such unity is present, even if the parties have been smaller.[19]

At the same time, ecclesial institutions of all the various communities would do well to recognize the value of unofficial contacts. As John Erickson points out, the origins of the ecumenical movement were not in ecclesial authority itself as much as in "parachurch groups and organizations . . . whose leaders—often lay men and women at some remove from the centers of church/denominational power—were deeply committed to the task of evangelization, mission, and the establishment of a better society on the basis of (Protestant) Christian principles."[20] These initiatives on the part of individuals and groups, though not forming part of the official framework of ecumenism, nonetheless continue to contribute in a significant way towards the realization of visible unity. An example from more recent times is the Princeton Proposal for Christian Unity, entitled *One Body through the Cross*, published in 2003. The document, while not forming part of an official dialogue, is the fruit of the work of sixteen theologians and ecumenists from various church traditions, who met over the course of three years in Princeton, New Jersey. The proposal, which is cited frequently in this work, offers valuable theological insights and practical suggestions aimed at giving a new impulse to ecumenism.[21]

17 David S. Yeago, "The Ecclesial Context of Ecumenical Reception: A Case Study," in Braaten and Jenson, *Ecumenical Future*, 41.
18 David S. Yeago, "Ecclesial Context of Ecumenical Reception," 42.
19 Cf., for example, the incorporation of smaller groups of Anglican faithful through *Anglicanorum coetibus*, discussed in pages 60–61, 159.
20 John H. Erickson, "The One True Church: Thoughts concerning an Ecumenical Conundrum," in Braaten and Jenson, *Ecumenical Future*, 154.
21 Braaten and Jenson, *Princeton Proposal*.

Such nonofficial activity reminds us that ecumenical activity, while institutional, can never be reduced to merely human institutions. Ecumenism should not lose sight of the original spiritual and evangelizing force behind institutions. While seeking to embody itself within the Church's institutional structure, "ecumenism in its essence is a charismatic phenomenon or process; it is constituted by the intention to receive the gift of unity bestowed on us by the Holy Spirit."[22] Otherwise this activity runs the risk of falling into the danger diagnosed by William J. Abraham: "the mechanisms invented have, as it were, taken on a life of their own and overshadowed the original vision; the instruments of renewal have become identified as mere instruments; the original vision of renewal is lost from view."[23]

A MISSIONARY TASK

One can consider the Church's mission from three different angles with regard to those who are the object of this mission. First, there is the pastoral aspect of mission which is *ad intra* and addressed to the Catholic faithful. In addition, mission has the *ad gentes* dimension which is *ad extra* and refers to the traditional sense of the missionary activity of the Church; this effort is addressed to non-Christians. Finally, the ecumenical aspect deals with non-Catholic Christians.

We find this distinction explicitly in *Ad Gentes*, the Second Vatican Council's Decree on Mission Activity in the Church. The documents states: "Missionary activity among the nations differs from pastoral activity exercised among the faithful as well as from undertakings aimed at restoring unity among Christians."[24] It is vital to understand ecumenism as a specific aspect of the Church's one mission. With this awareness, one can avoid confusing the means employed in the various areas of mission, which are different according to the particular case. Such an understanding is also essential for a correct theological consideration of the expression "other Christians." As explained in the Encyclical *Ut unum sint*, this phrase is undoubtedly better than that of "separated brothers."[25] Even if these Christians are not in the same ecclesial position as Catholic faithful, they cannot be considered "infidels" either.

These three aspects of mission have an essential unity. As the Decree *Ad Gentes* goes on to state, "these two [pastoral and ecumenical] ends are

22 Abraham, "Ecumenism and the Rocky Road to Renewal," 186.
23 Abraham, "Ecumenism and the Rocky Road to Renewal," 177.
24 Vatican Council II, Decree *Ad Gentes* (December 7, 1965), 6.
25 John Paul II, *Ut unum sint*, 42.

most closely connected with the missionary zeal."[26] Ultimately, ecumenism is an essential part of the Church's mission. If the Catholic Church were not ecumenical, she would betray her mission and the explicit will of the Lord, as manifest in John 17:21, in which Christ prays "so that they may all be one, as you, Father, are in me and I in you, that they also may be in us, that the world may believe that you sent me." John Paul II reaffirmed "*irrevocably*" the Church's commitment to ecumenism. [27]

Through ecumenical activity, the Church follows an explicit will of Christ; she seeks to overcome the scandal of divisions which lessen the credibility of the Church and undermine evangelization; she tries to offer to all the baptized the entire patrimony of salvific goods which she has received. The Church, who is a mother, cannot help but care for her children. In her ecumenical activity, she carries out a task which is constitutive of her own identity: "God gathers his people precisely in order to bring unity to a divided humanity."[28]

A GOAL STILL TO BE REACHED

Finally, we must not forget that the final goal of ecumenism is the *visible* unity of the Church: "one flock, one shepherd" (Jn 10:16).[29] Ecumenical activity is aimed at "full" or "perfect" communion among the churches in a structural sense: in "confessing the one faith, celebrating divine worship in common, and keeping the fraternal harmony of the family of God."[30] As the Princeton Proposal recalls, for Christians to realize the unity prayed for by Jesus they need "structures, institutions, and regular practices by which they are gathered together as one people of faith and have access to one another for the sake of mutual care, joint mission, and common service to the world's needs."[31]

The achievement of such institutional unity requires reestablishing among all Christian communities the three visible bonds of unity: a unity of creed, of liturgy, and of hierarchy. As stated by Kasper, "while there can be several intermediate steps on the level of spiritual and practical ecumenism, the ultimate goal is neither unity on the basis of the lowest common

26 *Ad Gentes*, 6.
27 John Paul II, *Ut unum sint*, 3.
28 Braaten and Jenson, *Princeton Proposal*, no. 19.
29 Kasper, *That They May All Be One*, 41.
30 *Unitatis Redintegratio*, 2.
31 Braaten and Jenson, *Princeton Proposal*, no. 9.

denominator, nor peaceful coexistence, nor uniformity, but visible full communion in faith, sacramental life, apostolic ministry and mission according to the image of the unity of the Father, Son and Holy Spirit within the Holy Trinity."[32] Visible unity, in fact, is not only considered helpful for the progress of the Church, but is inherent in the Church's "genetic code." This truth is evidenced by the New Testament Revelation regarding the life of the primitive Christian community: "They devoted themselves to the teaching of the apostles and to the communal life, to the breaking of the bread and to the prayers" (Acts 2:42).[33]

Properly speaking, full communion refers also, and above all, to intimate communion with God through Jesus Christ in the Holy Spirit, or what we might term "the state of grace." This perspective is not properly that of ecumenism. Nonetheless, interior communion is important to keep in mind within an ecumenical perspective, because of the close link which it has with structural communion.

For Catholic ecclesiology, the consideration of visible unity as both a gift and a task to be carried out is of great importance. One should not think of unity as a goal of ecumenism as if unity did not exist now, because ecumenism is not a matter of creating unity. Unity, in its deepest reality, can only be a gift granted by God to his Church in an irrevocable way. Trust in God's faithfulness and his gifts gives hope to ecumenism. Unity is given to the Church as an essential gift; therefore, true ecumenism does not try to create such unity as if it were not present. Rather, ecumenical activity seeks to discover unity in all the places where it is located, as well as to get rid of that which obscures it and which prevents the manifestation of its fullness. In this perspective, ecumenism is understood as an expansion of the unity already present, of "that unity which Christ bestowed on His Church from the beginning," and which "subsists in the Catholic Church as something she can never lose."[34]

Ecumenism must also avoid falling into the other extreme—for example by saying "in reality we are already united; the important unity is the spiritual unity of grace." According to such an understanding of ecumenism,

32 Kasper, *Harvesting the Fruits*, 205.

33 Many authors see in this text the three visible bonds of unity which have just been mentioned: regarding this topic, see Yves Congar, "Proprietà essenziali della Chiesa," in *Mysterium Salutis*, 3rd ed., vol. 7, *L'evento salvifico nella comunità di Gesù Cristo*, ed. Johannes Feiner and Magnus Löhrer (Brescia: Queriniana, 1981), 456–57.

34 *Unitatis Redintegratio*, 4.

which would be foreign to the Catholic understanding, ecumenism would simply serve to promote a renewal in faith and greater cooperation among Christians.[35] The theory of the three branches, proposed in the nineteenth century, might be considered as one instance of this conception. According to this theory, the Church of Christ is one while subsisting in the Catholic, Orthodox, and Anglican Churches, like three branches of the same tree.[36] This theory does not completely eliminate the significance of the visible aspect of the Church, although it does lessen the urgency for seeking genuine visible and structural unity. If anything, according to the theory there would only be the need for a step from "from unity to union," like the members of a family that have quarreled but whose vital bonds of origin cannot be erased.[37]

Today, many Christians perceive the unity of the Church to be the unity of those who accept the Bible and confess Jesus as Lord, or other particular ecclesial elements such as the sacraments, hierarchical structure, or a specific spiritual tradition.[38] However, the already-existing unity of the Church of Christ cannot be reduced to solely an invisible unity, nor to a weak grouping of churches, nor even to a particular set of ecclesial elements. In fact, as mentioned earlier in this chapter with regard to Acts 2:42, Revelation clearly shows the visible bonds of unity as something intrinsic to ecclesial communion.

Both of the aforementioned extremes—the denial of the existing unity on one hand and the affirmation of an already full unity on the other—have been rejected by the Church's Magisterium.[39] The historical nature of the Church, which is always in an eschatological tension during her pilgrimage on earth, allows us to affirm, without contradiction, that unity is a reality

35 Brian E. Daley, SJ, "Rebuilding the Structure of Love: The Quest for Visible Unity among the Churches," in Braaten and Jenson, *Ecumenical Future*, 82.

36 This was the position that was in the background of the *Association for Promoting the Union of Christendom*, which Anglicans and Catholics together founded in England in 1857. By decree of the Holy Office of September 16, 1864 (*Acta Apostolicae Sedis* 11 [1919], 310), the Holy See prohibited the participation of Catholics in this association. Thils, *Histoire doctrinale*, 241–42, 296–97.

37 George D. Rosenthal, "The Unity of the Church," in Anglo-Catholic Congress, *Report of the Anglo-Catholic Congress 1930* (London: Catholic Literature Association, 1930), 22–29.

38 Daley, "Rebuilding the Structure of Love," 82.

39 "The followers of Christ are therefore not permitted to imagine that Christ's Church is nothing more than a collection (divided, but still possessing a certain unity) of Churches and ecclesial communities. Nor are they free to hold that Christ's Church nowhere really exists today and that it is to be considered only as an end which all Churches and ecclesial communities must strive to reach." Congregation for the Doctrine of the Faith, Declaration *Mysterium Ecclesiae* (June 24, 1973), 1.

which the Church has already been given, and yet unity still needs to achieve its fullness. The Church finds herself in a state of journey between the redemption already carried out by Christ and the not-yet-realized eschatological recapitulation of all things.[40] Using a very expressive image, in 1957 Abbot Couturier said:

> The Roman Catholic Church affirms that the Unity of the Church already exists, that it is a revealed truth, it does not therefore deny that unity is still in the future. In a living organization, whatever it may be, the two apparently opposite terms of being and becoming co-exist harmoniously each in its own right. The whole unifying force of that which will become an oak tree, the unity of the oak tree itself, is already present in the acorn.[41]

Thus, the Church cannot be content merely to preserve the unity which she already has, since unity is a gift in eschatological tension towards its fullness. For this reason, putting a brake on ecumenism would be tantamount to stifling this tension, taking away from communion its intrinsic dynamism.

40 Christophe Jean Dumont, OP, *Les voies de l'unité chrétienne: Doctrine et spiritualité* (Paris: Cerf, 1954), 210–13.
41 Paul Couturier, "Prayer and Christian Unity," in Geoffrey Curtis, *Paul Couturier and Unity in Christ* (Westminster, Mass.: J. William Eckenrode, 1964), 337.

Chapter 4

Ecclesial Communion

Christians of various communities appreciate, more now than in the past, that divisions should be considered as wounds which harm an essential aspect of the Church's nature.[1] At the origin of these divisions, there have evidently been misunderstandings, wounded pride, and attitudes which were not always permeated by passion for the truth and God's glory. Moreover, as already mentioned, numerous other cultural or political factors have played a significant role. But if we limit ourselves to strictly ecclesiological motives, we can say that at the foundation of many deviations from Catholic communion, paradoxically, there is a desire for faithfulness to the substance of the Gospel, at least implicitly. This substance is seen to have been compromised and the separating party seeks to remedy the defect. One could summarize the history of divisions in terms of a different appreciation by the parties involved of what is substantial in the Church and what is secondary, accidental, and thus changeable according to the circumstances of time, place, or culture.

The theological study of ecumenism should thus be realized in the light of this historical experience. Such study should focus attention on the essential and distinguish that which is binding for all within ecclesial communion from what can instead be open to different viewpoints. In this manner, ecumenical theology can then engage the separated parties and work to reconstitute unity.

The necessary starting point for this effort can be nothing other than the Divine Revelation regarding the unity of the Church. Such is the perspective of the Decree *Unitatis Redintegratio*, which begins with a declaration of principles regarding the way in which the Church conceives her unity.[2] This text offers a specifically Catholic reflection on the unity of the Church and on ecumenism in general, which does not always coincide with—indeed, in some points it is also very distant from—the conception

1 Michael Root, "Essential Unity and Lived Communion: The Interrelation of the Unity We Have and the Unity We Seek," in Braaten and Jenson, *Ecumenical Future*, 122.
2 *Unitatis Redintegratio*, 2.

present among other churches and communities. In light of this situation, the question "What is the unity that we are looking for?" is one of the most burning questions of ecumenical theology.

To establish the essential starting point for ecumenism, in this chapter we will study in detail the text of *Unitatis Redintegratio* number 2, on the unity of the Church. The present chapter will seek to integrate this text within the context of other aspects of ecclesial unity present in *Lumen Gentium* and in the postconciliar Magisterium, so as to be able to better understand the ruptures of unity. In Chapter 5, we will examine the ecumenical principles that should guide the reestablishment of unity. In Chapter 6, we will study the concrete ways in which the ecumenical movement tries to apply these principles.

GOD'S LOVING PLAN FOR HIS CHURCH

The first paragraph of *Unitatis Redintegratio* number 2 is a synthesis of the essence of ecclesial communion and the fundamental elements of this communion. The language of the text is meant to be welcoming and persuasive. Even though the document is primarily addressed to the Catholic faithful—shepherds and ordinary faithful—it is also written with a non-Catholic audience in mind. The text of this initial paragraph reads:

> What has revealed the love of God among us is that the Father has sent into the world His only-begotten Son, so that, being made man, He might by His redemption give new life to the entire human race and unify it. Before offering Himself up as a spotless victim upon the altar, Christ prayed to His Father for all who believe in Him: "that they all may be one; even as thou, Father, art in me, and I in thee, that they also may be one in us, so that the world may believe that thou has sent me" (Jn 17:21). In His Church He instituted the wonderful sacrament of the Eucharist by which the unity of His Church is both signified and made a reality. He gave His followers a new commandment to love one another, and promised the Spirit, their Advocate, who, as Lord and life-giver, should remain with them forever.

A systematic study of the text reveals five aspects of particular relevance, as indicated by the numbers below. To begin with, the quotation of John 17:21 emphasizes the relationship between (1) *Trinitarian communion and ecclesial communion*, which will be discussed more extensively at the end of the section. The reference to (2) *the communal character of redemption* is more direct. In fact, the effects of redemption are described as both a regeneration and as a congregation. In the Church of Christ, being a Christian—being regenerated—coincides with being in communion or being gathered, because the grace that saves us is the same grace that unites us with one another.

Therefore, the opinion that the council abandoned the individualism characterizing the Christian life of the time so as to embrace indifferently a certain salvific collectivism is reductive. Such a view became quite widespread in the immediate postconciliar period. The reality is that, overcoming an artificial dichotomy, the council understands the Christian to be, at the most profound level of identity, a *person in communion.*

The (3) *pneumatological aspect* could not be absent from this first paragraph on the essential elements of ecclesial unity. The Holy Spirit, ultimately, is the force that makes communion possible. If the entire salvific plan of God is structured around love, having its root in the Trinitarian communion, it follows that the principle which expresses this love and realizes it is the Holy Spirit. As the bond of love within the Trinity, the Spirit is also the bond of love within the Church. In the hearts of believers, this presence of the Holy Spirit takes shape in (4) *the virtue of charity*, or the "new commandment." This is not simply one virtue among others; the unity of the Church, which is communion, is primarily a communion of love. The unity of faith is a premise of this communion, but in the eschatological perspective only charity will remain. Finally, (5) *the Eucharist* is a manifestation and a cause of unity. There exists a connection, suggested in the above text, between the Church's Trinitarian origin and the Eucharist. In her pilgrim state on earth, the Church's Trinitarian dimension is actualized in the Eucharist.

As it has been appropriately summarized, "the *convocatio*, therefore, of the Father ('the love of God for us'), as a task-gift to man of the intratrinitarian *communio* in the Paschal Mystery of his Son Jesus, generates a history of salvation that has its highest moment in the Eucharist of the Church, its principle of continuity in the Spirit, its expressiveness in the commandment of charity."[3] There are evidently other elements of ecclesial communion—the Roman primacy, the episcopal college, the three bonds of creed, liturgy, and hierarchy—and these will be discussed in the subsequent paragraphs. Here, we would like to emphasize those elements which correspond to the Church considered as *fructus salutis*—that is, not those elements at the service of communion, but rather communion in itself. The Eucharist, however,

3 Germano Pattaro, *Corso di teologia dell'ecumenismo* (Brescia: Queriniana, 1985), 152. Our translation.

participates in both of these two dimensions: it manifests communion and also builds communion.

In this number, the decree does not describe all of the aforementioned elements in an orderly and systematic way. Rather, the text simply dedicates the second paragraph to the Holy Spirit, then describes the visible aspect of the unity of the Church, and concludes by returning to the Trinitarian dimension. In keeping with the systematic nature of the present study, we will first examine the Trinitarian aspect, then the pneumatological one, and subsequently consider the visible aspect, integrating some points of the postconciliar Magisterium not explicitly present in *Unitatis Redintegratio.*

TRINITARIAN COMMUNION AND ECCLESIAL COMMUNION

The concept of communion is "the central and fundamental idea of the Council's documents."[4] Unfortunately, this term has often been used in a confused or superficial way. Such usage can have negative consequences. The value of the ecclesiology of communion becomes greatly diminished when this word is applied in indistinct and undifferentiated ways. Many have understood the term in an exclusively horizontal sense, while the fundamental and most important aspect is left in the shadows. Thus, it is necessary to go back to the original New Testament meaning of the word, and from there to examine its use within ecclesiology.

The term "communion" comes from the Greek root *koinon-*, used to express the most diverse relations of commonality, the common participation in one thing, as well as joint undertakings. *Koinonía* is used particularly to denote a close sharing of life.[5] In the New Testament, the word occurs nineteen times, of which fourteen are found in the writings of Paul. In these writings, the term expresses the bond of charity between different communities (2 Cor 9:13) and the union in faith with the Son (1 Cor 1:9), even in suffering (Phil 3:10).

The notion of communion becomes particularly strong in relation to the Eucharist (1 Cor 10:16). In fact, the apostle of the Gentiles affirms that communion in the one Eucharistic bread is the sign and source of communion in the ecclesial body. Communion has an explicitly mentioned

4 Synod of Bishops, "*Relatio finalis* from 2nd Extraordinary Assembly" (1985), II, C, 1, quoted in John Paul II, "Address to the Bishops of the United States of America" (September 16, 1987), 1.
5 F. Hauck, "*koinonós*," in *Grande lessico del nuovo testamento*, ed. Gerhard Kittel and Gerhard Friedrich (Brescia: Paideia, 1965–1992), 5:696–97.

pneumatological aspect (2 Cor 13:13) as object of God the Father's love. In Acts 2:42, the word appears in an explicitly ecclesiological context, in reference to the Church's faithful. Through such communion, the faithful are members of the same body and possess everything in common. In the Johannine writings, Trinitarian communion is connected with ecclesiological communion: explicitly in 1 John 1:3 and, without using the word, in John 17:21.[6] The Trinity itself is a communion of persons—the self-giving and self-communication of the Father and the Son and both of them in the Holy Spirit—and is the original source of all communion.[7]

The Letter *Communionis notio* of the Congregation for the Doctrine of the Faith from May 28, 1992, asserts the centrality of the concept of communion and affirms, quoting words of Saint John Paul II, that "the concept of communion lies 'at the heart of the Church's self-understanding,' insofar as it is the Mystery of the personal union of each human being with the divine Trinity and with the rest of mankind, initiated with the faith, and, having begun as a reality in the Church on earth, is directed towards its eschatological fulfilment in the heavenly Church." However, the letter goes on to add immediately afterwards that "if the concept of communion, which is not a univocal concept, is to serve as a key to ecclesiology, it has to be understood within the teaching of the Bible and the patristic tradition, in which communion always involves a double dimension: the vertical (communion with God) and the horizontal (communion among men)."[8]

The Church, therefore, is communion because she participates in the communion of God the Father, Son, and Holy Spirit. This is the doctrine summarized in John 17:21—a classic citation in ecumenical theology—and which needs to be understood above all in a theological manner and not just as an exhortation. In the Decree *Unitatis Redintegratio*, we find this foundational idea offered as a culmination of the introductory statements on the unity of the Church: "This is the sacred mystery of the unity of the Church, in Christ and through Christ, the Holy Spirit energizing its various functions. It is a mystery that finds its highest exemplar and source in the unity of the Persons of the Trinity: the Father and the Son in the Holy Spirit, one God."[9] In this way, the decree offers a summary of the teaching of the Constitution *Lumen Gentium* (numbers 2–4) on the Trinitarian origin of

6 Paolo Martinelli, "*Comunione*," in Pacomio and Occhipinti, *Dizionario dei teologi*.
7 Kasper, *That They May All Be One*, 58.
8 Congregation for the Doctrine of the Faith, *Communionis notio* (May 28, 1992), 3.
9 *Unitatis Redintegratio*, 2.

the Church, and alludes to Saint Cyprian's vision of the Church as "a people made one with the unity of the Father, the Son and the Holy Spirit."[10]

The Trinity, therefore, is not simply a model to be imitated. *Unitatis Redintegratio* speaks not only of "exemplar," but also of "principle"; ecclesial communion must not only be similar to the Trinitarian communion, but it also comes from and participates in this same Triune mystery. In an analogous sense, the expression *Ecclesia de Trinitate*—a summary of Cyprian's idea—not only refers to an ecclesial unity according to the exemplar of Trinitarian unity, but also emphasizes that the Church is the Church of God because it has its origin in him. The Church is *of* God because she is *from* God.[11]

From all these considerations we can say that Trinitarian communion is also the goal of ecclesial communion. The Trinitarian communion is therefore both a gift and a mission for the Church. Between ecclesial and Trinitarian communion there is a fourfold relationship of origin, model, participation, and goal:

> 1) *Origin*: This is because the Church has her beginning, as already mentioned, in the salvific decree of God the Father and in the missions of the Son and of the Holy Spirit. The Church, in her essential aspects, is an unfolding in time of the Trinitarian missions.
> 2) *Model*: The personal essence of each of the divine persons consists in being in communion with the others; each divine person is a "subsistent relation." In a similar way, within the Church, the fact of being a Christian—being regenerated—coincides with being in communion or being gathered. The same logic holds at the collective level. Indeed, being a particular church necessarily implies being in communion with the other particular churches.
> 3) *Participation*: This reflects the perspective used in John 17:21, "That they may all be one, as you, Father, are in me and I in you," also taken up in 1 John 1:3, "So that you too may have fellowship with us; for our fellowship is with the Father and with his Son, Jesus Christ." In a nonfigurative sense, we can say that the Church is an extension, in space and time, of the Trinitarian communion.

10 Cyprian, *De Oratione Dominica*, 23, cited in *Lumen Gentium* 4.

11 In good Latin usage, the preposition *de* adds something more than simply origin, which is better rendered by the preposition *a*; *de* can also indicate a relation or an imitation. *De unitate Patris et Filii et Spiritus Sancti adunata* should therefore be translated as "a people unified, starting from, and according to the model of unity" or "participating in the unity of the Father, the Son, and the Holy Spirit."

4) *Goal*: This characteristic distinguishes Christianity from the other monotheistic religions. The Christian faith does not remain at the mere threshold of the one God but penetrates into the intimacy of communion within the Trinity. At the end of time, when God will "be all in all" (1 Cor 15:28), ecclesial communion will become full participation in the Trinitarian communion while always preserving the creatural condition.

The concept of communion or *koinonia* has continued to reveal itself as an important theological framework for ecumenical dialogue, helping to offer a dogmatic foundation for unity which at the same time offers a basis for unity in its visible aspect. The statement of the World Council of Church's Seventh Assembly focuses on communion within the Trinity as the model for the unity to which the Church is called, in the variety of her theological and cultural traditions. In view of this identity, "the purpose of the Church is to unite people with Christ in the power of the Spirit, to manifest communion in prayer and action and thus to point to the fullness of communion with God, humanity and the whole creation in the glory of the kingdom." The Lutheran theologian Harding Meyer has similarly proposed *koinonia* or *communio* as a theological framework which can help advance the cause of unity.[12]

The use of this model offers a good basis for dialogue which grounds the Church within the Trinitarian mystery at her essence, while at the same time offering a concrete structure for an ecclesial life marked by diversity within the unity of communion. Such an emphasis can correct the temptation, at times present in the ecumenical movement, to neglect doctrine for the sake of common action in the world.[13] Meyer asserts that the perspective of communion, with its emergence in the ecumenical movement in the 1980s, has allowed for a genuine step forward in the understanding of unity among Catholics and Lutherans.[14] The concept continues to have great potential for advancing the cause of ecumenism, though it also requires each community "to affirm and correct their individual understandings of *koinonia/communio*."[15] The Catholic Church, "at the same time holy and always in need of being purified," also needs to seek to express the authentic

12 Harding Meyer, *That All May Be One: Perceptions and Models of Ecumenicity* (Grand Rapids, Mich.: Eerdmans, 1999), 63–72.
13 Meyer, *That All May Be One*, 153.
14 Meyer, *That All May Be One*, 71.
15 Rusch, "A Survey of Ecumenical Reflection about Unity," 9.

nature of communion ever more clearly, so as to overcome the misunderstandings which have arisen over the course of time and which are at times due to the weaknesses of her members.[16]

THE HOLY SPIRIT, THE PRINCIPLE OF UNITY

Returning to text of the decree, the second paragraph of *Unitatis Redintegratio* number 2 identifies the most profound cause of ecclesial unity: the Holy Spirit arising from within the Paschal Mystery. On the basis of what has just been said about the relationship between Trinitarian communion and ecclesial communion, one can more easily comprehend that the Spirit is a bond of communion both within the Trinity and within the Church, though in a different manner at each level. Referring to New Testament texts of great importance for this theme, the decree affirms:

> After being lifted up on the cross and glorified, the Lord Jesus poured forth His Spirit as He had promised, and through the Spirit He has called and gathered together the people of the New Covenant, who are the Church, into a unity of faith, hope and charity, as the Apostle teaches us: "There is one body and one Spirit, just as you were called to the one hope of your calling; one Lord, one faith, one Baptism" [Eph 4: 4–5]. For "all you who have been baptized into Christ have put on Christ . . . for you are all one in Christ Jesus" [Gal 3: 27–28].

This perspective, in which the unity of the Church rests on the unity of the Paschal Mystery and in which the sending of the Spirit constitutes a part of this same mystery, does not allow for the establishment of an opposition between the mission of Christ and the mission of the Spirit. Ecclesial unity is thus primarily a theological-dogmatic reality. This reality gives rise to a moral obligation to preserve and increase unity and reestablish it where it has been lost:

> The Spirit is the gift from the glorified Cross and the first and last legacy of the Paschal Mystery celebrated, in Him and with Him, by the Father for the good of the world. For this reason the Church, in Christ and by the Spirit, will always be one and singular. Thus, this oneness is by virtue of the Church's vocation of identity, and not by sociological or ethical decision.[17]

16 *Lumen Gentium*, 8.

17 Pattaro, *Corso di teologia dell'ecumenismo*, 152. Our translation.

Ultimately, the Church is one single body in Christ because she is vivified by the one Spirit in the unity of faith, hope, and charity.

Another noteworthy aspect of the decree is its simultaneously pneumatological and eschatological perspective. Ecclesial union concerns the glorious, risen Christ; therefore, the consummation of the Church will occur with the bodily resurrection of the dead. The Church, in fact, looks more to the future than to the past; she is "[Church] in the Spirit; as a consequence, she is rooted in the movement that makes her be from Christ, from whom she comes, and that opens her to Christ, who calls her from the future of his judgment."[18]

In the second part of the same paragraph, the conciliar text describes more directly the action of the Spirit within the Church:

> It is the Holy Spirit, dwelling in those who believe and pervading and ruling over the Church as a whole, who brings about that wonderful communion of the faithful. He brings them into intimate union with Christ, so that He is the principle of the Church's unity. The distribution of graces and offices is His work too, enriching the Church of Jesus Christ with different functions "in order to equip the saints for the work of service, so as to build up the body of Christ" [Eph 4:12].[19]

The parallelism with *Lumen Gentium* is more than evident. The latter document states:

> In order that we might be unceasingly renewed in Him [Eph 4:23], He has shared with us His Spirit who, existing as one and the same being in the Head and in the members, gives life to, unifies and moves through the whole body. This He does in such a way that His work could be compared by the holy Fathers with the function which the principle of life, that is, the soul, fulfills in the human body.[20]

The text of the decree, however, places more emphasis on the diversity proper to this communion generated by the Spirit. This accentuation has great relevance for ecumenism because it excludes uniformity as a necessary condition for unity. In keeping with this perspective, ecumenical theology today tends to speak of *communion*, rather than unity, as a goal of the ecumenical movement.

18 Pattaro, *Corso di teologia dell'ecumenismo*, 153. Our translation.
19 *Unitatis Redintegratio*, 2.
20 *Lumen Gentium*, 7.

That which is most important in this paragraph is also that which is most evident—namely, the fact that ecclesial communion is built up by the Spirit, "the principle of the Church's unity." In this manner, the conciliar text takes up the teaching of Saint Irenaeus, according to which, "where the Church is there is the Spirit of God; and where the Spirit of God is, there is the Church, and every kind of grace."[21] In the final analysis, the pneumatological aspect has an absolute priority to the institutional aspect of the Church. This institutional dimension must be understood as being at the service of the outpouring of the Spirit upon the ecclesial body. The Spirit moves from its invisible presence in the hearts of believers and seeks to incarnate itself in the concrete conditions of man's existence, and specifically within the unity of life in a community.[22]

An ever-increasing awareness of the role of the Holy Spirit has been an important recourse for ecumenical theology, as Telford Work points out.[23] The British theologian Lesslie Newbigin, in a series of lectures given in Scotland in 1952, argued that Catholics and Protestants need to appreciate once more the fundamental role of the Holy Spirit, along with Christ, in the life of the Church. He asserted that, in the search for the wholeness of the Church in the tension between the Catholic and Protestant elements, "there is a third term which both of them have tended to forget"—that is, the Risen Christ's gift of the Holy Spirit to the Church.[24] This perspective allows us to appreciate that the Church's life and fellowship can never be reduced to a set of doctrines or even to her faithfulness to the apostolic teaching, without considering that the Holy Spirit is "the abiding and indwelling principle of life in a fellowship."[25] While recognizing the value of each local community of faithful and the fears which Christians can have of a centralized structure, Newbigin asserts that such unity in the Spirit necessarily tends towards the fellowship of all Christians and a recognition of the priority of the whole body of the Church with regard to the local, following the example of the Council of Jerusalem.[26]

21 Irenaeus of Lyons, *Adversus haereses*, in *The Apostolic Fathers with Justin Martyr and Irenaeus*, trans. Alexander Roberts and William Rambaut, Ante-Nicene Fathers, ed. Alexander Roberts and James Donaldson, vol. 1 (Peabody, Mass.: Hendrickson Publishers, 1994), 3.24.1.
22 Root, "Essential Unity," 120.
23 Telford Work, "Speaking for the Spirit in the Time of Division," in Braaten and Jenson, *Ecumenical Future*, 203–7.
24 Lesslie Newbigin, *The Household of God: Lectures on the Nature of the Church* (New York: Friendship Press, 1954), 104.
25 Newbigin, *Household of God*, 115.
26 Newbigin, *Household of God*, 119.

A similar sentiment is to be found in the work of Robert Jenson (1930–2017), a leading ecumenical theologian in recent years. Jenson argued that both Protestant and Catholic ecclesiologies suffer from an overly rational vision of God, which paralyzes their dialogue. Jenson holds that "Catholics and Protestants alike think of time as outside God, a supposition that is plainly false."[27] He contends that an authentic understanding of the action of the Spirit in the Church, in the various aspects of the Church's life, would lead to a deeper awareness of the Church's identity in continuity not simply with her historical past, but also with her eschatological future.[28] This perspective would avoid the danger of understanding God's eternity in a static way, a conception proper to Hellenism, in which God's eternity would be seen as a passivity.[29]

Contrary to this static vision, a new appreciation of the Holy Spirit's dynamic protagonism within the Trinity would give a new vision of the Church's being:

> Eternity would be apprehended as the dramatic mutuality of Father and Spirit, of God as God's origin and God as God's goal, and therefore not as immunity to change but as *faithfulness* in action. Being would accordingly be apprehended not as persistence in what is but as *anticipation* of what is not yet. The Church would know herself as the temporal mission not of resistance to time but of faithful change in time, and know her own continuity in that mission not as hanging on to what is already there but rather as receiving what must come.[30]

Jenson expresses the hope that such a renewed dogmatic perspective can help to provide a necessary context to understanding the Church's institutional nature. While the full ramifications of this perspective remain to be fleshed out, Jenson's work is a pressing reminder of the importance of a deep understanding of the Trinity and specifically the Holy Spirit for the fruitfulness of ecumenical theology.

27 Robert Jenson, *Unbaptized God: The Basic Flaw in Ecumenical Theology* (Minneapolis: Fortress Press, 1992), 118. Special thanks to Blanche Jenson for her assistance.
28 Jenson, *Unbaptized God*, 137.
29 Jenson, *Unbaptized God*, 139.
30 Jenson, *Unbaptized God*, 138.

MINISTRY AT THE SERVICE OF UNITY

The decree, faithful to its intention to remain at a general level, dedicates the third paragraph of number 2 to the ministerial element, while in the next one it examines the relationship between the threefold office proper to ministers and the three bonds of communion within the people of God.

There are still many Christians who give credence to the saying of Loisy, according to which "Jesus foretold the kingdom, and it was the Church that came," as if the institutional element had been absent from the Lord's intentions.[31] The council does not hesitate to boldly affirm the contrary: "In order to establish this His holy Church everywhere in the world till the end of time, Christ entrusted to the College of the Twelve the task of teaching, ruling and sanctifying."[32] The text emphasizes the instrumental aspect of ministry, while the Church remains the substantial element at the service of which the pastoral office is carried out. Ministry is mentioned in its original phase, realized in the twelve apostles, in direct connection with the action of Christ himself. The concept of succession within this ministry is implied, since the ministerial mission concerns the Church "everywhere in the world till the end of time."

The decree affirms the collegiality of the original twelve apostles, while at the same time it describes the organization of this same apostolic college according to head and body. The Petrine primacy, in fact, immediately makes its appearance within the conciliar text:

> Among their number He selected Peter, and after his confession of faith determined that on him He would build His Church. Also to Peter He promised the keys of the kingdom of heaven, and after His profession of love, entrusted all His sheep to him to be confirmed in faith and shepherded in perfect unity. Christ Jesus Himself was forever to remain the chief cornerstone and shepherd of our souls.[33]

Even if no biblical quotations appear within this text, the references to the classic texts Matthew 16:13–19 and John 21:15–19 are evident. Here, *Unitatis Redintegratio* goes back to the teaching of *Lumen Gentium*, although

31 Alfred Loisy, *The Gospel and the Church*, trans. Christopher Home (New York: Charles Scribner's Sons, 1912), 166.
32 *Unitatis Redintegratio*, 2.
33 *Unitatis Redintegratio*, 2.

without explicitly mentioning it. In fact, affirming the election of Peter (and in him, also that of his successors) from among the apostles—parallel to the "chosen from among them" of *Lumen Gentium* number 19—the Petrine (and thus Roman) primacy is not understood as an external element, but as an apostolic function. Hence, this primacy is called to be exercised in communion with the other bearers of the apostolic ministry. The function of primacy can act on its own accord, but not separately from the college of bishops.[34] Due to the primarily apostolic nature of the Petrine primacy, the Petrine succession has an essentially episcopal character, and thus a sacramental instrumentality. On the basis of 1 Peter 5:4, the conciliar text affirms that Christ Jesus Himself remains forever "shepherd of our souls."

COMMUNION IN FAITH, WORSHIP, AND CHARITY

The decree describes the relationship between the pastoral function of ministers and the ecclesial communion of the faithful with precise wording:

> Jesus Christ, then, willed that the apostles and their successors—the bishops with Peter's successor at their head—should preach the Gospel faithfully, administer the sacraments, and rule the Church in love. It is thus, under the action of the Holy Spirit, that Christ wills His people to increase, and He perfects His people's fellowship in unity: in their confessing the one faith, celebrating divine worship in common, and keeping the fraternal harmony of the family of God.[35]

Authentic unity, though rooted in the ineffable eternal mystery of the Trinity, needs to be expressed with these concrete human forms of unity, which arise from the insertion of persons into the Mystical Body of Christ through baptism. Unity in the confession of faith is essential: "When truth and unity are played against one another, both are misrepresented."[36] The Church lives the confession of faith in her worship and in her life of fraternal communion.

An important characteristic of this text is the way it emphasizes that our Lord is the active subject. Preaching, worship, and government are fundamentally actions of Christ, in which ministers act in an instrumental role for the benefit of the faithful. The text under consideration manifests two

34 Gérard Philips, *L'Église et son Mystère au II Concile du Vatican* (Paris: Desclée, 1967), 293.
35 *Unitatis Redintegratio*, 2.
36 Braaten, *Princeton Proposal*, no. 47.

distinct triads, in reference to both the threefold aspect of ministry and the three aspects of unity within the ecclesial community as a whole. These triads are linked according to a relationship of means and end. With regard to the first triad, the original Latin text has the connotation of instrumentality when it describes Christ's action by means (*per*) of the apostolic functions.[37] The second triad makes specific reference to Christ's will. In this manner, the text emphasizes the priority of the communion of the faithful in unity, while at the same time affirming the will of Christ to reach this unity through the three offices of the apostolic ministry.

This text also accentuates the pneumatological aspect of ministry. Ministerial action takes place "under the action of the Holy Spirit." Ministry and the Holy Spirit are not in fact two parallel paths of sanctification. From the Church's beginning at Pentecost, the two are wondrously united.[38] Precisely because the Spirit edifies the unity of the Church by means of the ministerial function of pastors, "their preaching has its own distinctive quality and is not simply transmission of knowledge, the administration of sacraments is a gift of salvation and not just ritual, pastoral government is a service of communion and not simply socio-juridical power."[39]

The visible communion of the faithful in faith, worship, and charity offers a manifestation of the more interior and invisible communion. The unity between the visible aspect and the invisible aspect of ecclesial communion, only suggested in the text at hand, finds an explicit expression in the Letter *Communionis notio*:

> *Ecclesial communion is at the same time both invisible and visible.* As an invisible reality, it is the communion of each human being with the Father

37 The original Latin text of *Unitatis Redintegratio* 2 reads: *Iesus Christus per Apostolorum eorumque successorum, nempe episcoporum cum Petri successore capite, fidelem Evangelii praedicationem sacramentorumque administrationem, et per gubernationem in dilectione*.

38 "Christ has promised and sent two elements, though in different ways, to constitute his work, for the extension in time and over the earth of the Kingdom founded by him, and to gather redeemed humanity in his Church, his Mystical Body, so that it be his fullness, in expectation of his final and triumphant coming in the consummation of the time: the apostolate and the Spirit. The apostolate acts externally and objectively: it forms, so to speak, the material body of the Church to which it gives her visible and social structure; while the Holy Spirit acts within, in each person and also in the whole community, animating, vivifying, and sanctifying. These two agents, the apostolate, to which the sacred Hierarchy succeeds, and the Spirit of Jesus, which uses this same Hierarchy as an ordinary instrument in the ministry of the word and of the sacraments, act together: on the day of Pentecost they are united among each other in a marvelous way, when the great work of Christ begins." Paul VI, "Speech at the Inauguration of the Third Session of the Second Vatican Council" (September 14, 1964). Our translation from original in Latin.

39 Pattaro, *Corso di teologia dell'ecumenismo*, 163. Our translation.

> through Christ in the Holy Spirit, and with the others who are fellow sharers in the divine nature, in the passion of Christ, in the same faith, in the same spirit. In the Church on earth, there is an intimate relationship between this invisible communion and the visible communion in the teaching of the Apostles, in the sacraments and in the hierarchical order. By means of these divine gifts, which are very visible realities, Christ carries out in different ways in history his prophetical, priestly and kingly *function* for the salvation of mankind. This link between the invisible and visible elements of ecclesial communion constitutes the Church as the *Sacrament* of salvation.[40]

One should also keep in mind that *Unitatis Redintegratio* number 2 speaks of an increase and perfection in unity, in such a way as to link such growth and perfection with the institutional aspect (preaching, sacraments, government), but not in a mechanistic sense. The Church's aspect of mystery and her institutional dimension do not exist in parallel separation, nor do they relate to each other in a simply automatic fashion, but rather they have a dynamic relationship. Relevant here is the possibility, described in *Lumen Gentium* number 14, of being in the Church in body, but not in charity, as well as the absolute need of "possessing the Spirit of Christ" to be fully incorporated into the Church. The working of the Spirit, one should not forget, takes place according to *gift*, not the law. There can thus exist a gap between reality and the sign, between communion and the community, since the mystery of the Church will always transcend the institutional and visible aspect.

Here, too, one can appreciate the decree's continuity with the teaching of *Lumen Gentium*. Regarding this topic, the Dogmatic Constitution on the Church contains a text of great ecumenical importance, which is worth quoting in full:

> The society structured with hierarchical organs and the Mystical Body of Christ, are not to be considered as two realities, nor are the visible assembly and the spiritual community, nor the earthly Church and the Church enriched with heavenly things; rather they form one complex reality which coalesces from a divine and a human element. For this reason, by no weak analogy, it is compared to the mystery of the incarnate Word. As the assumed nature inseparably united to Him, serves the divine Word as a living organ of salvation, so, in a similar way, does the visible social

40 Congregation for the Doctrine of the Faith, *Communionis notio*, 4.

structure of the Church serve the Spirit of Christ, who vivifies it, in the building up of the body [Eph 4:16].[41]

In the above text, the succession of the three pairs describes, from different angles, the relationship between the divine and the human in unity. In particular, "the visible assembly and the spiritual community" will only fully be one at the final consummation of the world, yet still in the present they are part of one single entity. Their analogy with the Incarnate Word is not absolute, but it is, as the Latin text literally says, "not insignificant" (*non mediocrem analogiam*). One cannot separate the visible from the spiritual aspect, but neither do they correspond to each other as a single identical reality.

Once again, here the decree takes up the distinction between community and communion, even if their boundaries are not distinct; if such were the case, the distinction would become separation. Even if the two aspects present a possible divergence, one should not forget that, according to New Testament Revelation, communion with God and communion with pastors are shown to be mutually intertwined: "What we have seen and heard we proclaim now to you, so that you too may have fellowship with us; for our fellowship is with the Father and with his Son, Jesus Christ" (1 Jn 1:3). The effort to bring about the visible unity of the Church therefore passes along the line of intersection between these two poles.[42]

UNITY AND CATHOLICITY

The genuine nature of the Church as communion is made manifest in light of the Church's catholicity, which has emerged as a key concept for a theology of ecumenism. The concept of catholicity has come to encompass a set of connotations which prevent a unilateral interpretation. Catholicity derives from the Greek *katholou*. The term was used in Greek philosophy and made reference to the whole or to that which is universal.[43] From the patristic period onwards, the term came to describe both the universal breadth of human geography which the Church aims to reach as well as the all-embracing quality of the Church's doctrine. Saint Cyril of Jerusalem, in his classic formulation of this property, affirms that the Church is called "catholic" "because it extends over all the world, from one end of the earth

41 *Lumen Gentium*, 8.
42 Pattaro, *Corso di teologia dell'ecumenismo*, 163.
43 s.v. "καθόλου," in Franco Montanari, *The Brill Dictionary of Ancient Greek*, English ed., ed. Madeleine Goh and Chad Schroeder (Leiden: Brill, 2015), https://dictionaries.brillonline.com/montanari.

to the other; and because it teaches universally and completely one and all the doctrines which ought to come to men's knowledge."[44] In both of these senses, catholicity serves as a specific mark of distinction for the true Church of Christ.

With time, catholicity came to take on a more institutional sense, and served to identify the authentic Church of Christ within an apologetic perspective. This tendency, strongly present after the Reformation and reaching its culmination after the First Vatican Council, could lead to a purely institutional meaning of catholicity which would be indicative of uniformity. Without leaving behind the institutional dimension of catholicity, the renovation in ecclesiology of the nineteenth and twentieth centuries, as well as the Second Vatican Council, sought to recover the richness of the patristic sense of catholicity. The council desired that the description of the Church's catholicity, within the chapter on the people of God, be inseparable from the description of the Church's intimate nature.[45] In this perspective, catholicity appears as an essential characteristic of the people of God acting in history and a necessary aspect of the Church's mission.

In having recourse to this essential property and mark of the Church, *Lumen Gentium* gives expression to a concept which was vital to the council's vision of the Church and to the conciliar experience as a whole. The Second Vatican Council was itself an unprecedented experience of the Church's catholicity and various council fathers desired that this property of the Church be addressed in the exposition of the Church as people of God.[46] The council retained the traditional quantitative sense of catholicity as referring to the Church's universal geographic extension, by which she "is to be spread throughout the whole world and must exist in all ages" and whose actual universal spread throughout the world serves as a mark of her

44 Cyril of Jerusalem, *Catechetical Lectures*, in *St. Cyril of Jerusalem, St. Gregory Nazianzen*, trans. Edwin Hamilton Gifford. Nicene and Post-Nicene Fathers of the Christian Church, Second Series, 7, ed. Philip Schaff and Henry Wace (Buffalo, N.Y.: Christian Literature Publishing, 1894), 18.23, https://www.newadvent.org/fathers/310118.htm.

45 *Relatio* for chapter II of *Lumen Gentium*, in *Acta Synodalia Sacrosancti Concilii Oecumenici Vaticani II* (Vatican City: Typis Polyglottis Vaticanis, 1970–1976), 3/1:210.

46 G. Philips, *Conspectus Observationum Generalium in Totum Schema de Ecclesia*, Vatican Secret Archives, Second Vatican Council Fond, busto 766, Folder 295. A summary of the *Conspectus*, distributed to the council fathers, can be found in *Acta Synodalia* 2/1:74–78. For more extensive description of the importance of catholicity in the contributions of the Council Fathers and the elaboration of *Lumen Gentium*, see Joseph Thomas, "The Catholicity of the Church in the Second Vatican Council: The Theological Background, Conciliar Elaboration and Dogmatic Content of *Lumen Gentium* 13," Dissertationes Series Theologica 37 (Rome: Pontifical University of the Holy Cross, 2011).

divine origin.[47] At the same time, the council recognized a more qualitative sense of catholicity, by which the Church remains ever open to the greatest diversity of culture and thought even in the realm of religious practice.

This qualitative aspect of catholicity has great importance for ecumenical dialogue. It formed a central aspect of John Henry Newman's desire to chart a new path for Christian unity by purifying the Church of the human and cultural elements which hinder the manifestation of her essential catholicity.[48] The modern study of ecumenism emerged from an attempt to place a renewed emphasis on the Church's universal nature, so as to overcome the dichotomy between the origins of Christian missions in Western society and the developments of these societies in a more global context.[49] In 1968, the Assembly of the World Council of Churches at Uppsala focused its attention on this aspect of the Church, speaking of catholicity as the "fullness, the integrity, and the totality of life in Christ" and actualized by the Spirit.[50] The assembly urged a fresh understanding of this catholicity, so as to remove the national and cultural boundaries which can at times obscure the unity of the bride of Christ.[51] As we have seen, the sources of divisions among Christians have often been rooted in differences of culture, politics, and other legitimate differences which do not pertain to the essence of the Gospel or the Church.

The council's vision of catholicity was rooted in the Church's desire to elevate all authentic human values in Christ, in the framework of the theology of missions.[52] This vision had a myriad of precedents. In the great diversity of cultures and perspectives brought together in the Second Vatican Council, in a time of an increased sense of global identity, the Church came to a heightened awareness that catholicity forms an essential and primary property of her essence. The renewed appreciation of the lay vocation led to a renewed awareness of the Church's call to sanctify the totality of human realities in Christ. The council fathers came to see catholicity as a key way of

47 *Lumen Gentium*, 13.
48 Ian Ker, *John Henry Newman. A Biography* (New York: Oxford University Press, 1990), 209.
49 Barreto, "World Christianity," 4.
50 World Council of Churches, *The Holy Spirit and the Catholicity of the Church*, in *Official Report of the Fourth Assembly of the World Council of Churches, Uppsala, July 4–20, 1968*, ed. Norman Goodall (Geneva: World Council of Churches 1968) no. 7, https://archive.org/stream/wcca14/wcca14_djvu.txt.
51 World Council of Churches, *The Holy Spirit and the Catholicity of the Church*, no. 10.
52 Jean Daniélou, *Animadversiones ad novam ordinationem capitum Schematis De Ecclesia, 30 IX.1963*, Vatican Secret Archives, Second Vatican Council Fond, Busto 766, Folder 297, 2. The text is cited and discussed in Thomas, "Catholicity of the Church," 328–29.

expressing the authentic nature of the Church's mission, which seeks to respect and foster the authentic values and gifts proper to each culture.

In the development of this teaching on catholicity, the council was indebted to the renewed ecclesiology of the preceding decades. The council's understanding of catholicity has a particular resonance with the understanding outlined by Yves Congar, the likely writer—though not originator—of the final text of *Lumen Gentium* number 13. Congar, in continuity with the Catholic and Orthodox traditions, identified catholicity with the Church's capacity to assume the fullness of human realities. In this perspective, the Church possesses the fullness of catholicity as an interior property, a fullness which participates in the fullness or *pleroma* (cf. Col 1:19) of Christ. Through this essential catholicity of the Church, which Congar terms "the universal capacity of unity," the Church possesses the duty and capacity to assume and elevate all of the goods of humanity.[53] At the same time, while having this fullness, the Church is called to actualize her catholicity more fully through her mission of spreading the gifts of salvation.

The council desired to make universality a primary perspective within the council's entire view of the Church from the very beginning of *Lumen Gentium*, even if the topic of catholicity would be dealt with as a specific theme in number 13 of the dogmatic constitution. In the vision of the Church laid out by the Dogmatic Constitution on the Church, and later expressed in *Unitatis Redintegratio* and *Ad Gentes*, catholicity is not simply a quantitative indicator and apologetic reference for the Church but rather is inseparable from the key conciliar concepts of the Trinitarian dimension of the Church and people of God.

More specifically, in the point dedicated to catholicity, located in *Lumen Gentium*'s chapter on the people of God, catholicity appears as an immediate consequence of the Trinitarian design of salvation, expressed in the historical realization of this mission through the Church, the people of God and visible sacrament of salvation.[54] In line with the eternal plan of the Father, carried out in time through the mission of the Holy Spirit, *Lumen Gentium* number 13 locates the dogmatic foundation of the Church's catholicity in Christ, "heir of all things [Heb 1:2] . . . the head of the new and universal people of the sons of God." The Church's catholicity is rooted, as we have said, in her capacity to assume and purify all human realities, elevating them

53 Yves Congar, *Esquisses du Mystère de L'Église* (Paris: Cerf, 1941), 56. Our translation.
54 Thomas, *Catholicity of the Church*, 372–73.

to the order of redemption: "By reason of [the characteristic of universality] the Catholic Church strives constantly and with due effect to bring all humanity and all its possessions back to its source in Christ, with Him as its head and united in His Spirit."[55] This Christological conception of catholicity was important for the council's desire to express the authentic nature of the Church's mission in contemporary society. Completing this Trinitarian mission, the text recognizes the Holy Spirit as the power which maintains communion within diversity. The Paraclete is the one who "who brings together the whole Church and each and every one of those who believe, and who is the wellspring of their unity in the teaching of the apostles and in fellowship, in the breaking of bread and in prayers."[56]

While this dogmatic vision of catholicity implies the Church's openness to all authentic human values, this same vision also limits the identification of catholicity with the Church as visible institution. Avery Dulles sees *Lumen Gentium* number 8, with the words *subsistit in*, as extending the attribution of catholicity to the Church of Christ, rather than directly to the Roman Catholic Church.[57] From this perspective, ecumenism appears as a process aimed at a fuller manifestation of the Church's catholicity. As *Unitatis Redintegratio* affirms, the Church's ecumenical activity gives "better expression to the authentic catholicity and apostolicity of the Church."[58] Divisions, the text continues, prevent the Church from expressing "her full catholicity in all her bearings." This ecumenical realization of catholicity, connected to the essential mystery of the Church, defies any static classification: the Church is at once fully catholic, as she possesses the fullness of salvific gifts, and yet this very fullness leads her to seek a greater dynamic realization of her catholicity. Pope Paul VI described this reality in his speech during the solemn promulgation of *Lumen Gentium*, *Unitatis Redintegratio*, and *Orientalium Ecclesiarum*. He asserted that the decree on ecumenism, by manifesting more clearly the nature of the Church, did not restrict the multiple movements of her catholicity. He went on to note that this catholicity always moves forward, always receives.[59]

55 *Lumen Gentium*, 13.
56 *Lumen Gentium*, 13.
57 Avery Dulles, *The Catholicity of the Church* (Oxford: Clarendon Press at Oxford University Press, 1985), 21.
58 *Unitatis Redintegratio*, 4.
59 Pope Paul VI, "Speech at the Conclusion of the Third Session of the Second Vatican Council," 17.

Although the last century has seen a mutual appreciation of this property on the part of Catholics, Orthodox, and Protestants, one should be aware of the differences in understanding catholicity possessed by each party to ecumenical dialogue. The Orthodox, in keeping with the older patristic sense of catholicity, tend to view catholicity as an interior property of fullness but without a necessary reference to the visible, institutional, and missionary aspects of the Church. Congar argued that the Russian concept of *sobornost*, which can be translated as "catholicity," expresses the variety of functions present within the Church's unity. Still, he also saw the need for the concept to be freed of a certain antihierarchical understanding present in the Orthodox vision.[60] Protestant communities can similarly place more of an emphasis on the spiritual aspect of catholicity in opposition to the institutional aspect. The early Protestant Reformers saw their communities as possessing authentic catholicity, which they believed the Roman Catholic Church betrayed.[61] With regard to the Anglican Church, according to the traditional three-branch theory which has been important to this community, the Anglican, Orthodox, and Roman Catholic Churches would all be authentic expressions of the Church's catholicity.

The Catholic Church, while appreciating the qualitative aspect of catholicity as part of the interior richness of the Church, also has a long tradition of identifying catholicity as a visible and quantifiable mark of the Church of Christ. The members of the Church, as *Lumen Gentium* states, are "scattered . . . throughout the world" and constituted in organic unity under the governance of the college of bishops, headed by the Roman pontiff.[62]

As the text goes on to affirm, "within the Church particular Churches hold a rightful place; these Churches retain their own traditions, without in any way opposing the primacy of the Chair of Peter, which presides over the whole assembly of charity and protects legitimate differences, while at the same time assuring that such differences do not hinder unity but rather contribute toward it."[63] The particular or local churches, a key part of the council's vision of the Church, offer a tangible expression of the Church's capacity to assume and redeem the various human cultures and hence her catholicity. In a similar vein, the World Council of Churches' Assembly at Nairobi, in 1975, building upon the previous assembly focused on catho-

60 Yves Congar, *Jalons pour une Théologie du Laïcat* (Paris : Cerf, 1953), 386, 391–94.
61 Whitlock, *Divided We Fall*, 44.
62 *Lumen Gentium*, 13.
63 *Lumen Gentium*, 13.

licity, affirmed that "the one Church is to be envisioned as a *conciliar fellowship of local churches*."[64] *Lumen Gentium* emphasizes that the role of the Roman pontiff is not in any way opposed to this broader ecclesial communion, but rather at its service. Fostering this awareness of the Roman pontiff as guardian of authentic catholicity, and thus the guarantor of authentic diversity with the unity of faith, forms an important task for ecumenism.[65]

The consideration of the Church's catholicity, in its different aspects, thus remains an important incentive to the cause of Christian unity. An increasingly global society, in which the most varied human cultures continue to develop their own particular ways of living and expressing the Christian faith, offers a fresh impulse for the Church to renew her ecumenical efforts and language.[66] The field known as "World Christianity," which developed in the twentieth century, has sought to give greater expression to these diverse articulations of Christianity, especially in non-Western cultures. An authentic sense of catholicity implies an awareness of the totality of salvific gifts which the Church has received from Christ, as well as the totality of the human race, to whom the Church is called to bring these same gifts. This latter horizon, the goal of the salvation of all, has been and will always be an important driving force which propels the cause of unity forward. Saint Paul's affirmation that God wants all to be saved (1 Tm 2:4) "is an invitation not to devote ourselves exclusively to our own communities, but to open ourselves to the good of all, to the universal gaze of God who took flesh in order to embrace the whole human race and who died and rose for the salvation of all. If we, with his grace, can assimilate his way of seeing things, we can overcome our divisions."[67]

THE EUCHARIST, THE EPISCOPATE, AND THE UNITY OF THE CHURCH

The first paragraph of *Unitatis Redintegratio* number 2 mentions the sacrament of the Eucharist "by which the unity of His Church is both signified and made a reality," without adding more details. This mode of presentation

64 World Council of Churches, *Breaking Barriers, Nairobi 1975: Official Report, Fifth Assembly, World Council of Churches*, ed. David M. Paton, in *The Ecumenical Movement: An Anthology of Key Texts and Voices*, ed. Michael Kinnamon and Brian E. Cope (Grand Rapids, Mich.: Eerdmans, 1997), 110.
65 Congar, *Esquisses*, 56.
66 Barreto, "World Christianity," 5.
67 Pope Francis, "Homily for the Feast of the Conversion of St. Paul" (January 25, 2020).

is in keeping with the conciliar document's effort to offer a synthetic exposition of doctrine. The present study will seek to develop this important topic more extensively, drawing on other texts. The Eucharist cannot be separated from the theme of the episcopate, as shall be explained shortly. Nor can the discussion of this sacrament bypass the notion of the Church as a communion of churches, a topic which will be studied in more detail in the next section.

"The Church draws her life from the Eucharist. This truth does not simply express a daily experience of faith, but recapitulates *the heart of the mystery of the Church*."[68] The Eucharist not only manifests the Church; "*a causal influence of the Eucharist* is present at the Church's very origins."[69] From a more specifically communal perspective, the Letter *Communionis notio* deals with this topic:

> Ecclesial communion, into which each individual is introduced by faith and by Baptism, has its root and center in the Blessed Eucharist. Indeed, Baptism is an incorporation into a body that the risen Lord builds up and keeps alive through the Eucharist, so that this body can truly be called the Body of Christ. The Eucharist is the creative force and source of communion among the members of the Church, precisely because it unites each one of them with Christ himself: "Really sharing in the body of the Lord in the breaking of the Eucharistic bread, we are taken up into communion with him and with one another. 'Because the bread is one, we, though many, are one body, all of us who partake of the one bread' (1 Cor 10, 17)." Hence, the Pauline expression *the Church is the Body of Christ* means that the Eucharist, in which the Lord gives us his Body and transforms us into one Body, is where the Church expresses herself permanently in most essential form. While present everywhere, she is yet only one, just as Christ is one.[70]

On one hand, therefore, the unity partaken of here is that of the true Body (*Corpus verum*). This body is one and unique in the whole Church, present in its entirety in each singular realization: the Eucharist in each individual church is the same Eucharist among the different churches. Thus, the Eucharistic mystery is also an ecclesial mystery. Joining the Eucharistic

68 John Paul II, Encyclical Letter *Ecclesia de Eucharistia* (April 17, 2003), 1.
69 John Paul II, *Ecclesia de Eucharistia*, 21.
70 Congregation for the Doctrine of the Faith, *Communionis notio*, 5. Includes note on quote: "Const. *Lumen Gentium*, n. 7/b."

community, through participation in the true Body, implies at the same time a belonging to the universal Church. Thanks to communion in the one Body of Christ, the various Christian communities are in communion with one other. The Eucharistic mystery leads us to affirm a reciprocal inclusion of the local churches and of the universal Church. This is the perspective of *Communionis notio* number 11: "Indeed, the unicity and indivisibility of the eucharistic Body of the Lord implies the unicity of his mystical Body, which is the one and indivisible Church. From the Eucharistic centre arises the necessary openness of every celebrating community, of every particular Church; by allowing itself to be drawn into the open arms of the Lord, it achieves insertion into his one and undivided Body."[71]

However, if the idea of communion of particular churches were conceived of only on the basis of the Eucharist, such communion could easily be presented "in such a way as to weaken the concept of the unity of the Church at the visible and institutional level."[72] This is not because the Eucharist does not have the power in itself to bring about the entire unity of communion but because one cannot consider the Eucharist apart from the sacramental ministry along with its implicit requirement of hierarchical communion. A unilateral consideration of the Eucharist is not enough: "Unity, or communion, between the particular Churches in the universal Church, is rooted not only in the same faith and in the common Baptism, but above all in the Eucharist and in the episcopate."[73]

This reference to the episcopate deserves a deeper explanation. In the Eucharistic-ecclesiological context which has been delineated, the episcopal ministry is a service to the sacrament of unity, the Eucharist, and to the unity of communion brought about by the Eucharist. In this context, the episcopate is both the ministry of unity within a specific community, and at the same time the ministry of unity between that same community and the universal Church. This reality derives from the fact that the bishop is, simultaneously, head of the particular church and member of the episcopal college. When he acts as head of his church, he also acts as a member of this college. The fullness of the Eucharistic mystery requires that the individual—each single bishop—be in communion with the universal by means of the episcopal college.

In other words, one can say that there is an inseparable tie between the Eucharistic understanding of the mystery of the Church, in her pilgrim state

71 Congregation for the Doctrine of the Faith, *Communionis notio*, 11.

72 Congregation for the Doctrine of the Faith, *Communionis notio*, 8.

73 Congregation for the Doctrine of the Faith, *Communionis notio*, 11.

of growth, and the ecclesiological understanding of the mystery of the Eucharist, which is similarly in a state of development. The Eucharist is an ecclesial mystery because its fruit is a greater unity and communion in the Church, and also because the Church celebrates this sacrament within the already-existing unity and communion of the Church. In the second sense of the already-existing bonds, the bishop has the specific role of signifying the unity and communion of the Church which celebrates this sacrament. One cannot imagine a bishop remaining within the unity of the Church without also participating simultaneously in the unity of the episcopate. A bishop separated from his brothers in the episcopate would not be adequately integrated into the sacramental sign of the Eucharist because he would not be a sign of unity.

Since the unity of the episcopate has its center in the bishop of Rome, the bishop who celebrates the Eucharist needs to be in communion with the successor of Peter. This aspect completes the theological conception of the relationship between the Eucharist, the episcopate, and ecclesial unity. As *Communionis notio* number 14 explains in summary form:

> The unity of the Eucharist and the unity of the Episcopate with Peter and under Peter are not independent roots of the unity of the Church, since Christ instituted the Eucharist and the Episcopate as essentially interlinked realities. The Episcopate is one, just as the Eucharist is one: the one Sacrifice of the one Christ, dead and risen. . . . Every valid celebration of the Eucharist expresses this universal communion with Peter and with the whole Church, or objectively calls for it, as in the case of the Christian Churches separated from Rome.

THE CHURCH AS COMMUNION OF CHURCHES AND SYNODALITY

The particular relationship between the Eucharist, the episcopate, and the Church means that the Church exists as at once the communion of all the faithful—"the universal Church, that is, the worldwide community of the disciples of the Lord"[74]—and the communion of churches, or "the body of the churches" according to the language of *Lumen Gentium* number 23. Therefore, "it is possible to apply the concept of communion in analogous fashion to the union existing among particular Churches, and to see the universal Church as a Communion of Churches."[75] Between these dimensions,

74 Congregation for the Doctrine of the Faith, *Communionis notio*, 7.
75 Congregation for the Doctrine of the Faith, *Communionis notio*, 8.

universal and particular, there is a relationship which is not comparable to that of states or provinces with respect to a country, nor to that of a confederation of independent nations. Between the particular churches—"fashioned after the model of the universal Church"—and the universal Church there exists "a special relationship of 'mutual interiority' with the whole, that is, with the universal Church, because in every particular Church 'the one, holy, catholic and apostolic Church of Christ is truly present and active.'"[76]

The relationship of communion does not exist only between each particular church and the universal Church, but also among the different particular churches. As such, this aspect of communion adds to the notion of union the elements of diversity and dynamism. That means, in the first place, that unity does not imply uniformity. Indeed, diversity, which is not the same as division, is a source of mutual enrichment within communion: "The universality of the Church involves, on the one hand, a most solid unity, and on the other, a plurality and a diversification, which do not obstruct unity, but rather confer upon it the character of 'communion.'"[77] Secondly, the elements of ecclesial communion—persons, institutions, and so on—within the particular churches have a reciprocal, dynamic relationship with one another, rather than just having a static union. Ultimately, these elements of ecclesial communion, although different, not only coexist peacefully but live within a constant and mutual exchange of self-giving.

This vision of communion among the churches must be completed by considering the priority of unity with respect to diversity. This seems, in fact, to be the most adequate way to frame the relationship between the universal Church and particular churches. In the relationship between these two dimensions, which we might term "perichoretic"[78] or marked by mutual interiority, "the unity of the Church takes precedence over the diversity of the local Churches," as Walter Kasper has affirmed.[79] In this

76 *Lumen Gentium*, 23; John Paul II, "Speech to the Roman Curia" (December 20, 1990), 9; Congregation for the Doctrine of the Faith, *Communionis notio*, 9. The final citation includes note on quote: "Decr. *Christus Dominus* n. 11/a."

77 Congregation for the Doctrine of the Faith, *Communionis notio*, 15.

78 An expression borrowed from Trinitarian theology, which indicates the mutual presence and interpermeation of the Divine Persons.

79 This author has shown himself to be very critical of the priority of the universal Church, especially in controversy with then-Cardinal Ratzinger. On the debate, see Kilian McDonnell, "The Ratzinger/Kasper Debate: The Universal Church and Local Churches," *Theological Studies* 63, no. 2 (2002): 227–50. It is therefore particularly interesting that the universal-local binary does not indiscriminately relate to the unity-diversity binary.

manner, there is still room for acknowledging certain ways in which the local aspect of the Church can be prioritized with respect to the universal—for example, the Eucharist from the celebrative point of view. Such an awareness does not contradict the teaching of *Communionis notio*, according to which the universal Church "is a reality ontologically and temporally prior to every individual particular Church."[80] Given that in some cases the local aspect takes priority while in others the universal does, one would be correct to affirm a "mutual priority." However, this would be an "asymmetric" mutual relationship which favors the universal aspect, as appears above all in the historical and theological analysis of apostolic succession.[81]

A correct understanding of this communion among churches takes on paramount importance in the context of reestablishing ecclesial unity.[82] The various churches, and their own groupings, relate to each other within a legitimate diversity. In this context, the Constitution *Lumen Gentium* speaks positively of the "various churches, established in various places by the apostles and their successors," that "have in the course of time coalesced into several groups, organically united, which, preserving the unity of faith and the unique divine constitution of the universal Church, enjoy their own discipline, their own liturgical usage, and their own theological and spiritual heritage." Far from constituting a danger for ecclesial communion, "this variety of local churches with one common aspiration is splendid evidence of the catholicity of the undivided Church."[83]

The emphasis on synodality in recent years is a manifestation of this perspective of communion, characteristic of the ecclesiology of the last ecumenical council. A recent document of dialogue affirms, with regard to this concept, that "the term comes from the word 'council' (*synodos* in Greek, *concilium* in Latin), which primarily denotes a gathering of bishops, under the guidance of the Holy Spirit, for common deliberation and action in caring for the Church. Broadly, it refers to the active participation of all

80 Congregation for the Doctrine of the Faith, *Communionis notio*, 9.

81 The topic goes beyond the space allotted in these pages. For an analysis of the key issues, see Philip Goyret, "Ermeneutica conciliare ed ecclesiologia contemporanea," *Annales Theologici* 23, no. 2 (2009): 405–40. For a more thorough examination, see Goyret, *Dalla Pasqua alla Parusia: La successione apostolica nel "tempus Ecclesiae"* (Rome: Edusc, 2007), 301–74.

82 "I think I am able to say in conclusion that the deepening and the working towards a balanced presentation of an ecclesiology of communion is a great possibility, perhaps the greatest possibility for tomorrow's ecumenism." Johannes Willebrands, "The Future of Ecumenism," *One in Christ* 11 (1975): 323.

83 *Lumen Gentium*, 23.

the faithful in the life and mission of the Church."[84] Both dimensions of synodality have been manifested, among other ways, by the practice of the ordinary synods of bishops. These synods are a vestige of Vatican II aimed at preserving a collegial approach to addressing specific pastoral issues.

Although the practice of synodality has had its challenges, through this praxis the Church manifests in a tangible way that her unity is not uniformity and that her hierarchical structure does not diminish the legitimate variety present in the Church's myriad traditions. She demonstrates more clearly that all the faithful walk together in the one journey of the people of God, and that the presence of authority in the Church does not diminish this truth.[85] As the aforementioned document on synodality notes, the concept recalls the great heritage of synodality present in the Church of the East and West over the course of the first millennium. Such a heritage "constitutes a necessary reference point and a powerful source of inspiration for both Catholics and Orthodox as they seek to heal the wound of their division at the beginning of the third millennium."[86]

Synodality must be carefully distinguished from collegial forms of government found in human society, however valuable such institutions can be. A synod "is not a parliament; it is not a parlour; it is not demonstrating who has more power in the media and who has more power on the web, in order to impose some idea or some plan."[87] Rather, a synod is a process of dialogue and discernment which the Church undertakes, trusting in the guidance of the Holy Spirit. Agreement comes about not simply through compromise and negotiation, but through the power of the Paraclete "who helps to overcome closure and tension and works within hearts so that they may achieve unity in truth and goodness."[88] The experience of the Council of Jerusalem, as recounted in Acts of the Apostles chapter 15, is a fundamental reference point. The Church, in keeping with her nature as communion, expresses her unity through a dialogue of diverse perspectives. In the Catholic perspective, an adequate theological appreciation of the bishop

84 Commission between the Catholic Church and Orthodox Church, *Synodality and Primacy*, 3, http://www.vatican.va/roman_curia/pontifical_councils/chrstuni/ch_orthodox_docs/rc_pc_chrstuni_doc_20160921_sinodality-primacy_en.html.

85 Anglican-Roman Catholic International Commission, *The Gift of Authority* (November 3, 1998), 34–40, http://www.vatican.va/roman_curia/pontifical_councils/chrstuni/documents/rc_pc_chrstuni_doc_12051999_gift-of-autority_en.html.

86 Commission between Catholic Church and Orthodox Church, *Synodality and Primacy*, 21.

87 Pope Francis, "Greeting at Opening of Synod of Bishops for the Pan-Amazon Region" (October 7, 2019).

88 Pope Francis, "General Audience" (October 23, 2019).

as foundation of unity within each particular church, and hence of the special role of the episcopate as a manifestation of catholicity, is another significant pillar for the concept of synodality.[89]

Synodality takes on a different character when carried out within the Catholic Church and between the Catholic Church and communities which lack full communion with her. Still, there is room for common ground. Among Protestants there is the awareness of a formal process of dialogue through which the Christian community, under the guidance of the Holy Spirit, comes to discern and proclaim the Gospel truth in each time period.[90] Such a process, according to the Protestant perspective, would not require a hierarchically mediated apostolic structure. Nonetheless, the development of theologies of synodality within both Catholic and Protestant circles offers a solid theological basis for authentic ecumenical dialogue, rooted in the essential nature of the Church. Such a perspective is important for an adequate understanding of authority in the Church, a difficult issue in ecumenical dialogue but fundamental for the Church's identity: "Normative teaching and authorized ways of ordering common life are necessary and essential elements of the church's apostolic existence."[91]

THE INDEFECTIBILITY OF THE CHURCH: CONTENT AND CONSEQUENCES

The indefectibility of the Church, emphasized in *Unitatis Redintegratio*, requires mention within these reflections on the unity of the Church. The goal of the ecumenical movement, in fact, consists in achieving "that unity which Christ bestowed on His Church from the beginning," a unity which "subsists in the Catholic Church as something she can never lose."[92] The decree expresses the hope that this unity "will continue to increase until the end of time."[93]

The present work has already noted the dynamic character of unity, as both simultaneously subsisting in the Church and yet at the same time in tension towards its fullness. This unity has an indefectibility which is a consequence of the Church's more general aspect of indefectibility. The latter qual-

89 *Lumen Gentium*, 23. See also Thomas, *The Catholicity of the Church*, 485.
90 Work, "Speaking for the Spirit," 204–5. Work cites John Howard Yoder, "The Hermeneutics of Peoplehood: A Protestant Perspective," *The Priestly Kingdom: Social Ethics as Gospel* (Notre Dame, Ind.: University of Notre Dame Press, 1984), 26–28.
91 Braaten and Jenson, *Princeton Proposal*, no. 37.
92 *Unitatis Redintegratio*, 4.
93 *Unitatis Redintegratio*, 4.

ity has a solid Christological foundation in Matthew 16:18—"the gates of the netherworld shall not prevail against it"—and belongs to the deposit of faith.

The theological tradition has developed the concept of indefectibility according to a threefold meaning: "1) The Church will never perish; 2) The Church will never fail in her duty; and 3) the Church will subsist until the end, just as Christ willed her and established her, without undergoing substantial changes, which would be practically equivalent to her disappearance."[94] The third aspect implies that none of the essential elements of the Church will be lacking. Indefectibility, moreover, concerns the Church in both her aspects of being a means of salvation and being herself a fruit of salvation: "The Church is undoubtedly 'pure' (holy) already, insofar as she is the body of Christ; and Christ is present in her, acts in her, through the apostolic ministry, the sacraments it administers. . . . She is also pure to the extent that this Spirit takes hold of our being and makes us 'holy.'"[95]

At a deeper theological level, the indefectibility of the Church's unity has its roots in the theology of the covenant. According to this theology:

> Already now and for all of the rest of history, there will be a community in whose bosom there is offered to God, in an objective and indubitable way, the *hesed* [enduring love] of the man Christ Jesus, who redeems us, and in which God offers to men, by means of Christ Jesus, the eternal *hesed* of God. In other words, the indefectibility of the Church means that, across time and space, the institutional and visible structure of the Christian community, which makes possible the bloodless renewal of the sacrifice of Christ according to the will of God, will remain unalterable despite the attacks of the enemy.[96]

Such continuity can be a challenge in an age of "church-shopping," in which believers can be tempted to choose a church which fits their own preferences and desires.[97] Nonetheless, in keeping with Christ's promise, the Church cannot fail to be faithful to the deposit which she has received.

94 Paul Faynel, *L'Église* (Paris: Desclée, 1970), 2:21. Our translation.
95 Louis Bouyer, *The Church of God: Body of Christ, and Temple of the Spirit*, trans. Charles Underhill Quinn (Chicago: Mayer, 1982), 495.
96 Rodríguez, *Iglesia y ecumenismo*, 130–31. Our translation.
97 Braaten and Jenson, *Princeton Proposal*, no. 39.

SINS AGAINST COMMUNION

Every sin damages ecclesial communion: besides being an offense against God, sin always has a divisive effect. However, there are certain actions or positions that directly harm the visible bonds of ecclesial communion. Such actions can be carried out either by individuals or entire communities. Ecumenical theology is particularly interested in the latter aspect.

The teaching regarding the divisions that wound the unity of the Body of Christ typically focuses on heresy, apostasy, and schism.[98] In addition to these traditional themes, ecumenical theology needs to also examine the phenomenon of sects and some aspects of the notion of excommunication. The latter phenomenon, strictly speaking, is not the action of someone who breaks communion but rather the resulting ecclesiological status of such a break, habitually accompanied by the corresponding canonical penalty.

From a canonical point of view, heresy is defined as "the obstinate denial or obstinate doubt after the reception of Baptism of some truth which is to be believed by divine and Catholic faith."[99] From this point of view, heresy negates doctrine, while at the same time sharing with doctrine a verbal, objective, public, and external aspect which makes it more than simply an interior conviction.[100] Heresy is distinguished from schism in that heresy has a direct reference to the faith, which, in theory, schism does not.

Heresy is distinct from apostasy in that the latter involves the total abandonment of the Church. In heresy, by contrast, the difficulty concerns only a part of the truths of faith. In fact, "the genesis and development of a heretical doctrine are almost always due to the choice (*hairesis*) of a single statement of Revelation, which is asserted in an absolute way and thereby distorted."[101] Some of Pascal's considerations are still relevant: "For the most part it happens that, unable to conceive the relation of two opposite truths, and believing that admission of one involves the exclusion of the other, they [the heretics] embrace the one and exclude the other, thinking that we, on the other hand, take the contrary position. . . . Their fault is not that they follow an error, but

98 This is also the terminology in the *Catechism of the Catholic Church*, 817, in *Code of Canon Law* (1983), 751 and 1364, and in the *Code of Canons of the Eastern Churches* (1990), 1436–37.
99 *Code of Canon Law*, 751.
100 Giampero Bof, "*Unità*," in *Teologia*, ed. Giuseppe Barbaglio, Giampero Boff, and Severino Dianich (Cinisello Balsamo: Edizioni San Paolo, 2002), 1807.
101 G. B. Sala, "Ortodossia," in *Nuovo dizionario di teologia*, ed. Giuseppe Barbaglio and Severino Dianich (Cinisello Balsamo: Edizioni San Paolo, 2000), 991. Our translation. This theme was studied in great depth by John Henry Newman, as is shown in Jean Guitton, *La philosophie de Newman: Essai sur l'idée de développement* (Paris: Bovin et Cie, 1933), 79–80, 114–15.

that they do not follow another truth."[102] Finally, one should keep in mind that heresy, besides being an error with regard to the content of faith, involves a certain pertinacity: "there is no sin of heresy unless the one who professes an error in doctrinal matters refuses to let himself be instructed and corrected by the Church, and insists on holding his personal opinion against her."[103]

In the case that heresy becomes schism, one should keep in mind the more unified theological sense which these two concepts originally had. According to Congar, "there was from the beginning and during the first millennium a concept of heresy which was more ecclesiological than dogmatic," such that it was not clearly distinguished from schism.[104] Unity of the Church was thought of above all as unity in the order of holiness; the schismatic "is a person who, lacking the sanctity of communion, lays the premise to fail in the purity of faith; the heretic only failed in doctrine because he failed in communion."[105]

Fundamentally, the difficulty of distinguishing the different possible ways of breaking unity was rooted in the interdependent nature of the various types of ecclesial bonds of unity, such that the doctrinal and disciplinary realms could not be separated. As Möhler wrote with great insight, "since [the early Church] saw the principle that begot faith and that which formed the community as the same principle in the fullest sense, she necessarily deduced . . . that those who did not have the first in a general way, could only have the second in a troubled way, and vice versa."[106] Only in late Scholasticism, and especially during the Counter-Reformation, would the faith of the Church more clearly classify the different types of doctrinal truths and define heresy by its opposition to the established faith.[107] Something of the more unified sense of heresy and schism is still perceptible today, since, in light of the dogmatic definition of the Roman primacy, in principle schism always implies a heresy.

Schism, from the Greek *schisma*, meaning "separation," refers to a rupture of the bonds of hierarchical communion at an institutional level.

102 Blaise Pascal, *The Thoughts of Blaise Pascal*, trans. Charles Kegan Paul (London: George Bell and Sons, 1901), 274.
103 Congar, "Proprietà essenziali della Chiesa," 523. Our translation.
104 Congar, "Proprietà essenziali della Chiesa," 518. Our translation.
105 Antonio Acerbi, "Ortoprassi," in Barbaglio and Dianich, *Nuovo dizionario di teologia*, 1008–9. Our translation.
106 Johann Adam Möhler, *Unity in the Church or the Principle of Catholicism: Presented in the Spirit of the Church Fathers of the First Three Centuries*, trans. Peter C. Erb (Washington, D.C.: The Catholic University of America Press, 1996), 144.
107 Acerbi, "Ortoprassi," 1009.

Extra-ecclesial motives have often played a significant role in this type of division. While heresy is more directly concerned with the truth of faith, in schism the motive for breaking ecclesiastical communion often comes from the civil sphere and more concretely from nationalisms and regionalisms. The catholicity represented in the see of Rome is considered to be an invasion of the particularity and autonomy of both the local church as well as the human community in its political and cultural dimension.[108] In not a few cases, ecclesiastical schism is a consequence of the political schism.

The notion of apostasy should not be omitted here, as it is the broader sin against communion. From the point of view of ecumenical theology, however, apostasy is not a theme of much interest, since the apostate departs intentionally and entirely from ecclesial communion. From the ontological point of view, the apostate retains the indelible character of baptism within his or her soul, which constitutes the "structural" bond of communion. At the same time, however, in this condition the person does not possess even the minimum of faith by which this character can be raised to the reality of ecclesial communion.

Consequently, the apostate differs from one who is excommunicated in that the latter does not so much leave the Church but is rather "pushed out." This removal from ecclesiastical communion takes place even if the person still professes the entire truth of the faith or a great portion of it. Thus, the person who is excommunicated does not seek such a sanction, at least in theory, but rather receives it. Moreover, even though both the apostate and the excommunicated person retain the baptismal character in their souls, their personal situation separates them from the means of salvation offered by the Church.

In regard to excommunication, one should not lose sight of the original meaning of this word. Etymologically, "excommunication" refers to one who is excluded from eucharistic communion. This exclusion was the consequence of a wound or rupture in ecclesial communion, either on the moral or on the doctrinal level. The notions of schism and excommunication overlapped inasmuch as the first was conceived as "raising an altar against altar." In this sense, Augustine said with regard to the followers of Parmenian that "they erected their altar of schism."[109]

108 On this theme, see the different historical examples cited in Congar, *Proprietà essenziali della Chiesa*, 515.
109 Congar, *Proprietà essenziali della Chiesa*, 505–6.

Excommunication, in addition to being pronounced at the individual level, can be declared among the churches and specifically among bishops. Such action excluded any kind of Eucharistic intercommunion between the relevant faithful and pastors. Only later, with the development of canon law in the second millennium, would the juridical aspect take on great prominence. Excommunication increasingly came to be seen as a juridical penalty imposed by ecclesiastical authority, which involved the exclusion from certain rights or activities of the Church, as well as effects in the civil sphere.[110]

In examining this topic, one should keep in mind that canonical excommunication does not necessarily coincide with a partial or total lack of theological and ecclesial communion. Relevant here is the previously mentioned "nonmechanistic" character of the relationship between the visible and invisible elements in the Church. Also, as the next chapter will emphasize, ecclesial communion is a reality that admits of gradualness, a quality which is not possible in the context of canonical excommunication.

Ecclesial communion, finally, can also be damaged by sects and a sectarian mentality. The terminology has undergone considerable change on this issue. Ecclesiastical writings sometimes used the term "sect" with reference to a non-Catholic Christian community, in addition to the non-Christian sects. Lutherans and the Reformed, for example, were therefore included among the sects. On this point, these writings would contrast the universality of Catholic truth with the supposed sectarianism of the truths professed by these other groups. Although the etymological sense of the term evokes the idea of secession (from *secare*, "to cut"), the present meaning can no longer be applied to churches and the other ecclesial communities which have developed over the course of the centuries.[111] Nor does the term "sect" properly apply to groups which are more recent in origin yet claim to possess a certain catholicity.

To avoid confusion, the distinction introduced by Ernst Troeltsch between "church" and "sect" was common up until the 1970s. Both "church" and "sect" were considered to be "religious groups," but while the former existed in harmony with society as a whole, the latter group rejected or even opposed such coexistence.[112] The life of Christian sects, however, has evolved,

110 Giovanni Cereti, "Comunione," in Barbaglio, Boff, and Dianich, *Teologia*, 265.
111 The word also goes back to the idea of following (from *sequi*, "to follow"). See Robert Bergeron, "Christian Sects," in Latourelle and Fisichella, *Dictionary of Fundamental Theology*, 967–71.
112 Massimo Introvigne, "Le 'nuove religiosità' e la religione," in *La verità della religione*, ed. Giovanni Tanzella-Nitti and Giulio Maspero (Rome: Cantagalli, 2007), 139–40.

and today the vast majority of them are neither at the margins nor in opposition to civil society. Therefore, from the 1980s to the 1990s the terminology underwent a further change. Today, we speak about "new religions" and "new religious movements," given the somewhat derogatory connotation of the term "sect."[113] Another common term today is "cult," understood by some as "deviant religious groups within a deviant tradition," although their distinction with respect to sects has been subject to much discussion.[114]

Beyond the terminological issue, the theological meaning of sects is not easy to characterize with precision.[115] Their specific identity is not simply that of dissent, nor of an antagonistic attitude towards the established Church. According to Cardinal Christoph Schönborn, in Catholic theology today "a sect is characterized by estrangement from the common biblical-apostolic truth and the central contents of faith."[116] For others, the defining characteristic of the sect would result from the combination of a radical eschatological perspective and a strong sense of enlightenment, which ends in dualism, fideism, and a radical ethic.[117]

For scholars of ecclesiology, today's concept of Christian sects implies a rejection of the properly ecclesial character of the Christian community. In a sect, one accepts the Gospel, but not the Church. According to such a group, the Church would be neither founded nor desired by Jesus. Among the other characteristics frequently linked to a sectarian mentality are the following:

> Some traditional articles of faith are so overemphasized that they squeeze Christ and his gospel out of the central place in the faith; new doctrines and forms of belief, which are beyond the Bible and Church tradition, acquire central importance and they become a means of distinguishing the members from all other Christians. . . . The sectarians are detached from the world and exclusive, and their group-related self-understanding makes church fellowship impossible and often creates social isolation.[118]

113 Francis Arinze, "The Challenge of New Religious Movements," in *Today's Destructive Cults and Movements*, ed. Lawrence J. Gesy and Carol Giambalvo (Huntington, Ind.: Our Sunday Visitor, 1993).

114 Introvigne, "Le 'nuove religiosità' e la religione," 140–41. Our translation.

115 We must keep in mind that there are also sociological and juridical criteria for defining the concept of sect. On this, and for a more general overview of the theme, see Eugenio Fizzotti and Sergio Tapia, "Sette e nuovi movimenti religiosi," in Calabrese, Goyret, and Piazza, *Dizionario di ecclesiologia*, 1321–29.

116 Christoph Schönborn, "Are There Sects in the Catholic Church," *L'Osservatore Romano: Weekly Edition in English* 13, no. 20 (August 13, 1997): 3.

117 Bergeron, "Christian Sects," 967–71.

118 Hans D. Reimer, "Sects," in *Dictionary of the Ecumenical Movement*, ed. Nicholas Lossky et al. (Grand Rapids, Mich.: Eerdmans, 1991), 914.

Usually, the sect limits salvation to a certain number of persons who belong to the respective group. Thus, sects are the opposite of the major churches. The sects, in light of this tendency and the larger picture outlined above, are phenomena which remain outside the ecumenical movement.

Chapter 5

Catholic Principles of Ecumenism

Chapter 3 described the elements that define ecumenism, distinguishing this theme from other activities or realities and situating ecumenism in the context of the Church's mission. Chapter 4 examined the Catholic vision of ecclesial communion, focusing also on the types of divisions that wound Church unity. We will now analyze Catholic thought on the reestablishment of unity—that is, on ecumenism in the proper sense.[1]

The present study seeks to offer a Catholic consideration of ecumenism. Such a perspective does not entirely match, and at times is very different from, the conception of ecumenism on the part of other churches. In spite of this divergence, ecumenism as such, as a movement aroused by the Holy Spirit, retains an essential unity. The Spirit who breathed upon Protestant and Anglican circles at the beginning of the twentieth century, igniting in them a desire for unity, is the same Spirit who also breathed in the Catholic Church later on, inspiring her to be integrated into the ecumenical movement. In light of this perspective, the council fathers decided to modify the title of chapter 1 of the Decree *Unitatis Redintegratio* from "Principles of Catholic Ecumenism" to the definitive "Catholic Principles on Ecumenism."[2]

After a brief look at the situation in the preconciliar period, this chapter will analyze the specific theological principles of ecumenism. We will then consider these principles in the context of the various situations of relationship with the one Church, so as to shed light on the path to reestablishing full communion. Finally, some proposed models of unity will be examined in view of the teaching on ecclesial unity developed after Vatican II.

1 As a general bibliography for this chapter, see the following: Battista Mondin, *L'ecumenismo nella Chiesa Cattolica prima, durante e dopo il concilio* (Rome: Herder, 1966); Pattaro, *Corso di teologia dell'ecumenismo*; Rodríguez, *Iglesia y ecumenismo*; Luigi Sartori, *Teologia ecumenica* (Padua: Libreria Gregoriana Editrice, 1987); Jean-Marie-Roger Tillard, *Church of Churches: The Ecclesiology of Communion* (Collegeville, Minn.: Liturgical Press, 1992); Jos Vercruysse, *Introduzione alla teologia ecumenica* (Casale Monferrato: Piemme, 1992); José R. Villar, *Eclesiología y ecumenismo: Comunión, Iglesia local, Pedro* (Pamplona: Ediciones Universidad de Navarra, 1999).

2 Vatican Council II, *Relatio super Schema Emendatum Decreti de Oecumenismo* (Vatican City: Tipografia Vaticana, 1964), 6.

FROM "NO SALVATION OUTSIDE THE CHURCH" TO THE QUESTION OF "MEMBERS"

The most widespread ecclesiology from the period prior to Vatican II went back to the Counter-Reformation and was deeply imbued with the model of the Church as a society. Within such a perspective, one could not adequately articulate the specific nature of the ecumenical movement. To understand this difficulty, here we shall retrace, briefly, the long road that led from the patristic axiom "no salvation outside the Church" (*extra Ecclesiam nulla salus*) and arrived at the more modern issue of "members" of the Church.[3]

The first explicit formulations of this patristic principle appear almost simultaneously in the East with Origen and in the West with Cyprian. In his homilies on Joshua, Origen, in debate with the Jews, comments on the episode of Rahab. Rahab offers a hiding place for the scouts sent to Jericho, obtaining in return salvation for herself and for all those who take refuge in her house. In this context, Origen affirms: "Let no one deceive himself. Outside this house, that is, outside the Church, no one is saved."[4]

In order to grasp Origen's thought correctly, one should not lose sight of the fact that "from a typological perspective, Origen connects profoundly the exploits of Joshua with the salvific events carried out by Christ, events in which the mediating function is rooted, a function which is absolutely singular for the attainment of salvation."[5] For his part, Cyprian emphasizes the unicity of the Church against any form of schism. Any such division would diminish the exclusivity of the salvific mediation of the Church.[6] In this context, Cyprian warns that outside of the Church one cannot have life,[7] since the house of God is uniquely one and "no one can be saved except in the Church."[8] Elsewhere he adds, with reference to intra-ecclesial life,

3 For a more in-depth treatment, see Yves Congar, "Hors de l'Église, pas de salut," in *Catholicisme Hier Aujourd'hui Demain*, ed. Gabriel Jacquemet, vol. 5 (Paris: Letouzey et Ané, 1962), 948–56; Bernard Sesboüé, *"Hors de l'Église, pas de salut:" Histoire d'une formule et problèmes d'interprétation* (Paris: Desclée de Brouwer, 2004); Giacomo Canobbio, *Nessuna salvezza fuori della Chiesa? Storia e senso di un controverso principio teologico* (Brescia: Queriniana, 2009).

4 Origen, *Homilies on Joshua*, trans. Barbara J. Bruce, Fathers of the Church 105 (Washington, D.C.: The Catholic University of America Press, 2002), 3.5, citing Joshua 2:17–21.

5 Sandra Mazzolini, "*Extra Ecclesiam nulla salus*: Prospettiva patristica," *Annales Theologici* 25 (2011): 322–23. Our translation.

6 Cyprian of Carthage, *Epistulae*, 4.4.

7 Mazzolini, "*Extra Ecclesiam nulla salus*," 324.

8 *Nemini salus esse nisi in Ecclesia possit*. Cyprian of Carthage, *Epistulae*, 62.4.

that for the heretics baptism and martyrdom do not bring salvation, "because salvation does not exist outside the Church."[9]

Saint Augustine's teaching follows along the same lines as Saint Cyprian's, but with a greater openness in debate with the Donatists. For the bishop of Hippo, the Donatists have the sacraments, the Gospel, faith in the Trinity, but not salvation, because "salvation does not exist outside the Church."[10] Those who sin against the Spirit and remain outside the unity of the Church until the end of their life cannot be saved, because the Holy Spirit does not give life to anyone outside the body of Christ.[11] However, for Augustine, there are baptized Catholics who are, in reality, not truly within the ark of salvation because they are in the Church physically but not with the heart.[12] At the same time, there are baptized persons outside the visible bounds of the Church who are actually within this ark "with their heart but not with the body."[13]

After Saint Augustine, the bond between salvation and the Church tightens even more and takes on an increasingly exclusivist bent. In the *Ancient Statutes of the Church*, from around 475 AD, the principle "outside the Catholic Church no one is saved"—expressed in absolute terms—forms part of the doctrinal test for those promoted to the episcopate.[14] Saint Fulgentius of Ruspe radicalizes this absolute formulation still further when he writes to Peter, a pilgrim departing to Jerusalem and eager to be enlightened with true faith. Fulgentius affirms: "Hold most firmly and never doubt that not only all pagans but also all Jews and all heretics and schismatics who finish this present life outside the Catholic Church will go 'into the eternal fire which has been prepared for the devil and his angels.'"[15]

In similar terms, this type of radical negation is present in the later professions of faith: in that prescribed by Innocent III to the Waldensians, in that of the Fourth Lateran Council, and in the bull *Unam Sanctam* of Bon-

9 *Quia salus extra Ecclesiam non est.* Cyprian of Carthage, *Epistulae*, 73.21.

10 *Salus extra Ecclesiam non est.* Augustine, *De baptismo*, in *Polemica contro i Donatisti*, ed. Agostino Trapé, Opere di Sant'Agostino, vol. 15 no. 1 (Rome: Citta Nuova, 1998), 4.17.24.

11 Augustine, *Epistulae*, in *Le lettere*, ed. A. Trapè, Opere di sant'Agostino 23 (Rome: Citta Nuova, 1974), 185.49–50.

12 *Corde sed non corpore.*

13 Augustine, *De baptismo*, in *Polemica contro i donatisti*, ed A. Trapè, Opere di sant'Agostino, vol. 15, no. 1 (Rome: Citta Nuova, 1998), 5.28.39.

14 Denzinger, *Enchiridion symbolorum*, 325.

15 Fulgentius of Ruspe, *De fide ad Petrum*, in *Fulgentius: Selected Works*, trans. Robert B. Eno, Fathers of the Church 95 (Washington, D.C.: The Catholic University of America Press, 2002), 38.81.

iface VIII.[16] This progressive exclusivism reaches its culmination with the bull *Cantate Domino* of the Council of Florence from 1442, regarding union with the Coptic and the Ethiopian Church. This document incorporates the expression of Saint Fulgentius, giving it magisterial strength: "[The Church] firmly believes, professes and preaches that all those who are outside the catholic church, not only pagans but also Jews or heretics and schismatics, cannot share in eternal life and will go into the everlasting fire which was prepared for the devil and his angels [Mt 24:41], unless they are joined to the Catholic Church before the end of their lives."[17]

One can easily understand how these expressions, when interpreted in an overly rigid manner, led to criticism due to their harshness. However, as Gérard Philips has emphasized, "out of respect for objectivity, one cannot lose sight of either the source of the text nor the general problematic of the time. One continues reading and realizes that the decree only contemplates those persons who are conscious of tearing the seamless tunic, by refusing to remain in the one Catholic Church."[18] Other authors bring to light different nuances to be considered with regard to the Council of Florence. In Ángel Antón's view, one must keep in mind the prevailing conviction, present at the time, of the widespread diffusion of the Gospel throughout the whole world. This context would make nonadhesion to the faith inexcusable.[19] Giacomo Canobbio sees the decree as being particularly addressed, in a polemical way, towards the bishops still remaining in Basel and loyal to the antipope Felix V.[20] Finally, Joseph Ratzinger interprets the Florentine decree as the universal formulation of a principle which had been initially addressed to schismatics and heretics of the first centuries and, more particularly, to those who sought to alter the structure of the Church from within. According to the latter view, *extra Ecclesiam nulla salus*, originally an exhortation addressed to Christians themselves, becomes in Florence a theological formula valid for all.[21] The atypical nature of this particular

16 Denzinger, *Enchiridion symbolorum*, 791; 802; 870.

17 *Cantate Domino*, in Tanner, *Decrees of the Ecumenical Councils*, https://www.papalencyclicals.net/councils/ecum17.htm.

18 Philips, *L'Église*, 192. Our translation.

19 Ángel Antón, *El misterio de la Iglesia* (Madrid: Biblioteca de Autores Cristianos, 1986), 1:339.

20 Giacomo Canobbio, "*Extra Ecclesiam nulla salus*: Interpretazioni e prospettive," *Annales Theologici* 25 (2011): 296–97. Union with the Orthodox and with the Armenians had been already reached with the previous bulls *Laetentur coeli* and *Exultate Deo* of the year 1439, though the former proved ephemeral.

21 Joseph Ratzinger, *Das neue Volk Gottes: Entwürfe zur Ekklesioloigie* (Düsseldorf: Patmos-Verlag, 1972), 159.

council should not be lost sight of for a correct interpretation of the dictum at hand: Florence was a true council of union, in which Greek and Latin fathers took part together.[22]

With the European arrival in America in 1492 and with maritime journeys to the American and Asian continents, the cultural context of theological reflection greatly changed. A new awareness emerged of the existence of large groups of persons who had never been evangelized. Saint Robert Bellarmine explicitly addresses this topic and admits the possibility of a certain adherence to the Church, or *votum Ecclesiae*, among such persons. Bellarmine understands this possibility as a belonging to the soul of the Church but not to her body.[23] This possibility parallels the scholastic conception of the reception of baptism by desire (*in voto*) as opposed to the normal administration of this sacrament *in re*.[24]

The Magisterium itself has, on more than one occasion, denounced as erroneous a literal reading of *extra Ecclesiam nulla salus*. Alexander VIII condemned the Jansenist teaching which rejected the action of Christ's grace outside the visible confines of the Church.[25] Pius IX assumes the concept of invincible ignorance, until then a concept exclusive to moral theologians, in order to apply it to this theme:

> There are, of course, those who are struggling with invincible ignorance about our most holy religion. Sincerely observing the natural law and its precepts inscribed by God on all hearts and ready to obey God, they live honest lives and are able to attain eternal life by the efficacious virtue of divine light and grace. Because God knows, searches and clearly understands the minds, hearts, thoughts, and nature of all, his supreme kindness and clemency do not permit anyone at all who is not guilty of deliberate sin to suffer eternal punishments.[26]

Although Pius IX's teaching represents an important step forward in the theological subject at hand, he does not yet speak of the bond between the Church and such persons outside the visible Church.

22 Miguel De Salis, "*Extra Ecclesiam nulla salus*: Prospettiva conciliare," *Annales Theologici* 25 (2011): 354.

23 Bellarmine, *De controversiis christianae fidei adversus huius temporis haereticos*, Seconda Controversia Generalis, Liber 3, *De Ecclesia militante*, caput II, 75.

24 Giacomo Canobbio, "Necessità," in Calabrese, Goyret, and Piazza, *Dizionario di ecclesiologia*, 948.

25 *Decree of the Holy Office* (December 7, 1690), 5, in Denzinger, *Enchiridion symbolorum*, 2305.

26 Pius IX, Encyclical Letter *Quanto conficiamur moerore* (August 10, 1863), 7, https://www.papalencyclicals.net/pius09/p9quanto.htm.

In the encyclical *Mystici Corporis*, from 1943, Pius XII counts among the actual members of the Church those who have received baptism and maintain the bonds of faith and communion.[27] At the same time, the pontiff addresses those who have not been enlightened by Gospel truth or who, by breaking faith or unity, have separated from the Catholic Church. The pontiff asks these persons to "seek to withdraw from that state in which they cannot be sure of their salvation. For even though by an unconscious desire and longing [*inscio quodam desiderio ac voto*] they have a certain relationship with the Mystical Body of the Redeemer, they still remain deprived of those many heavenly gifts and helps which can only be enjoyed in the Catholic Church."[28] Finally, the Letter of the Holy Office to the Archbishop of Boston in 1949, against the excessive rigor of Father Leonard Feeney, manifests a development with regard to the desire or *votum* by which one adheres to the Church. The letter states that "this desire need not always be explicit, as it is in catechumens; but when a person is involved in invincible ignorance God accepts also an implicit desire."[29]

On one hand, one might aptly affirm:

> At around the middle of the twentieth century, two themes come to be distinguished, which until then had been closely connected with one another: the question of belonging to the Church . . . and the study of the axiom being analyzed here. . . . *Extra Ecclesiam*, in fact, progressively becomes a principle more objective than personal: it does not indicate so much who is saved, as much as the way in which those who come to salvation are saved.[30]

On the other hand, however, the accumulated patrimony of doctrine, even with the various clarifications, still presented many problematic aspects. The consideration of Catholics as the only "actual" (*reapse*) members of the Church did not leave room for appreciating the ecclesial status of non-Catholic Christians. Such a vision would suggest an unhealthy separation between being a Christian and being in the Church. Furthermore, the distinction between "actual" members and members by "desire" would imply that non-Christians and non-Catholic Christians would be viewed as theo-

27 Pius XII, Encyclical Letter *Mystici Corporis* (June 29, 1943), 22.
28 Pius XII, *Mystici Corporis*, 103.
29 Holy Office, *Letter to the Archbishop of Boston* (August 8, 1949), https://www.ewtn.com/catholicism/library/letter-to-the-archbishop-of-boston-2076.
30 Miguel De Salis, "*Extra Ecclesiam*," 359. Our translation.

logically equivalent, with regard to the relationship of these respective groups with the Church. Finally, the possibility of salvation through desire (*votum*) refers exclusively to the realm of individuals. Thus, such a conception fails to appreciate the existence of objective and ecclesial means of grace and salvation among non-Catholic Christians.

The aforementioned difficulties are challenging and delicate issues. At the same time, those who would seek to be faithful to the entire truth could not ignore such topics. This is the perspective from which one must understand the doctrinal development of the Second Vatican Council. Although carried out in continuity with the traditional doctrine, the conciliar teaching is an authentic step forward.[31]

THE GRADUALNESS OF ECCLESIAL COMMUNION

We can now fully address the first of the principles that arise from the council's teaching. This principle was already mentioned in the previous chapter and will now be discussed within its specifically ecumenical context. This principle consists in understanding ecclesial communion as a gradual reality. Such a vision is based on an approach that comes, necessarily, from the way in which the very notion of communion is conceived—that is, as a participation in the Trinitarian communion. This means that one can be more or less in communion with the Church, both from the point of view of the individual as well as at the level of organized community. This is expressed by *Unitatis Redintegratio* when the decree affirms that those "who believe in Christ and have been truly baptized are in communion with the Catholic Church even though this communion is imperfect."[32] As was said over the course of the council, "communion among the faithful of Christ can be perfect or less perfect."[33]

Therefore, communion varies *gradually* from nonexistence to full realization. The possibility of such an imperfect structural communion is due to the fact that the three visible bonds of unity—creed, liturgy, and hierarchy—can exist separately from one another, although this possibility would represent an anomalous situation. Each one of these bonds, furthermore, can exist in an incomplete way. This vision leads to the notion of full (perfect) or incomplete (imperfect) communion or incorporation in the

31 Rodríguez, *Iglesia y ecumenismo*, 141–54.
32 *Unitatis Redingratio*, 3.
33 *Communio inter christifideles perfecta vel minus perfecta esse potest. Acta Synodalia*, 3/7, 25.

Church. An ecclesiology of communion makes possible this flexible understanding of belonging to the Church. On the other hand, the notion of imperfect communion is difficult to understand if one solely considers the Church as the Mystical Body of Christ or as a "perfect society" (*societas perfecta*), both of which only admit the alternatives of member or nonmember.

THE RELATIONSHIP BETWEEN "THE CHURCH OF CHRIST" AND THE CATHOLIC CHURCH

Lumen Gentium states that the "one Church of Christ" which is "constituted and organized in the world as a society, subsists in [*subsistit in*] the Catholic Church, which is governed by the successor of Peter and by the Bishops in communion with him, although many elements of sanctification and of truth are found outside of its visible structure." This affirmation, in which *subsistit in* describes the relationship between the Church of Christ and the Catholic Church, is the object of the present section. This assertion is the foundation upon which the entire ecumenical structure of the conciliar teaching rests.[34] To understand the significance of the famous expression *subsistit in*, it is necessary to go back—even if only in a summary way—to its origins within the proceedings of the council.[35]

In the first draft of *Lumen Gentium*, the parallel text—then number 7—took up the teaching of *Mystici Corporis* on the identity between the Catholic Church and the Mystical Body, citing Pius XII's encyclical explicitly in a footnote.[36] According to this first draft, "only the Roman Catholic [Church] is

34 With the words of then-Cardinal Joseph Ratzinger, "we find the entire ecumenical problematic in the difference between '*subsistit*' and '*est*.'" Joseph Ratzinger, "L'ecclesiologia della *Lumen gentium*," *La comunione nella Chiesa* (Cinisello Balsamo: San Paolo, 2004), 155–56. Our translation.

35 Even in the years immediately after the promulgation of *Lumen Gentium*, Gérard Philips foretold with certainty that this expression would lead to "rivers of ink flow." Philips, *L'Église*, 119. Our translation. For an overview of the publications on this topic, see Philippe Molac, "La réception du 'subsistit in': Une premièrè étape: Du concile Vatican II à l'encyclique Ut unum sint," *Bulletin de Litterature Ecclesiastique* 107, no. 1 (2006): 23–50; among the literature still abundant even after the encyclical *Ut unum sint*, Reinhard Knittel, "Il '*Subsistit in*' di *Lumen Gentium* 8 e la permanenza indeffettibile della Chiesa pellegrinante," *Divinitas* 44, no. 3 (2001): 253–71; Pedro Rodríguez and José R. Villar, "Las Iglesias y comunidades eclesiales separadas de la Sede Apostólica Romana," *Diálogo Ecuménico* 39 (2004): 537–623; and Donato Valentini, "Subsistit in," in Calabrese, Goyret, and Piazza, *Dizionario di ecclesiologia*, 1383–1408, with a long bibliography.

36 Francisco Gil Hellín, *Constitutio dogmatica de ecclesia* Lumen Gentium (Vatican City: Libreria editrice Vaticana, 1995), 62. Some years after the publication of *Mystici Corporis*, Pius XII himself reaffirmed this position in the encyclical *Humani generis*, when he said: "Some say they are not bound by the doctrine, explained in Our Encyclical Letter of a few years ago, and based

rightly called Church."[37] In the second draft, there appears a reference to "many elements of sanctification" which can be found outside the visible structure of the Catholic Church.[38] This draft expressed the relationship of identity between the Church of Christ and the Catholic Church with the expression "this Church (of Christ) is then the Catholic Church."[39] The third draft makes the affirmation that "this Church . . . subsists in the Catholic Church."[40] The doctrinal commission of the council explained that the phrase "subsists in" was used in place of "is" so that the expression might be more in accord with the ecclesial elements found outside the Catholic Church.[41]

The Catholic teaching on the specific relationship between the Church of Christ and the Catholic Church rests on certain assumptions and has a broad set of implications which we will now examine. First of all, as should be clear and as Pope John Paul II has authoritatively confirmed, outside the visible confines of the Catholic Church not all is simply "ecclesial vacuum."[42] This teaching had already been anticipated by Pope Pius XI, who affirmed that "stones detached from a gold-bearing rock are also gold-bearing."[43] The principle finds confirmation in the validity of the sacraments conferred outside the visible confines of the Catholic Church. A longstanding tradition recognizes this validity.[44]

The conciliar magisterium would reaffirm and build upon this ecclesiological vision. With regard to separated churches and communities, the council states that "the Spirit of Christ has not refrained from using them

---

on the Sources of Revelation, which teaches that the Mystical Body of Christ and the Roman Catholic Church are one and the same thing." *Humani generis* (August 12, 1950), 27.

37 *Sola iure Catholica Romana nuncupatur Ecclesia.* Gil Hellín, *Constitutio dogmatica de ecclesia:* Lumen Gentium, 64.

38 *Elementa plura santificationis.* Gil Hellín, 64.

39 *Haec igitur Ecclesia (Christi) est Ecclesia catholica.* Gil Hellín, 64.

40 *Haec Ecclesia (. . .) subsistit in Ecclesia catholica.* Gil Hellín, 64.

41 *Loco 'est' dicitur 'subsistit in,' ut expressio melius concordet cum affirmatione de elementis ecclesialibus quae alibi adsunt.* Gil Hellín, 64. The Doctrinal Commission explained the motivation of the paragraph as that of describing the intimate mystery of the Church, in her perpetual unity with Christ and his work. This mystery, as the commission goes on to explain, is concretely found on earth in the Catholic Church. The commission went on to further emphasize that the Church is one and unique and is present on earth in the Catholic Church: *Intentio [Lumen Gentium 8] autem est ostendere, Ecclesiam, cuius descripta est intima et arcana natura, qua cum Christo Eiusque opere in perpetuum unitur, his in terris concrete inveniri in Ecclesia catholica. (. . .) Ecclesia est* unica, *et his in terris adest in Ecclesia catholica. Acta Synodalia*, 3/1, 176–77.

42 John Paul II, *Ut unum sint*, 13.

43 Pius XI, "Speech" (January 10, 1927).

44 On the question of the validity of baptism conferred outside of the Catholic Church, see the long list of magisterial documents compiled by Congar, *Chrétiens désunis*, 288.

as means of salvation which derive their efficacy from the very fullness of grace and truth entrusted to the Church."[45] The same document notes that "the written word of God; the life of grace; faith, hope and charity, with the other interior gifts of the Holy Spirit, and visible elements too" are among the "elements and endowments" which can be found "outside the visible boundaries of the Catholic Church," and which serve "to build up and give life to the Church itself."[46]

Such affirmations should not harm the relationship of identity between the Church of Christ and the Catholic Church. The *subsistit in* of *Lumen Gentium* 8 simply places this relationship in the context of a *nonexclusive* identity, in such a way as to place the various ecclesial elements in relation with the Church. At the same time, the council reaffirms the essential identity between the Church founded by Christ and the Catholic Church as we find it today, "governed by the successor of Peter and by the Bishops in communion with him."[47] In fact, despite the sad divisions and the lack of faithfulness to the Gospel shown on several occasions by her children, the Church of Christ still subsists—that is, she continues to exist—in the Catholic Church. In this sense "the continuity of existence involves a substantial identity of essence."[48]

Recently, this principle of identity has been authoritatively confirmed by the Congregation for the Doctrine of the Faith, which stated that "in number 8 of the Dogmatic Constitution *Lumen gentium* 'subsistence' means this perduring, historical continuity and the permanence of all the elements instituted by Christ in the Catholic Church."[49] The same document reiterates that "the use of this expression [*subsistit in*], which indicates the full identity of the Church of Christ with the Catholic Church, does not change the doctrine on the Church."

The council's teaching here does not blur the Catholic teaching on the oneness of the Church. In fact, *Unitatis Redintegratio* does not affirm the existence of other churches which are complete in themselves. Rather, the decree simply recognizes that the aforementioned "elements of sanctification and of truth" from *Lumen Gentium* number 8 including the sacraments,

45 *Unitatis Redintegratio*, 3.
46 *Unitatis Redintegratio*, 3.
47 Rodríguez and Villar, *Las Iglesias y comunidades eclesiales separadas de la Sede Apostólica Romana*, 596–97. Our translation.
48 Umberto Betti, "Chiesa di Cristo e Chiesa Cattolica: A proposito di una espressione della '*Lumen Gentium*,'" *Antonianum* 61 (1986): 743. Our translation.
49 Congregation for the Doctrine of the Faith, *Responses to Some Questions Regarding Certain Aspects of the Doctrine on the Church* (June 29, 2007).

Sacred Scripture, ministry, and liturgy—also exist and act efficaciously among other Christians within their own communities. The Church is truly complete in herself only when she possesses the totality of ecclesial elements. Along this line of reflection, John Paul II states in the encyclical *Ut unum sint* that the Church has already been given her eschatological fullness. In accord with this vision, which is attested to by the fathers of the East and West, the pontiff goes on to assert that "the elements of this already-given Church exist, found in their fullness in the Catholic Church and, without this fullness, in the other Communities."[50] Therefore, only the Catholic Church is the "universal sacrament of salvation," to use the expression from the Second Vatican Council.[51] The fullness of the means of salvation, through which God comes to encounter the human person, are found in this Church.[52]

The oneness of the Church and fullness of ecclesial elements are therefore inseparably linked to each other and thus exclude the possibility of another subsistence of the Church of Christ elsewhere, either fully or partially. On this question, the Congregation for the Doctrine of the Faith made a specific clarification with regard to an affirmation of Leonardo Boff in his book *Church: Charism and Power*. According to Boff, *Lumen Gentium* number 8 would imply that "it (sc. the sole Church of Christ) may also be present in other Christian Churches." Citing this position, the congregation maintained that "the Council had chosen the word *subsistit*—subsists—exactly in order to make clear that one sole 'subsistence' of the true Church exists, whereas outside her visible structure only *elementa Ecclesiae*—elements of Church—exist."[53]

The concept of subsistence, as already mentioned, certainly does imply a continuity of existence over the course of time. However, beyond this continuity, subsistence also indicates a very specific way of being. As Ratzinger notes, "*Subsistere* is a special case of *esse*. It refers to existence in the form of an individual subject."[54] The concept implies a "being-in-itself," as

50 John Paul II, *Ut unum sint*, 14.

51 *Lumen Gentium*, 48.

52 *Unitatis Redintegratio*, 3.

53 Congregation for the Doctrine of the Faith, *Notification on the Book "Church: Charism and Power" by Father Leonardo Boff O.F.M.* (March 11, 1985). See also Congregation for the Doctrine of the Faith, *Dominus Iesus* (June 16, 2000), 16: "The Church of Christ, despite the divisions which exist among Christians, continues to exist fully *only* in the Catholic Church."

54 Joseph Ratzinger, "*Deus locutus est nobis in Filio*: Some Reflections on Subjectivity, Christology, and the Church," in *Proclaiming the Truth of Jesus Christ: Papers from the Vallombrosa Meeting* (Washington D.C.: United States Catholic Conference, 2000), 27.

opposed to a "being-in-another." This explains why in other churches and communities, even though they possess some, or even many, ecclesial elements, the Church of Christ does not subsist even partially. These ecclesial elements "derive their efficacy from the very fullness of grace and truth entrusted to the Church": the original Latin text refers to "the Catholic Church."[55] All of this renders illegitimate any form of "ecclesiological relativism."[56] According to such relativism, any particular church or community would have the same value as another, to the point that membership in a specific Christian community, including the Catholic Church, would become irrelevant.

The conciliar notion of *subsistit in* presupposes an understanding of the indefectibility of the Church's unity, which is inseparably linked to the Church's oneness. *Unitatis Redintegratio* speaks of the unity of the Church of Christ which "subsists in the Catholic Church as something she can never lose."[57] Indefectibility is based directly on New Testament Revelation. In fact, "the promises of the Lord that he would not abandon his Church (cf. Mt 16:18; 28:20) and that he would guide her by his Spirit (cf. Jn 16:13) mean, according to Catholic faith, that the unicity and the unity of the Church—like everything that belongs to the Church's integrity—will never be lacking."[58] Therefore, we can affirm that "there is an historical continuity—rooted in the apostolic succession—between the Church founded by Christ and the Catholic Church."[59] Hence, one cannot hold that unity has subsisted in the Catholic Church up until a certain moment but either now subsists in another church or will do so in the future.

The concept of indefectibility places the Catholic position on ecumenism on the foundation of an already-existing unity. A Catholic vision of ecumenism "does not start with the differences in order to reach unity, but presupposes a given unity within the Catholic Church and its partial communion with the other churches and church communities in order to reach full communion with them."[60] With this perspective, we arrive at an aspect of ecumenism which we have already spoken of before: that of dilating the communion which is already present. Such communion already exists, as

55 *Virtus derivatur ab ipsa plenitudine gratiae et veritatis quae Ecclesiae catholicae concredita est. Unitatis Redintegratio*, 3.
56 Ratzinger, "*Deus locutus est nobis in Filio*," 3.
57 *Unitatis Redintegratio*, 4.
58 Congregation for the Doctrine of the Faith, *Dominus Iesus*, 16.
59 Congregation for the Doctrine of the Faith, *Dominus Iesus*, 16.
60 Kasper, *That They May All Be One*, 68.

has been noted, outside the boundaries of the Catholic Church, even if not fully. Ecumenism thus requires, as a starting point for dialogue, an accurate appreciation of the ecclesial situation of each party involved.

In light of the preceding analysis, we can now identify the limits of the so-called ecclesiology of sister churches. The expression "sister churches," present in some ecclesiastical documents of the fifth century and of the Middle Ages, recurs frequently in the ecumenical dialogue of the twentieth century, especially between Catholics and Orthodox. Frequently, the phrase has often been used in the hope for a fraternal relationship among the churches, without claiming to offer theological rigor. From a more systematic perspective, however, the council recalls that "a matter of primary concern and care among the Easterns, in their local churches, has been, and still is, to preserve the family ties of common faith and charity which ought to exist between sister Churches."[61] The conciliar text offers an adequate framework for this expression, specifying its use to express the relationship among particular churches—even of different denominations—as that of sisters, having as mother the universal Church.

At the same time, it does not seem ecclesiologically coherent to speak of sister churches to express the existing relationship between the Catholic Church, taken as a whole, and another church, such as the Orthodox Church, also taken as a whole. This language would suppose that the one Church of Christ subsists fully in these other churches, apart from the Catholic Church. In such a case, as has been explained in this section, the unicity of the one Church of Christ would be lacking. The Congregation for the Doctrine of the Faith in the *Note on the Expression "Sister Churches,"* from the year 2000, reaffirmed that this expression should be limited exclusively to the relationship between particular churches of the same communion, whether Catholic or not.[62]

61 *Unitatis Redintegratio*, 14.

62 Congregation for the Doctrine of the Faith, *Note on the Expression "Sister Churches"* (June 30, 2000). One should keep in mind that in the Orthodox sphere there is, at the official level, a rather critical attitude with respect to the ecclesiology of sister churches. See Jubilee Bishops' Council of the Russian Orthodox Church, "Basic Principles of the Attitude of the Russian Orthodox Church toward the Other Christian Confessions, 08–14–2000," *One in Christ* 41, no. 2 (April 2006): 88 100; also the refusal of the Sacred Synod of the Greek Orthodox Church to consider the Catholic Church "sister" of the Orthodox Church, an Italian translation of which can be found in Yannis Spiteris, "L'ecclesiologia della *Dominus Iesus* e il dialogo ecumenico," *Path* 1 (2002): 364.

THE ELEMENTS OF THE CHURCH

A historical look at the antecedents of the concept of the "elements of the Church" (*elementa Ecclesiae*), a concept which we have already touched upon, can help to better clarify its meaning. In the nonpolemic writing of the Middle Ages, the "attributes"—especially those of the Church—were mainly dealt with under the category of "conditions" (*conditiones*). This word comes etymologically from the verb *condere*, meaning "to found, to create, to institute." Hence, this notion was meant to indicate something inherent and belonging to the essence of a thing. A condition referred to something which was both constitutive of a thing itself, as an essential part of it, as well as a constituent part within that thing itself.[63]

The Protestant tradition, especially that of Calvinist origin, speaks instead of *vestigia* or "traces" of the Church. This term privileges the Church in the form of a confessing church. According to this Protestant view, the Church, in the present historical phase, can never fully express the richness of the Church of Christ.[64] The mystery of the Church would remain hidden until the eschatological consummation; in the present moment, the Church is manifested only through *vestigia*.

On the opposite extreme to this view of the Church as veiled in mystery is the Catholic notion of the notes or marks of the Church. This concept is important in polemical ecclesiological literature. The marks offer a sure sign of the presence of the Church of Christ. The *via notarum*, or demonstration of the Church by means of the marks, was based on the scholastic concept of a note (*nota*). The note was understood as a specific phenomenon, apt for mediating the knowledge and identification of a given reality. The demonstration of the truthfulness of the Catholic faith during the Counter-Reformation can be briefly described in the following words:

> On the basis of the New Testament testimonies, it is first of all shown that Christ Jesus has willed for his Church the four distinctive and permanent notes of unity, holiness, catholicity and apostolicity. To this major premise follows the minor, which highlights the undeniable and exclusive presence of these four characteristics in the Roman Catholic Church. On the other

63 Marcello Semeraro, *Mistero, comunione e missione: Manuale di ecclesiologia*, 2nd ed. (Bologna: Dehoniane, 1998), 129.

64 Pattaro, *Corso di teologia dell'ecumenismo*, 170–71. John Calvin, *Institution de la religion chrétienne* (Geneva: Labor et Fides, 1958), 4.2.11–12.

hand, these notes are lacking and do not present themselves in an equally clear and definite form in the other Christian confessions.[65]

The theological reflection on unity, holiness, catholicity, and apostolicity of the Church developed later within the notion of *proprietas* or "property." In this manner, the language shifted from an apologetic-defensive position, focused on the difference of the Catholic Church from realities external to it, towards the more theological realm of the Church's own inner being. Strictly speaking, however, the notion of property does not express the whole of this essential being. From an epistemological point of view, that which is *proprium* or "proper" to a thing is distinguished from the essence of that thing, even though the proper maintains an indissoluble relationship with the essence.[66] While these properties form a valuable part of the development of ecclesiology and are very present in the council's teaching, history has also manifested the difficulties in discerning the marks and properties of the Church in her pilgrim state: "Anyone who reflects on church life in the time and space of this present age cannot but be aware of division where there should be unity; sinfulness where there should be holiness; partiality where there should be catholicity, wholeness, and universality; and deviation where there should be faithfulness to the apostolic preaching of the gospel."[67]

In choosing the path of the "goods or elements of the Church" (*bona seu elementa Ecclesiae*)—which we can describe as the third principle of ecumenism—the council goes back to the most ancient framework of the conditions. The communities arising from the Reformation have a certain reserve towards this perspective. In their view, the Catholic sense of the elements of the Church would seem to imply a "making of the Church," in a mechanistic sense, as if this were an acquired right. Such an emphasis among Catholics would, according to this perspective, fail to adequately grasp the elements of the Church as gifts of the Spirit. Nonetheless, the Catholic Church's explicit recognition of the presence of these elements, even outside its visible borders, is very important for the cause of ecumenism.

65 Semeraro, *Mistero, comunione e missione*, 131. Our translation. At the beginning, the defenders of the Roman Church would enumerate as many as seven, ten, fifteen, and even one hundred notes. On the reduction to the four notes (and no more) the authority of the Nicene-Constantinopolitan Creed had its influence and, subsequently, the metaphysical justification that brought together the four notes with the four Aristotelian causes. See Semeraro, *Mistero, comunione e missione*, 131.

66 Semeraro, *Mistero, comunione e missione*, 131–32.

67 Erickson, "The One True Church: Thoughts concerning an Ecumenical Conundrum," 146.

One must take adequate account of the value of such recognition of ecclesial elements for non-Catholics. Among these, the council mentions "the written word of God; the life of grace; faith, hope and charity, with the other interior gifts of the Holy Spirit, and visible elements too" as well as "many liturgical actions of the Christian religion."[68] However, the decree does not seek to make an exhaustive list. In reality, everything that manifests or produces ecclesiality—apart from the primacy of the bishop of Rome—can also be found outside the institutional boundaries of the Catholic Church.

The decree affirms, in relation to the liturgical actions carried out outside the Catholic Church, that these "most certainly can truly engender a life of grace in ways that vary according to the condition of each Church or Community. These liturgical actions must be regarded as capable of giving access to the community of salvation."[69] With this statement, the council definitively abandons the idea of the sanctification of non-Catholic Christians "by desire" (*ex voto*), due to their nonculpable ignorance and their desire to carry out the will of God. Instead, the council recognizes that the sanctification of these non-Catholic communities does not occur in spite of their specific confession of faith, but rather in and through this confession.[70] As the decree notes immediately afterwards, "the separated Churches and Communities as such, though we believe them to be deficient in some respects, have been by no means deprived of significance and importance in the mystery of salvation. For the Spirit of Christ has not refrained from using them as means of salvation which derive their efficacy from the very fullness of grace and truth entrusted to the Church."[71]

The "elements" referred to in the decree are elements of the Church (*elementa Ecclesiae*); this means that they not only manifest ecclesiality but also make the Church. In other words, the efficacy of these elements is not limited to individual sanctification alone but also includes the communitarian aspect. Those who receive the effects of these elements, even outside the

68 *Unitatis Redintegratio*, 3.

69 *Unitatis Redintegratio*, 3.

70 Johann Adam Möhler Institut, *Le chiese cristiane nel Duemila*, 75–76. One may consider the position of Martin Jugie as an example of the attitude of Catholic theology before Vatican II. Speaking of the Orthodox Churches, he states that they are "entirely worthless for attaining salvation" (*sunt omnino ad salutem consequendam inutiles*); the Orthodox Christian of good faith can reach eternal life "by accident" (*per accidens*). The dissident Church is perhaps used "as a pure instrument or conduit" (*tanquam merum instrumentum vel canalis*) of the grace which "flows from the true Church" (*ex vera Ecclesia manat*). Our translation from the Latin. See Jugie, *Theologia dogmatica christianorum orientalium*, vol. 1 (Paris: Letouzey et Ané, 1926), 39.

71 *Unitatis Redintegratio*, 3.

Catholic Church, are sanctified and united in a church or community. These effects are none other than consequences of the nature of grace, as mentioned in the preceding pages: the grace that saves persons is the same grace that unites them.

It is necessary to now add that, according to Catholic ecclesiology, the various Christian communities outside the Catholic Church are not a homogeneous whole. The greater or lesser possession of the "elements and endowments which together go to build up and give life to the Church itself," or the "elements of sanctification and of truth" of which *Lumen Gentium* number 8 speaks, determines the ecclesial density of a given community.[72] Within this range of ecclesiality there also exist "leaps of quality," so to speak, with respect to ecclesial status. Therefore, the degree of communion with the Catholic Church is not the same among the various communities.[73]

Moreover, the possession or lack thereof of the episcopate—and with it, of the Eucharist—leads to a substantial qualitative difference, and not only a proportional one, with respect to the other communities. Only those groups which possess the episcopate and the Eucharist would, strictly speaking, be considered "churches." With such an assertion, Catholic theology does not intend to offend other communities. Rather, such terminology directly emerges from the Catholic consideration of the concept of Church, as theology takes it from Revelation.

The term "Church," in fact, comes from the Greek *ekklesia*, from *ek-kalein*, meaning "to summon." The word is used in reference to the community of believers in Christ in the New Testament, while the term *synagogé* is reserved for the people of Israel. In the Greek version of the Old Testament, the Septuagint, both these terms are used to translate the Hebrew word *qahal*, though the first one appears much more often. The Hebrew term refers to the convocation of a community in an ordered assembly for the celebration of worship.

Synagogé is most often used to translate the Hebrew *edah*. This Hebrew word has a broader reference to the people as a whole, considered as the community of the covenant.[74] *Ekklesia*, therefore, specifically indicates "the assembly of the Chosen People before God, above all for their assembly on Mount Sinai where Israel received the Law and was established by God as

72 *Unitatis Redintegratio*, 3.

73 Thils, *Histoire doctrinale*, 257.

74 Lorenzo De Lorenzi, "Chiesa," in *Nuovo Dizionario de Teologia Biblica*, ed. Pietro Rossano, Gianfranco Ravasi, and Antonio Girlanda (Cinisello Balsamo: San Paolo, 1988), 251–52.

his holy people. By calling itself 'Church,' the first community of Christian believers recognized itself as heir to that assembly."[75] This Christian community emerges from the Paschal Mystery and is built up by God through the sacrifice of the Body and Blood of Christ, the sacrifice of the new covenant. The sacrifices of the Old Law, with which the word *ekklesia* was associated, prefigure this new and eternal worship.

Hence, the name "Church" suggests the Christian people—understood as an assembly dedicated to worship—which has its source and culmination in the Eucharistic celebration.[76] Recently, the Magisterium has even affirmed that "*a causal influence of the Eucharist* is present at the Church's very origins."[77] In this perspective, the title of "Church" does not apply to a community of believers in Christ which does not validly celebrate the Eucharistic sacrifice.

Such is the situation of nonepiscopal Christian communities. Although their members are inserted into the body of Christ by baptism, these communities do not have the ecclesial density which comes from the Eucharist. The Catholic Church considers such groups "ecclesial communities," which "are not Churches in the proper sense."[78] Again, such classification need not be seen as offensive towards the communities in question. These same communities do not want to be considered a church in the same sense with which the Catholic Church understands the term. In any case, when one does not seek to speak with absolute theological precision, such groups can be designated as churches, in part because these communities frequently use this term in their official title.

With a few exceptions, history shows that those Christian communities which are most theologically distant from full communion are also those which are most susceptible to experiencing further divisions. This phenomenon offers historical support for the teaching regarding the elements of the Church. These elements, as constituent elements of ecclesiality, confer and reinforce internal unity; the diminution of these same elements weakens unity. This is to say that the ecclesial elements have their full meaning in

75 *Catechism of the Catholic Church*, 751.
76 Vatican Council II, *Sacrosanctum Concilium* (December 4, 1963), 10.
77 John Paul II, *Ecclesia de Eucharistia*, 21.
78 Congregation for the Doctrine of the Faith, *Dominus Iesus*, 17. It is worth repeating that this Church-ecclesial community distinction is not original to this document. It is present in the Second Vatican Council, but also in previous ecclesiastical documents, as highlighted by Congar in Appendix IV (already cited) "sur les termes employés dans les documents catholiques officiels récents pour désigner les dissidents" in *Chrétiens désunis*, 381–82.

their mutual relationship with one another. As affirmed by Congar: "Together they form the one soul of the one Church, because they are an ordered fullness, living and organic, rather than a collection of diverse elements."[79] They therefore are "forces impelling toward catholic unity," and if such momentum is not followed, there is a risk of disintegration.[80]

This ontology of the ecclesial elements is of great importance for properly understanding the search for full ecclesial communion. The ecclesial elements that a given community possesses partially, to the extent that the community authentically assimilates and develops such elements, should lead to the fullness of communion. This is because these elements, by their very nature, are meant to exist not separately but together.[81] Ecclesial unity is not a mere sum of ecclesial elements, but rather consists of an organic whole.[82] Therefore, the goal of full communion can be realized by an increase of the partial communion which is already present.

There is a further substantial difference in ecclesiality among the churches which have a valid episcopate—and hence the Eucharist—on one hand, and the Catholic Church on the other. This difference cannot be reduced to one more element, the primacy of the pope, which distinguishes the Catholic Church. The subsistence, the cohesion, and the efficacy of each of these elements is at stake in the difference between having almost all the ecclesial elements and having them all. Being Church, in the fullest sense of the word, refers to the complete possession of these elements. This is because the ecclesial elements, as has been pointed out, are not realities which were intended to be isolated and independent from one other. The attainment of full communion—and therefore the possession of the totality of the ecclesial elements—is like the placement of the cornerstone in ancient buildings. Though being just one more stone, it is the one which supports

79 Congar, *Divided Christendom*, 227.

80 *Lumen Gentium*, 8.

81 On the individual level it seems appropriate to quote the testimony of Heinrich Schlier on his conversion from Lutheranism to Catholicism: "The New Testament led me to inquire whether the Lutheran Confession and more specifically modern protestant faith, which has so widely deviated from its original form, is in agreement with its own testimony. Gradually I became convinced that the Church which I had in mind was the Roman Catholic Church. Hence it was, if I may say so, an authentic Protestant path which took me to the Church; a path which is actually provided for in the Lutheran confessional writings, although naturally not expected. In that context I must still mention something else. What led me to the Church was the New Testament as it presented itself to unbiased historical interpretation." "Kurze Rechenschaft," in *Bekenntnis zur katholischen Kirche*, ed. Karl Hardt, SJ (Würzburg: Echter-Verlag, 1956), 176; English translation in Hans Küng, *Structures of the Church* (London: Burns and Oates, 1965), 141.

82 *Acta Synodalia*, 3/7, 31.

everything.[83] As the doctrinal commission reaffirmed during the preparation of the decree *Unitatis Redintegratio*, unity is not a question of simply an addition of elements but rather an organic whole.[84] As the document states, the elements of the Church "together go to build up and give life to the Church."[85]

In her very essence, we repeat, the Church is more than the mere mathematical sum of ecclesial elements which are present in her. The Church, as a communion with God and among persons, is a complex reality, rooted above all in faithfulness to the Word of God. With great courage, Pope John Paul II did not hesitate to say that, in other Christian communities, "certain features of the Christian mystery have at times been more effectively emphasized."[86] Such a reality is a serious challenge for the Catholic Church, as Gustave Thils points out: "It would be intolerable that Catholics, proclaiming that they possess the entirety of the elements of the Church, imagine that they possess them *ipso facto* in their perfection, in their fullness, in their maximum vitality."[87] Ultimately, we cannot forget that "in a situation of division, unity in the Catholic Church is not concretely realized in all its fullness; the divisions remain a wound for the Catholic Church too."[88]

BAPTISM BY WATER AND THE CHURCH

"Finally those who have not yet received the Gospel are related in various ways to the people of God."[89] With these words, the council's Constitution on the Church introduces its section on the relationship of the Church with non-Christians. Here, the question is not one of imperfect communion, since non-Christians are not imperfectly incorporated to the Church. Rather, non-Christians are *ordered* to the Church, since all persons are des-

83 The following comment of Cardinal Willebrands is quite relevant: "But it would be to seriously misunderstand the thought of the Second Vatican Ecumenical Council if we were to consider this 'fullness' as something that springs only from juridical and canonical communion with the bishop of Rome. It is conditioned by this communion, but it is not reducible to it. It is essentially a communion in the total economy of the means of grace." "Chiesa, Corpo di Cristo, comunione nel Concilio Vaticano II," in *Una sfida ecumenica: la nuova Europa (discorsi)* (Verucchio: Pazzini Editore, 1995), 94. Our translation.
84 *Non agi de mera additione elementorum, sed de toto organico*. Francisco Gil Hellín, *Decretum de oecumenismo* Unitatis redintegratio (Vatican City: Libreria editrice Vaticana, 2005), 37.
85 *Unitatis Redintegratio*, 3.
86 John Paul II, *Ut unum sint*, 14.
87 Thils, *Histoire doctrinale*, 257. Our translation.
88 Kasper, *That They May All Be One*, 67.
89 *Lumen Gentium*, 16.

tined to communion with God.[90] That which distinguishes the situation of incorporation from that of such ordering is very visible and concrete, namely the baptism of water. "In explicit terms He Himself affirmed the necessity of faith and baptism [cf. Mk 16:16; Jn 3:5] and thereby affirmed also the necessity of the Church, for through baptism as through a door men enter the Church."[91]

In fact, the New Testament affirms that the Church is "one body and one Spirit," as there exists "one Lord, one faith, one baptism" (Eph 4:4–5). More specifically, Paul states that "in one Spirit we were all baptized into one body" (1 Cor 12:13). The salvific significance of baptism is therefore closely connected to its intrinsic ecclesiological dimension. Baptism is one of the principal foundations of the unity of the Church, although the sacrament performs this function in an instrumental manner. Christians become members of Christ by means of the gift of the Spirit received in baptism, through which personal faith becomes ecclesial faith. Being in Christ through baptism thus coincides with being members of his body, the Church.

The meaning of baptism is a matter of great ecumenical importance. It is precisely this reality of faith—the validly conferred baptism, which incorporates one into the Church—which drives the Catholic Church to seek full communion with those who are not perfectly united with her. Therefore, "Christian ecumenism is always baptismal ecumenism."[92] In this sphere, one cannot admit any kind of doubt regarding the validity of baptism.[93] This sacrament "establishes a sacramental bond of unity which links all who have been reborn by it."[94] Even when conferred outside the Catholic Church, baptism always remains one of the "gifts belonging to the Church of Christ," and a force "impelling toward catholic unity."[95]

In the case of the Christian life lived within the Catholic Church, this sacrament of faith constitutes a permanent call to full identification with

90 For a deeper examination of the notion of "ordering" to the Church, and of its origin and development in the council until its final elaboration in *Lumen Gentium* 16, see José Antonio Gil Sousa, "Ordenados a la Iglesia," *Aurensia* 5 (2002): 61–99.

91 *Lumen Gentium*, 14.

92 Kurt Koch, "Sviluppi ecumenici e nuove sfide," *Studi Ecumenici* 29, no. 2 (2011): 199. Our translation.

93 Therefore, the attitude of some Orthodox Churches that, in the case of conversions, confer baptism anew (cf. Koch, "Sviluppi ecumenici e nuove sfide," 200) is troubling, as is that of some Christian communities that do not consider the Trinitarian formula to be essential for this sacrament. See Kasper, *Harvesting the Fruits*, 191.

94 *Unitatis Redintegratio*, 22.

95 *Lumen Gentium*, 8.

Christ and thus to holiness. Baptism conferred outside the visible institution of the Catholic Church "envisages a complete profession of faith, complete incorporation in the system of salvation such as Christ willed it to be, and finally complete ingrafting in Eucharistic communion."[96]

Faith in baptism, the sacrament which serves as the door of the Church (*ianua Ecclesiae*) must be in harmony with the Church's unicity. In other words, there do not exist as many Churches as there are valid baptisms. In the face of the divisions which arose in the church of Corinth, in which some members professed to belong to Paul, Apollos, Cephas, or Christ, the apostle reaffirms that Christ is the absolute point of reference: "Is Christ divided? Was Paul crucified for you? Or were you baptized in the name of Paul?" (1 Cor 1:13). Christians are therefore always "baptized into Christ" (Gal 3:37, Rom 6:3) and thus incorporated into the one Church, "which is his body" (Eph 1:23). This incorporation takes place in such manner that the multiplicity of baptisms, whether implemented according to a Catholic rite or not, do not imply a multiplicity of churches. Rather, the baptized are inserted into one single reality, the Church founded by Christ, which subsists only in the Catholic Church.[97] In the "one baptism" spoken of in the Letter to the Ephesians (4:5), "'one' is understood not in contrast to a baptism that is repeated, but in the sense of a unique and unifying baptism, which, by virtue of the one Spirit, incorporates all the faithful in the one body of the Lord."[98]

The passage of *Lumen Gentium* number 14 quoted in the first paragraph of this section implies not only the necessity of baptism and faith but also the necessity of the Church. We will now take up this subject and examine how Vatican II has linked salvation and the Church. The complete text, which is found in chapter 2, on the people of God, and focuses on the Catholic faithful, says:

> This Sacred Council wishes to turn its attention firstly to the Catholic faithful. Basing itself upon Sacred Scripture and Tradition, it teaches that the Church, now sojourning on earth as an exile, is necessary for salvation. Christ, present to us in His Body, which is the Church, is the one Mediator and the unique way of salvation. In explicit terms He Himself affirmed

96 *Unitatis Redintegratio*, 22.
97 Congregation for the Doctrine of the Faith, *Dominus Iesus*, 16.
98 Heinrich Schlier, *Der Brief an die Epheser: Ein Kommentar* (Düsseldorf: Patmos, 1962), 188. Our translation.

> the necessity of faith and baptism and thereby affirmed also the necessity of the Church, for through baptism as through a door men enter the Church. Whosoever, therefore, knowing that the Catholic Church was made necessary by Christ, would refuse to enter or to remain in it, could not be saved.

Three aspects of the above text are particularly relevant for the topic under consideration. First of all, the council takes up the patristic dictum *extra Ecclesiam nulla salus*, though not in a literal sense, and states the principle in a positive way. The emphasis is not on the condemned but on the saved. Furthermore, the text places the assertion in an eminently Christological perspective. The Church is necessary not in and of herself, but because Christ, mediator and way of salvation, is present in his Body which is the Church. Finally, the expression is used according to the original patristic intention. That is to say, it is addressed above all to those who, aware of the truth of the Gospel, do not seek to enter the Church, or who, belonging to the Church, might seek to depart from its fold, attracted by heresy or schism.

The following statement from *Lumen Gentium* number 16, which implicitly recalls the magisterium of Pius IX and of the Holy Office, completes this conciliar teaching on salvation and the Church: "Those also can attain to salvation who through no fault of their own do not know the Gospel of Christ or His Church, yet sincerely seek God and moved by grace strive by their deeds to do His will as it is known to them through the dictates of conscience." In any case, one should not lose sight of the reality that salvation is a free gift, and grace by its very nature always has an ecclesial dimension. Grace is at once salvific and ecclesial, since we receive salvation by incorporation into the body of Christ, which is the Church.

The ideas mentioned in this section converge in the rich conciliar expression "universal sacrament of salvation" applied to the Church.[99] The Church does not produce salvation, but rather she transmits it or at least accepts the justified within herself because salvation—as we have said—always has an ecclesial aspect. To say that the ecclesial nature of salvation is of a sacramental type implies that salvation comes from Christ by means of the Church as the Lord's instrument, or at least that this salvation always has an objective reference to the Church.

The possible connection of the nonbaptized with the Church has an ordering towards the visible aspect of the Church, even if, in the subjectivity

99 *Lumen Gentium*, 48.

of the justified, there is no explicit contact. Such contact is not easy to grasp but is of great importance, especially in light of the current reality in which two-thirds of the world's population have not received baptism. A courageous statement made by Vatican II, in the Constitution *Gaudium et Spes*, counterbalances the stark theological reality of the great number of the nonbaptized: "For, since Christ died for all men, and since the ultimate vocation of man is in fact one, and divine, we ought to believe that the Holy Spirit in a manner known only to God offers to every man the possibility of being associated with this paschal mystery."[100]

In conclusion, looking at Christianity from within, we find the whole of the baptized; looking to the outside, we enter the territory of non-Christian religions and of nonbelievers. The former realm corresponds to ecumenical dialogue, while the latter pertains predominantly to interreligious dialogue. The distinction between these two spheres was discussed in Chapter 3 and is a matter of vital importance in ecumenical theology. Between a Christian and a non-Christian, even if both are destined for communion with God, one finds the decisive event of incorporation into Christ, "present to us in His Body, which is the Church . . . the one Mediator and the unique way of salvation."[101]

THE ECCLESIAL "STATUS" OF THE VARIOUS CHRISTIAN COMMUNITIES

That which we have studied in this chapter can be summarized as follows: The Church is a communion of persons with God and with one other. This communion is, by its nature, a reality that allows for gradualness: one can be more or less in communion, both on a personal level—the life of grace is gradual—and on an institutional level—an ecclesial community can lack full communion with the Catholic Church, depending on the ecclesial elements present in each case. These principles lead us to the affirmation that the ecclesial status of the baptized is not an either-or, in which one belongs or does not belong to the Church. Such belonging is a gradual condition. The Christian, starting from baptism, can progress from an imperfect incorporation into the Church—that is, a state of communion which is partial or gradual—until he or she reaches perfect incorporation, or full communion.

100 Vatican Council II, *Gaudium et Spes* (December 7, 1965), 22.
101 *Lumen Gentium*, 14.

One can thus describe the *ecclesial status* of Christian communities on the basis of their different degrees of communion with the Church.[102] Such a characterization is an important starting point for a healthy and balanced ecumenism. Before initiating a process of reestablishing communion, there is a need to identify the extent of the existing separation. One should also keep in mind that communion with the Church can be structural, in the sense of visible union, or on the other hand interior, which refers to the life of grace. Such communion can either be personal, referring to each believer in his or her individuality, or institutional, in reference to a broader community. Properly speaking, and holding to what was said previously regarding the theological framework of ecumenism, ecumenical theology is specifically concerned with structural-institutional communion. However, without doubt, reality goes beyond such rigid schemes. Thus, in light of the varying situations of communion, inevitably the distinct levels will intersect.

One can speak of a *situation of full incorporation* to indicate that of the faithful, or the baptized, who retain the triple bond of creed, liturgy, and hierarchy with the Catholic Church and also partake of the life in the Spirit by being in the state of grace. This is, in short, the teaching of *Lumen Gentium* number 14.

The *situations of imperfect incorporation* are very complex. Here, first of all, one should identify the Catholic faithful who have lost the life of grace because of sin. As long as these Catholics remain in this state, they cannot be saved. However, from the *structural* or institutional point of view, the condition of these faithful with respect to the Catholic Church is one of full communion since they maintain the triple bond of unity. "The Church, embracing in its bosom sinners, at the same time holy and always in need of being purified, always follows the way of penance and renewal."[103]

Quite distinct is the situation of those "who are born into these [non-Catholic] Communities and who grow up believing in Christ." These persons "cannot be accused of the sin involved in the separation, and the Catholic Church embraces upon them as brothers, with respect and affection. For men who believe in Christ and have been truly baptized are in communion with the Catholic Church even though this communion is imperfect."[104]

102 Pedro Rodríguez, "Ordenación e incorporación a la Iglesia. Síntesis doctrinal," *Teología Espiritual* 17 (1972): 353–66.
103 *Lumen Gentium*, 8.
104 *Unitatis Redintegratio*, 3.

In this area, one must take care to distinguish the episcopal churches, which possess the valid Eucharist, from the nonepiscopal ecclesial communities, which do not possess this sacrament. The presence of the Eucharist is not simply one more element in the life of the Church but is "the font from which all her power flows" and the root of all ecclesial communion.[105] Indeed, those who do not participate in a valid Eucharist acquire ecclesial communion through an explicit or implicit desire for the Eucharist. Such desires come at least from the reception of baptism, which always has an objective ordering towards the Eucharist. Since "the Most Blessed Eucharist contains the entire spiritual boon of the Church," one cannot imagine an ecclesial situation which is completely independent of this sacrament.[106]

The situation of those who have *voluntarily* separated themselves from the Catholic Church through the sins of heresy, schism, or apostasy, or who have been excommunicated, is a very particular one. These persons have been baptized, but the type of sin they have committed generates a subjective situation which renders the means of salvation inoperative. This status corresponds to the minimum degree of incorporation.

Finally, the situations of *ordering* towards the Church include all the nonbaptized. These persons are ordered to the Church but not incorporated to her either fully or imperfectly. In any case, the Church does not measure these persons according to a uniform standard but distinguishes those who are closest to the Church from those farthest from her. These groups go from the catechumens, who possess the "baptism of desire" and with this a desire for the Church, to the Jewish people, Muslims and members of the other monotheistic religions, and finally all other persons, who also are the object of God's saving will.

In distinguishing these myriad levels of communion, one must always keep in mind the absolute sovereignty of God, whose power is not bound by the elements of ecclesial communion, and "who wills everyone to be saved and to come to knowledge of the truth" (1 Tm 2:4). As previously mentioned, visible communion in the Church reflects the invisible communion of those who are justified, but such signification does not work in a mechanical or automatic way. "God alone knows what goes on in the heart of each man, and he does not deal with souls *en masse*, but one by one. No

105 *Sacrosanctum Concilium*, 10.
106 Vatican Council II, *Presbyterorum Ordinis* (December 7, 1965), 5.

one on this earth can make a judgement about the eternal salvation or condemnation of any individual."[107]

ECUMENISM IN A MISSIONARY PERSPECTIVE

The aforementioned classification is consistent with the triple aspect of the Church's mission as described in Chapter 3. The Church's pastoral care is aimed at those who are fully incorporated to her, so that they might preserve this state and grow in perfection. This pastoral solicitude is also directed to those Catholics who are only imperfectly incorporated—that is, those who are in a state of sin. In the case of such persons, the Church desires that their personal situation of communion might correspond with the fullness of institutional communion that they do not cease to possess. The Church admonishes this latter group by reminding them that "he is not saved, however, who, though part of the body of the Church, does not persevere in charity. He remains indeed in the bosom of the Church, but, as it were, only in a 'bodily' manner and not 'in his heart.'"[108] The council then addresses all Catholics, those in the state of sin and those in the state of grace, saying: "All the Church's children should remember that their exalted status is to be attributed not to their own merits but to the special grace of Christ. If they fail moreover to respond to that grace in thought, word and deed, not only shall they not be saved but they will be the more severely judged."[109]

The Church's missionary activity to all nations (*ad gentes*) is directed to those in a situation of ordering to the Church. The aim of this action is that these persons might enjoy, as soon as possible, communion with God in God's Church. To bring about their incorporation into Christ's body, the Church seeks to bring such persons to the waters of baptism and to the development of the visible and invisible bonds of communion.

In addition to these activities of the Church, ecumenical activity is directed to those persons who are in a situation of imperfect incorporation into the Church, so that they might reach full communion. For those Christian communities which do not possess a valid episcopate, part of this process is the recognition of the sacramental nature of the Church.[110] This aspect

107 Josemaría Escrivá, "The Supernatural Aim of the Church," *In Love with the Church*, trans. Fundación Studium (London: Scepter, 1989), 25, http://www.escrivaworks.org/book/in_love_with_the_church.htm.

108 *Lumen Gentium*, 14.

109 *Lumen Gentium*, 14.

110 Even if the document of the Joint Lutheran/Roman Catholic Study Commission, *Church and Justification: Understanding the Church in the Light of the Doctrine of Justification* (Wurzburg,

of the Church was brought into greater relevance during the middle of the twentieth century by the work of Otto Semmelroth (1912–1979) and especially in the ecclesiology of the Second Vatican Council. Indeed, the opening lines of the Dogmatic Constitution on the Church proclaim the Church to be "in Christ like a sacrament or as a sign and instrument both of a very closely knit union with God and of the unity of the whole human race."[111] The Church is sacrament not simply in her ministry of the seven sacraments, but rather her whole being, activity, and governance derive from these sacraments as efficacious signs of grace. Such a perspective, Susan Wood asserts, makes more evident the authentic nature of the Church and her mystery, and of her authority as being "personal, collegial, and communal."[112]

Beyond the various areas of disagreement, such a recognition of the Church's sacramental nature is a step of great importance from an institutional-theological point of view. A community which only conceives the Church as a community of the saved, without this vision of the Church's mediating role, will find it difficult to perceive the need for visible unity. From the perspective of Church as sacrament, the Church of Christ subsists in a concrete, permanent, and ministerially structured reality which has a necessarily *institutional* dimension. This institutional aspect does not exclude the charismatic aspect. A nonsacramental framework, on the other hand, privileges the notion of the Church as an *event*. Within such a viewpoint, the Church is "the assembly of all believers among whom the gospel is preached in its purity and the holy sacraments are administered according to the gospel," as stated in article 7 of the Augsburg Confession.[113]

Within the nonsacramental perspective, the role of the minister is absolutely secondary and not essential. As a "creature of the Word" (*creatura verbi*), according to an expression dear to Luther,[114] the assembly of believers is understood purely in terms of the proclamation and acceptance of the

---

1993) has led to advancement in this area, the road ahead is still long. As Donato Valentini said towards the end of the last century, "the sacramentality of the Church is the decisive point in Catholic-Lutheran dialogue." Quoted by Walter Kasper in "La successione apostolica nel ministero episcopale come problema ecumenico," *Salesianum* 59, no. 3 (1997): 399. Our translation.

111 *Lumen Gentium*, 1.

112 Susan K. Wood, "Issues and Perspectives in Roman Catholic Ecclesiology Today," in Braaten and Jenson, *Ecumenical Future*, 133.

113 "The Augsburg Confession," in Pelikan and Hotchkiss, *Creeds and Confessions*, 2:62; Kasper, *Harvesting the Fruits*, 204.

114 Cf, for example, *Ecclesia nata ex verbo. Genesisvorlesung (cap. 1–17)*, D. Martin Luthers Werke: Kritische Gesammtausgabe 42 (Weimar: Böhlau, 1911), 334.

Word in a context of faith; this Word has a singular manifestation in the sacraments.[115] Within such a perspective, the meaning of sacramental reality, whether in relation to the sacraments themselves or as a dimension of the Church herself, has been a fundamental problem.[116]

The churches with a valid episcopate should reflect on the nature of the episcopacy which they already possess. In the examination of this sacramental ministry, they can discover the primacy of the Roman pontiff as something intrinsic to the episcopate. Such reflection brings to the fore the importance of the principle of apostolic succession, within which the succession of the see of Peter is essential.

Indeed, a valid episcopate is not of itself a sufficient criterion to constitute a church. A bishop always exercises his ministry in communion with the other bishops. This communion is not simply affective but theological and hierarchical, deriving from the reality that the whole episcopal college succeeds the entire apostolic college.[117] Thus, on the one hand, one is a bishop only within the episcopal college, and this is so from the moment of ordination: "It pertains to the bishops to admit newly elected members into the Episcopal body by means of the sacrament of Orders."[118] At the same time, the episcopal ministry must be carried out "in hierarchical communion with the head and members of the college."[119]

This reality leads Catholic ecclesiology to consider the existence of a valid episcopate outside the episcopal college as a serious anomaly that requires remedy. Furthermore, the collegial aspect of apostolic succession implies the permanence of the structure of the apostolic college—head and members—within the episcopal college: "Just as in the Gospel, the Lord so disposing, St. Peter and the other apostles constitute one apostolic college, so in a similar way the Roman Pontiff, the successor of Peter, and the bishops, the successors of the apostles, are joined together."[120] Being a member of the episcopal college, therefore, cannot exclude the acceptance of the presiding role of the successor of Peter, and for this reason the Catholic Church cannot exclude the question of Roman primacy from ecumenical dialogue.

115 Martin Luther, *The Babylonian Captivity of the Church*, translated by Albert T. W. Steinhaeuser, in *The Works of Martin Luther* (Philadelphia: A. J. Holman, 1915), 2:186.
116 Kasper, *Harvesting the Fruits*, 154.
117 Goyret, *Dalla Pasqua alla Parusia*, 317–18.
118 *Lumen Gentium*, 21.
119 *Lumen Gentium*, 21.
120 *Lumen Gentium*, 22.

The third situation of imperfect incorporation—those who have voluntarily separated from the Church by heresy, schism, or apostasy—is difficult to classify. For those who have left this world, only the help of prayer remains for perfecting communion. For those who are still pilgrims on this earth, the doors of reconciliation with the Church remain open. These persons could be accepted into communion only on an individual level since they have personally excluded themselves from ecclesial communion. This acceptance of persons individually, as in the case of conversions, can be considered ecumenism only in a broad sense.

In light of the situation outlined above, can we say that the ultimate goal of ecumenism is the unity of all Christians in the Catholic Church? The answer is positive if the final step toward which ecumenism aims is the full communion of all Christians in a Church which has been profoundly purified. This renewed Church would possess a catholicity which is not simply a name but above all a theological property "with a new vital balance, a new doctrinal equilibrium, a renewed physiognomy, in short, in the spiritual fullness of a perfectly developed catholicity."[121] On the other hand, the answer to the question would be negative if ecumenism were only a strategy to hide an attempt to convert the interlocutor. The validity and specificity of ecumenism, formally different from individual reception into Catholic communion, must be taken seriously.

The Catholic perspective on ecumenism, therefore, is not to be thought of as being like a solar system, with the Catholic Church at the center and the other churches and communities orbiting in concentric circles, gradually drawing closer to the "sun." Instead, Catholic ecumenism is a *common path* towards an objective which is yet to be attained. The final goal is the full communion of all in Christ and must be reached by means of a mutual process of conversion and renewal, involving all the parties in dialogue. As Walter Kasper has affirmed, "the ecumenical endeavor is a common pilgrimage to the fullness of catholicity which Jesus Christ wants for his Church."[122] In other words, "the very essence of unity understood as full communion is catholicity not in its confessional but in its original and qualitative meaning as the full realization of all the gifts that the local and confessional churches have to contribute."[123]

121 Thils, *Histoire doctrinale*, 296.
122 Kasper, *That They May All Be One*, 67.
123 Kasper, *That They May All Be One*, 68.

MODELS OF UNITY

In addition to a starting point for ecumenism, which the previous pages have sought to describe, one also needs to clarify an endpoint of the ecumenical process. This final goal consists, as we would expect, in the attainment of visible communion. However, one can conceive of this visible unity according to different models. The official Catholic position in this regard is that developed in Chapter 4 of the present work, along the lines of *Unitatis Redintegratio* number 2. There are also other proposals, from inside and outside the Catholic Church, for visible unity which are worth examining.[124] The model of peaceful coexistence between the different churches and communities will not be taken into consideration here. Such coexistence is a necessary premise for ecumenism but does not constitute a goal.

The model of *reconciled diversity* comes from the Protestant sphere and begins from the assumption that "'the variety of denominational heritages (is) legitimate' and forms part of 'the richness of life in the church universal.' When 'in the open encounter with other heritages' the existing traditions and denominations lose their 'exclusive' and 'divisive' character, there emerges a vision of unity that has the character of a 'reconciled diversity.'"[125] Thus, the unity desired by Christ, far from implying the destruction or the overcoming of the different denominational identities, would support acceptance of such identities and consequent mutual enrichment. Underlying this vision is the notion that each single church is derived not from a division of the body of Christ, but from a particular manifestation of fidelity to the word of God. Divisions, reconciled by means of a common reference to the core Christian message of salvation and faith, would be transformed into legitimate diversity.

Reconciled diversity requires an ecclesiology that does not give too much importance to the visible element of the Church. One needs, in fact, to distinguish between legitimate diversity in the expression of the one faith and the contradiction between opposing positions. Such contradictions

124 Pontifical Council for Promoting Christian Unity, *The Ecumenical Dimension in the Formation of Those Engaged in Pastoral Work* (1997), II.B.c; Vercruysse, *Introduzione alla teologia ecumenica*, 106–18; Angelo Maffeis, "Modelli di unità della Chiesa nella storia del movimento ecumenico e nel dibattito teologico recente," *Teologia* 19, no. 1–2 (1994): 62–93; 109–50.

125 Lutheran-Roman Catholic Commission on Unity, *Facing Unity: Models, Forms and Phases of Catholic-Lutheran Church Fellowship* (March 3, 1984), 32. The document quotes from "The Ecumenical Role of the World Confessional Families in the One Ecumenical Movement," *LWF World Report* no. 15 (June 1983): 27–28. The latter is a discussion paper from two consultations with representatives from world confessional families.

would remain as irreconciled diversity and, therefore, manifest a union of churches without real unity. Rather than authentic unity, this model offers peaceful coexistence, or communion among denominations disguised as full communion.[126]

Reconciled diversity was achieved between the Lutheran Churches of Europe and the Reformed Churches with the Concord of Leuenberg in 1973.[127] Both traditions give less importance to the institutional dimension of the Church than does the Catholic Church. Ecclesial communion, in the context of the agreement, is conceived of as a communion of the pulpit and of the Lord's Supper. The respective churches remain autonomous and distinct from one another from the doctrinal point of view as well. In such a perspective, division becomes diversity without change in the original positions. Unity and diversity would coexist, as would be implied by the genuine sense of communion. However, in this particular case, the emphasis is on the *diversity* in unity, leaving in shadow the *unity* in diversity.

The model of reconciled diversity could perhaps be considered suitable as a *method* of ecumenism, but not as its goal.[128] Some would propose to leave unity at an apostolic core, absent the doctrinal elaborations which would allegedly be the source of division. However, in such a perspective, "nothing theologically decisive can be said about the ecclesial identities of divided churches, or division will be re-justified rather than overcome."[129] As we have previously seen, the World Council of Churches affirmed in its Fifth General Assembly, held in Nairobi, Kenya in 1975, that:

> [The one Church] is to be envisioned as a conciliar fellowship of local churches which are themselves truly united. In this conciliar fellowship, each local church possesses, in communion with the others, the fullness of catholicity, witnesses to the same apostolic faith, and therefore recognizes the others as belonging to the same Church of Christ and guided by the same Spirit.... Each church aims at maintaining sustained and sustaining relationships with her sister churches, expressed in conciliar gatherings whenever required for the fulfillment of their common calling.[130]

126 Kasper, *That They May All Be One*, 3–4.

127 See the text in Pelikan and Hotchkiss, *Creeds and Confessions of Faith in the Christian Tradition*, 3:744–52.

128 Joseph Ratzinger seems to move in this direction: "On the Progress of Ecumenism: A Letter to 'Theologische Quartalschrift', a periodical published in Tübingen," *Church, Ecumenism and Politics: New Essays in Ecclesiology* (San Francisco: Ignatius Press, 2008), 133–142.

129 R. R. Reno, "The Debilitation of the Churches," in Braaten and Jenson, *Ecumenical Future*, 65.

130 World Council of Churches, *Breaking Barriers*, 110.

This perspective rests upon the principle of diversity in faith. Visible unity would exist as a reality primarily in certain "conciliar gatherings," while in a habitual manner unity would be realized exclusively by means of mutual "sustained and sustaining relationships." The constitutive weakness of this form of unity is evident.

The model of *total organic unity*, on the other hand, "reflects a thinking which regards the existence of different confessional churches as a decisive obstacle to attaining true Christian unity and therefore takes the view that unity can be realized only by surrendering traditional ecclesial and confessional allegiance and identity."[131] According to this vision, churches which enter the process of unification are invited to cease their existence as autonomous bodies so as to create a totally new ecclesial body. In this way, the churches would reject the hypothesis of an absorption of one church in the other. Ordained ministry, specifically the episcopate, would be one of the fundamental elements of the united church.

A central part of this model, methodologically, is the further affirmation that union on the doctrinal level cannot be achieved through an a priori and rigid imposition of a single belief but rather through a process which follows the very act of reunion. Becoming part of the united church thus means loyalty to this new church and an abandonment of the preceding tradition. The process requires a definitive will that the previous ecclesial communities, as separate entities, definitively cease to exist.

In its main features, the model of total organic unity was applied in 1947 in the south of India between Congregationalists, Presbyterians, Methodists, and Anglicans. The new ecclesial body formed by the union is the Church of South India (CSI).[132] However, this particular experience was not repeated elsewhere.

This model is very pragmatic but lacks a theological appreciation of unity as an already-existing, even if not fully realized, aspect of the Church. Hence, in this approach pragmatism takes precedence over the search for the truth. The parties, realizing that they cannot agree when they dialogue as separate entities, decide to renounce their specific denominational positions and start over again.

The vision described here evidently contrasts with the vision of reconciled diversity. Many of the unionist attempts move between two extremes.

131 Lutheran-Roman Catholic Joint Commission, *Facing Unity*, 17.
132 Villain, *Introducción al ecumenismo*, 114–16.

On one hand, the churches completely eliminate their particular tradition to create a completely new reality. On the other, there is an attempt to reach a communion among churches with their existing traditions. Such communion is sought without asking for a change in the existing institutions or overcoming doctrinal differences, as long as the fundamental nucleus of apostolic Revelation is respected.

To complete this overview of the models of ecclesial unity, we should also speak of the *federations of churches*, though this model does not hold up to a serious theological analysis. The federation approach imitates a model that is valid in political society, but whose ecclesial substance goes no further than a common witness, a forum for dialogue, and a decision-making body. The federated churches continue to be separate churches, not the one Church.

More theologically substantive is the model proposed from the Orthodox sphere, and specifically from a *Eucharistic ecclesiology*. The Church, according to this view, is fully the Church when she validly celebrates the Eucharist. This affirmation is explicitly stated in the biblical text: "The cup of blessing that we bless, is it not a participation in the blood of Christ? The bread that we break, is it not a participation in the body of Christ? Because the loaf of bread is one, we, though many, are one body, for we all partake of the one loaf" (1 Cor 10:16–17).

Communion in the one Eucharistic bread is therefore a sign and source of communion in the one body of the Church; participation in the Eucharistic Body of Christ serves to increase unity in Christ's ecclesial body. For this reason, according to the model under consideration, every local church that celebrates the Eucharist, presided over by the bishop, is a church in the full sense. In any case, there do not exist as many churches as there are Eucharistic celebrations. In reality, the Eucharistic Body of the Lord is one and the same in all places. Accordingly, again according to this model, every church that recognizes the Eucharistic ecclesiality of other churches is in communion with these churches. Eucharistic *koinonia*—that is, communion—would be sufficient as a bond of unity.

Eucharistic ecclesiology has an important place in the Catholic sphere and for the future of ecumenism. As Brian E. Daley points out, the reestablishment of authentic unity without uniformity will require recovering, "in appropriately new terms, the sense of sacramental mystery that characterized the Christian understanding of both Scripture and church in the patristic age."[133] The build-

133 Daley, "Rebuilding the Structure of Love," 104.

ing up of the Church—the *aedificatio Ecclesiae*—is in fact realized when, by means of the episcopal and priestly ministry, the faithful are nourished by the Eucharist. Through this contact with Christ's Eucharistic Body, the faithful of the Church become the Mystical Body of Christ. According to the expression of Henri de Lubac, the Church is "the Body of Christ realized" (*Ecclesia Corpus Christi effecta*).[134] As a result, the particular churches are truly Eucharistic communities, with a unity modeled according to that of the true Eucharistic Body. This Eucharistic Body, as stated, is one and unique in the whole Church, present in its entirety in each of its singular realizations. Likewise, the one Church is present in each of the churches.

A Eucharistic understanding of the mystery of the Church goes hand in hand with an ecclesiological understanding of the mystery of the Eucharist. The Eucharist is an ecclesial mystery both because its fruit is ecclesial communion and also because it is celebrated within ecclesial communion. This reality has a direct consequence for the episcopal ministry, understood as both the ministry of unity for a community itself as well as the ministry of unity between each community and the entire universal Church.[135] As mentioned previously, the complete mystery of the Eucharist requires that each individual bishop be in communion with the universal Church through union with the episcopal college.

The Eucharist makes the Church, but one should also not forget that the Church makes the Eucharist. According to the latter axiom, the episcopal ministry signifies the unity of communion, on the part of the celebrating Church, as a reality prior to the unity of communion which is a fruit of the Eucharist. Therefore, a bishop separated from his brothers in the episcopate would not fit adequately into the sacramental sign of the Eucharist because he would no longer be a sign of unity. Ultimately, the episcopal mission entails a double dimension, which involves both the universal episcopate and each single bishop. This twofold aspect is in direct relationship to that twofold aspect of the Eucharist by which the one and entire Christ is present in each of his sacramental realizations. Both of these realities—the Eucharist and the episcopate—come together in the edification of the Church, or *aedificatio Ecclesiae*. This convergence gives the Church herself two distinct

134 Henri de Lubac, *Corpus Mysticum: L'Eucharistie et l'Église au moyen age: Étude historique*, 2nd ed. (Paris: Aubier Montaigne, 1949), 103.

135 Joseph Ratzinger, *Theologische Prinzipienlehre: Bausteine zur Fundamentaltheologie* (Munich: Wewel, 1982), 266.

facets, both universal and particular, in which unity becomes plurality without destroying itself.[136]

In light of the aforementioned understanding of the Eucharist and the episcopate, one can understand why the Orthodox version of this model does not find acceptance from a Catholic perspective. As the Letter *Communionis notio* states, "it is precisely the Eucharist that renders all self-sufficiency on the part of the particular Churches impossible. Indeed, the unicity and indivisibility of the eucharistic Body of the Lord implies the unicity of his mystical Body, which is the one and indivisible Church."[137] The same document adds that "the unity of the Church is also rooted in the unity of the Episcopate," and, within it, in the Roman primacy: "The unity of the Episcopate involves the existence of a Bishop who is Head of the *Body or College of Bishops*, namely the Roman Pontiff."[138]

From all this, it follows that "the unity of the Eucharist and the unity of the Episcopate with Peter and under Peter are not independent roots of the unity of the Church, since Christ instituted the Eucharist and the Episcopate as essentially interlinked realities."[139] Eucharistic ecclesiology of Orthodox origin, however, reduces ecclesial communion to the sole recognition of the ecclesiality of the other churches, in addition to the reality of interior communion. The universal dimension of the one Church, as the entire congregation of faithful presided over by a single episcopal college, disappears in the consideration of the communion of churches. This view does not give adequate attention to universal structures of communion.

These models of unity, in the final analysis, draw from ecclesiologies which are not able to express the mystery of the Church in her fullness. The models tend to replace the goal of full communion with the more accessible aim of ecclesial intercommunion, even if such an aim is not explicitly stated. These paradigms could serve as a methodological starting point for ecumenism but not as the definitive goal of ecclesial unity.

As we have mentioned, theologians today often speak of an 'Ecumenical Winter' to describe a present cooling of relations, after an initial enthusiasm in the decades immediately following the Second Vatican Council. At the same time, however, one can see signs that the ecumenical bases placed by

136 Philip Goyret, *El obispo, Pastor de la Iglesia: Estudio teológico del munus regendi en* Lumen gentium *27* (Pamplona: Ediciones Universidad de Navarra, 1998), 275–83.
137 Congregation for the Doctrine of the Faith, *Communionis notio*, 11.
138 Congregation for the Doctrine of the Faith, *Communionis notio*, 2.
139 Congregation for the Doctrine of the Faith, *Communionis notio*, 14.

the Conciliar teaching are only beginning to bear their full fruits. Stephen Lopes, Bishop of the Personal Ordinariate "Chair of Saint Peter" for faithful coming from Anglicanism or Episcopalianism in the United States and Canada, has asserted that the Apostolic Constitution *Anglicanorum coetibus* constitutes a breakthrough in ecumenism. He has stated that the Constitution is a "realized ecumenism," in which the Church accepts the Anglican heritage as part of the full catholic union.[140] The constitution, promulgated by Benedict XVI on November 4, 2009, provides for the reception of groups of Anglican faithful into full Catholic communion while preserving their proper liturgical tradition.

As *Anglicanorum coetibus* points out, the foundation for this new step in Christian unity is none other than a set of ecclesiological principles enumerated in the Second Vatican Council's Dogmatic Constitution on the Church. These principles include: the Church's Trinitarian origin, which demands the permanent search for full unity; the need for visible communion to complement invisible unity; and the recognition—in *Lumen Gentium* number 8—of "elements of sanctification and of truth" outside the visible confines of the Catholic Church, which impel her towards Catholic unity. The complementary norms issued on March 19, 2019, explicitly recognize the Anglican liturgical patrimony as part of the Catholic faith and an element pushing towards unity.

In light of this new pastoral phenomenon, we can see a concrete realization of the Church's catholicity, through which the one faith comes to be more deeply expressed through a specific cultural and liturgical tradition. Only the future can tell to what extent *Anglicanorum coetibus* might serve as a model for the full incorporation of other traditions not yet in full catholic communion. In any case, in these steps we can see the Church more fully realizing her authentic catholicity, seeking to affirm all that is valid among the various liturgical and cultural traditions, and eliminating artificial barriers to unity.

140 Stephen Lopes, "Unity in Diversity: Towards a New Ecumenical Springtime" (Lecture, Aquinas Institute for Catholic Life, Princeton University, Princeton, N.J., March 7, 2019).

Chapter 6

Ecumenism in Practice

In light of the principles examined in the previous chapters, ecumenism is to be understood as the sum of the efforts undertaken to lead all Christian communities to the condition of full, visible communion in the one Church of Christ. These efforts take place on different levels, which will now be studied.[1]

SPIRITUAL ECUMENISM

Spiritual ecumenism is "the soul of the whole ecumenical movement."[2] As Walter Kasper's *A Handbook of Spiritual Ecumenism* points out, "it is significant that Jesus did not primarily express his desire for unity in a teaching or in a commandment to his disciples, but in a prayer to his Father. Unity is a gift from above, stemming from and growing toward loving communion with the Father, Son and Holy Spirit."[3] In this context, ecumenism is a search for unity that is understood as the acceptance of a divine gift and not as a reality constructed by human beings. From this perspective, one can appreciate how an ecumenical spirituality and faithfulness to one's own tradition of faith cannot be separated. Hence, one needs to avoid understanding spiritual ecumenism in "a merely emotional sense as an escape from, and a substitute for, an objective confession of faith.... Such a tendency, which seeks a spirituality apart from the objective faith of the churches, sooner or later becomes empty and void; it cannot help the churches to overcome their differences and it becomes ecumenically useless."[4]

This same *Handbook* insists that "since unity is a gift, it is fitting that Christians pray for it together."[5] *Unitatis Redintegratio* focuses on the foun-

1 Lucia Antinucci, *Ecumenismo* (Casale Monferrato: Piemme, 1991); Pontifical Council for Promoting Christian Unity, *Directory for the Application of Principles and Norms on Ecumenism* (March 25, 1993) and *The Ecumenical Dimension in the Formation of Those Engaged in Pastoral Work* (1997).
2 *Unitatis Redintegratio*, 8.
3 Walter Kasper, *A Handbook of Spiritual Ecumenism* (Hyde Park, N.Y.: New City Press, 2007), no. 4.
4 Kasper, *That They May All Be One*, 158.
5 Kasper, *Spiritual Ecumenism*, no. 5.

dation of this truth: "Such prayers in common are certainly an effective means of obtaining the grace of unity, and they are a true expression of the ties which still bind Catholics to their separated brethren. 'For where two or three are gathered together in my name, there am I in the midst of them' [Mt 18:20]."[6]

With theological finesse, John Paul II emphasized the special value of prayer among Christians of distinct communities: "Prayer, the community at prayer, enables us always to discover anew the evangelical truth of the words: 'You have one Father' (Mt 23:9)." He later adds: "'You have one teacher, and you are all brethren' (Mt 23:8). 'Ecumenical' prayer discloses this fundamental dimension of brotherhood in Christ, who died to gather together the children of God who were scattered."[7] We have already mentioned the historical origins of the Week of Prayer for Christian Unity. Christians of different communities, including Catholics, can also meet to pray together on other occasions.[8] In these gatherings, as in other types of interdenominational activities, one should avoid both instrumentalizing the event for proselytism as well as apathy towards the existing differences.[9]

Spiritual ecumenism does not only consist in private and public prayer for the unity of Christians, but above all in "change of heart and holiness of life."[10] One cannot forget that at the root of every lack of unity sin is always present. As a consequence, the most efficacious means for overcoming divisions and reestablishing communion will always be those which seek most directly to eliminate sin through conversion of heart. Only such a true attitude of conversion, of individuals and of institutions, can serve to overcome the ever-present obstacles to unity and allow for true change in the current situation. As the New Delhi Assembly of the World Council of Churches observed, "the achievement of unity will involve nothing less than a death and rebirth of many forms of church life as we have known them . . . nothing less costly can finally suffice."[11] This is the direction of the council's teaching when it states: "All the faithful should remember that the more effort they

6 *Unitatis Redintegratio*, 8.
7 John Paul II, *Ut unum sint*, 26.
8 Regarding Catholics, see Pontifical Council for Promoting Christian Unity, *Directory for the Application of Principles*, nos. 108–15. See also nos. 26–31 of Kasper, *Spiritual Ecumenism*, which suggests various times and formats for these prayer meetings.
9 Pontifical Council for Promoting Christian Unity, *Directory for the Application of Principles*, 23.
10 *Unitatis Redintegratio*, 8.
11 World Council of Churches, *New Delhi Statement on Unity* (December 31, 1961), 3.

make to live holier lives according to the Gospel, the better will they further Christian unity and put it into practice."[12]

The personal holiness of the faithful will therefore be the most powerful means to reconstitute unity. This is because love and truth converge, and, in the short or long term, end up coming together. Furthermore, "the need for interior conversion" for the practice of true ecumenism needs to be understood in all of its profundity, in such a way as to include forgiveness—both asked for as well as received—for the offenses of each party.[13] This process of reconciliation includes "the *necessary purification of past memories*" which John Paul II greatly insisted on in the final years of his pontificate.[14] The pardon of sins looks not simply to one's own sins, but also to those of previous generations of Christians. This is especially true when these past sins have taken shape in structures of sin which have contributed to or furthered divisions in the Church. In the homily given at the Mass of the "Day of Pardon" for the Great Jubilee, on March 12, 2000, John Paul courageously affirmed that "we cannot fail to recognize the infidelities to the Gospel committed by some of our brethren, especially during the second millennium. Let us ask pardon for the divisions which have occurred among Christians, for the violence some have used in the service of the truth."[15]

Full communion, therefore, is not only a matter of doctrinal and institutional agreement but also of profound conversion at both the personal and communal levels.[16] Ecumenical theology must ever keep in mind that "thought should not try to solve a problem that can be solved only by conversion."[17] Conversion helps free ecumenism from a disordered desire for monopoly or domination and from the danger of indifferentism. Instead, an attitude of conversion endows ecumenical activity with the touchstone of right intention, which implies the sincere desire to communicate to all Christians the entire patrimony of salvific goods.

The courageous confession of Gospel truth even to the shedding of blood, particularly frequent during the persecutions of Christians of the

12 *Unitatis Redintegratio*, 7.
13 John Paul II, *Ut unum sint*, 15.
14 John Paul II, *Ut unum sint*, 2.
15 "Homily on the Day of Pardon" (March 12, 2000), 4. On the culpability for the divisions of Christians and the resulting violence, and on the coherence of asking forgiveness today for acts committed in the past, see International Theological Commission, Document *Memory and Reconciliation: The Church and the Faults of the Past* (March 7, 2000), 5.2–5.3.
16 John Paul II, *Ut unum sint*, 15.
17 Root, "Essential Unity," 125.

various communities over the course of the twentieth century, has given rise to an awareness of an "ecumenism of the martyrs." Such ecumenism draws from the awareness that the full communion existing among the martyrs in heaven has been preceded by their personal faithfulness to the Christian faith to the extent of martyrdom. Indeed, and again in the words of John Paul II, we can say that "perhaps the most convincing form of ecumenism is the ecumenism of the saints and of the martyrs." This is because "the *communio sanctorum* speaks louder than the things which divide us."[18]

Personal holiness, combined with a fervent love for the truth, necessarily leads towards catholicity. As we have seen, one can understand catholicity in both a quantitative sense, involving the desire to bring all persons closer to Christ without any discrimination, as well as in a qualitative sense, which implies the universal openness of revealed truth. In light of this reality, an important goal for conversion is the development of a mindset which is truly catholic, universal, and open to the good to be found in other Christians spread throughout the world. As we have seen, many of the divisions among Christians have been the result of the exaltation of national or other particular identities at the expense of the universal. The words of Pope Francis on the occasion of the five hundredth anniversary of the Reformation, with regard to Catholics and Lutherans, are sadly true with regard to a wider horizon of divisions: "Certainly, there was a sincere will on the part of both sides to profess and uphold the true faith, but at the same time we realize that we closed in on ourselves out of fear or bias with regard to the faith which others profess with a different accent and language."[19]

In contrast to past provincialism, in an ever-more global world, Christians are called to recognize that their vocation to Christ unites them to the whole of the Mystical Body of Christ, spread out over both space and time. Only such a truly universal horizon can overcome the narrower concerns at the root of division: "Until leaders of local churches see their members as baptized into the whole people of God, there will be no visible unity of all in each place."[20]

18 John Paul II, Apostolic Letter *Tertio millennio adveniente* (November 10, 1994), 37.
19 Pope Francis, "Common Prayer at Lund."
20 Braaten and Jenson, *Princeton Proposal*, no. 53.

KNOWLEDGE OF OTHER COMMUNITIES, MUTUAL RELATIONS, AND INSTITUTIONAL COLLABORATION

While, in the view of many, the recent years have not seen great advances in ecumenism, the last decades have consolidated a greater mutual understanding and commitment to working together in the task of living the Gospel message. As Pope Francis has noted, Christians of various communities recognize that they must "journey together," trusting in the action of the Holy Spirit.[21]

Journeying together implies an effort to foster a deeper trust and knowledge of other communities. This attitude of mutual collaboration requires the study of the origins and the current situation of other Christian communities, free from prejudice and outside of a polemic-apologetic viewpoint. Journeying together also implies the need for sincerely appreciating the positive values present in other communities. Such an attitude means avoiding discriminatory intolerance and narrow-mindedness, but also being vigilant against an undifferentiated syncretism and the confusion of denominational boundaries.[22] Personal and institutional relations with other Christians must be treated not simply as a question of courtesy. Rather, these relations are a consequence of an already existing, though imperfect, communion; they reflect the relations of fraternal charity proper to Christians. As Telford Work comments, "nothing breaks down barriers like truly shared lives."[23] In this regard, the so-called Lund Principle, articulated at the Third Faith and Order Conference of 1952, has served as an important reference point for ecumenical activity. The principle calls churches to "act together in all matters except those in which deep differences of conviction compel them to act separately."[24]

This relationality would be superficial if ecumenical formation did not permeate all of one's theology and spirituality. Ecumenism needs to shape a mindset which is open to other traditions without betraying one's own. In this way, it is possible to avoid the danger of a potential rift between theology and ecumenical practice. Such is the orientation of the 1997 document published by the Pontifical Council for Promoting Christian Unity, entitled *The Ecumenical Dimension in the Formation of Those Engaged in Pastoral Work*.

21 "General Audience" (June 5, 2019).
22 Pontifical Council for Promoting Christian Unity, *Ecumenical Dimension in Pastoral Work*, 7.
23 Telford Work, "Speaking for the Spirit," 212.
24 Third World Conference on Faith and Order (Lund, Sweden, 1952).

At an official level, the now-regular encounters between members of the Catholic and Orthodox Churches, as well as between Catholic and Anglican bishops, offer a lived expression of the unity which already exists in an imperfect way. At the same time, unofficial engagements also offer an important opportunity for the growth in mutual relations between Christian communities.[25] Over the first two decades of the twenty-first century, *The Global Christian Forum* has offered an important manifestation of collaboration and dialogue. The forum was first proposed by Rev. Dr. Konrad Raiser, then General Secretary of the World Council of Churches, as an independent space for dialogue. The forum is not intended as an avenue of official theological dialogue. Rather, it offers an open space in which members of different Christian communities can get to know one another, pray and reflect together, and engage in common initiatives.[26]

In addition, the development of "receptive ecumenism" in the past two decades represents an important manifestation of an ecumenical attitude within the secular academy. This approach, developed by the British theologian Paul D. Murray, seeks to foster a positive attitude of self-examination. Such an attitude involves realizing that "the primary call is to take responsibility for one's own and one's own community's learning in the face of the other, without first demanding that the other does likewise."[27] This approach has given rise to a large body of scholarly work which has served to deepen ties between ecclesial communities and brought about a deeper understanding of the respective ecclesial identities. An important part of the success of this movement is its inward-looking focus, in contrast with critical and polemical attitudes of the past. Receptive ecumenism "invites us to ask not '*What do we have to tell, or learn about, the other?*, but rather '*What do we need to learn from the other?*'"[28] From a Catholic point of view, such an attitude is in keeping with the Church's essential catholicity. As Michael Root points out, "We need a living sense that we are more Catholic, not less Catholic, in giving attention to what can be authentically received from the Orthodox and Protestant traditions."[29]

25 Michael Root, "Normal Ecumenism: Ecumenism for the Long Haul," *Pro Ecclesia: A Journal of Catholic and Evangelical Theology* 28, no. 1 (February 2019): 76.
26 "About Us," Global Christian Forum, https://globalchristianforum.org/introduction/how-the-gcf-engages-with-participants/.
27 Murray, "Receptive Ecumenism," 17.
28 Vicky Balabanski and Geraldine Hawkes, "Introduction," in *Receptive Ecumenism: Listening, Learning and Loving in the Way of Christ*, ed. Vicky Balabanski and Geraldine Hawkes (Australia: ATF, 2018) viii, http://www.jstor.org/stable/j.ctvjdzcmh.3.
29 Root, "Normal Ecumenism," 76.

In the face of an aggressive wave of secularism and, at times, open persecution, the topic of collaboration between the various churches and ecclesial communities has acquired an even greater relevance. In calling for such cooperation of witness and service, the Princeton Proposal for Christian Unity notes that collaboration between Evangelicals and Roman Catholics in the promotion of human life "has done more to break down old habits of hostility than any theological discussion." The document further notes that "the increasing secularity of Western societies is making re-evangelization a common Christian project that transcends historical divisions and theological differences."[30]

An important step has been taken, in the European ambit, with the *Charta Oecumenica: Guidelines for the Growth of Collaboration between the Church in Europe*, published on April 22, 2001. This document was jointly issued by the Conference of European Churches—to which most of the Orthodox, Anglican, Reformed and Old Catholic Churches belong—and the Council of the Bishops' Conferences of Europe, which brings together Catholic Bishops. In the *Charta*, the churches and communities involved commit themselves to work together to promote, among other things, religious freedom, the rights of minorities, the fundamental values at Europe's roots, the nonviolent solution of conflicts between nations, and the safeguarding of creation. The parties also vow to counteract all forms of anti-Semitism.

At the local level, collaboration between Christians of different denominations can take shape by means of various types of joint initiatives. These can include the exchange of information, works of charity, the defense of public morality, and other possibilities which are spoken of in numbers 45 to 48 of *A Handbook of Spiritual Ecumenism*.

The great sensitivity to the environment, an important issue today, has also formed a means for common concern which can help to overcome past divisions. In the first-ever encyclical dedicated to environmental concerns, Pope Francis chose to incorporate the teachings of the Ecumenical Patriarch Bartholomew, "with whom we share the hope of full ecclesial communion."[31] Some theologians argue that, alongside the political and scientific factors, the environmental crisis "demands a systematic theological perspective to appeal to spiritual and psychological dimensions of human

30 Braaten and Jenson, *Princeton Proposal*, no. 50.
31 Pope Francis, Encyclical Letter *Laudato si'* (May 24, 2015), 7.

thinking regarding our biological and physical environments."[32] From this perspective, the collaborative efforts of Christians in this area offer an important evangelizing opportunity.

Such collaborative actions in the various ambits of society, however praiseworthy they might be, should not lose sight of the communion in faith which should inspire and guide them. Losing this authentically Christian vision of faith has been a temptation in the past decades of ecumenical activity. Communities must keep in mind that without such a supernatural outlook, grounded in Christ, "mutual witness and service can disintegrate into mere ideological commonality rather than genuine Christian cooperation."[33]

INSTITUTIONAL RENEWAL

The journey towards unity concerns all the groups involved, in the sense that all—the Catholic Church included—must reform those elements which are obstacles to true unity.[34] For a fruitful ecumenism oriented outward (*ad extra*), a healthy ecumenism oriented towards the inside (*ad intra*) is essential. Such *ad intra* ecumenism entails the purification and renewal of one's own institution.

Such change is not a matter of carrying out diplomatic reforms according to a policy of mutual concessions in order to reduce differences. Rather, a double movement needs to be initiated which might seem contradictory, but which actually embodies the authentic concept of *living tradition*. Institutional reform implies "re-form," a return to the original form, and at the same time applying this early framework to the current circumstances. Reform, in its essence, simultaneously looks backward and forward, and the correctness of each movement towards reform is measured by faithfulness to the original form. As *Unitatis Redintegratio* points out, "every renewal of the Church is essentially grounded in an increase of fidelity to her own calling."[35]

This fidelity looks to the Gospel as its unique and perennial source but also to contemporary man. If each party to ecumenism made the effort to go back to the origins, one might think that all Christians would be united

32 Maryamossadat Torabi and Seyed Masoud Noori, "Religious Leaders and the Environmental Crisis: Using Knowledge and Social Influence to Counteract Climate Change," *The Ecumenical Review* 71, no. 3 (July 2019): 345. http://dx.doi.org/10.1111/erev.12434.
33 Braaten and Jenson, *Princeton Proposal*, no. 51.
34 *Unitatis Redintegratio*, 6 and John Paul II, *Ut unum sint*, 16.
35 *Unitatis Redintegratio*, 6.

at the ultimate source of our faith. Contemporaneous to this movement of return, the current needs of the Church's mission spur Christians forward, so as to find the most appropriate present-day forms to carry out this mission with efficacy.

Often, as attested by history, the divisions in the Church are the consequence of long periods of resentful impatience, pastoral paralysis, corruption, and situations in need of reform. These problems continue to the point that the separating party loses hope that any real improvement of the situation will take place. In light of this reality, Vatican II wisely spoke of a Church "always in need of being purified."[36] With this constant purification, one can prevent pernicious elements from taking root. In contrast to such continual progress, singular reforms of extreme magnitude risk leading to schism, because such changes can obscure the continuity with the past and generate a feeling of rupture.

In this regard, Congar's description of four conditions for authentic reform without schism, contained in his famous work *True and False Reform in the Church*, remains valid. In such a reform, the Church must privilege the pastoral dimension, without allowing the reformist motivation to arise from mere theoretical speculation. Additionally, communion with the whole of the Church must be maintained, "not something servile or mechanical, but a living relation to the apostolic authority given by the Lord to structure his church, both at the local and universal level."[37] Thirdly, reform requires patience and not allowing oneself to be tempted by the quicker path of simply accepting certain situations as *faits accomplis*. Finally, the principle of tradition must be respected. Tradition implies progress towards the good by a double movement. On one hand, there is a return to the sources of faith; on the other, a development in continuity takes place. In this manner, authentic reform does not introduce novelties which are completely disconnected with the past. An abrupt change which lacked this continuity would produce an artificial rather than a natural adaptation, which in the end would prove harmful.[38]

One should also keep in mind that reform is not just a necessary remedy to eliminate or curb the consequences of sin. Rather, reform arises spontaneously from the reality of the Church as an institution which is pres-

36 *Lumen Gentium*, 8.
37 Yves Congar, *True and False Reform in the Church*, trans. Paul Philbert (Collegeville, Minn.: Liturgical Press, 2011), 235; original title: *Vrai e fausse réforme dans l'Eglise* (Paris: Cerf, 1950).
38 Congar, *True and False Reform*, 229–307.

ent in history.[39] Reform therefore does not concern that which comes from God, but that in the Church which comes from man; "it is the Church, insofar as she is an institution which is also human and earthly, that must be reformed."[40] Possible aspects for reform may include moral conduct, traditional practices and liturgy, more generalized habits of behavior, canonical discipline, and ecclesiastical law. Such efforts must always keep in mind that institutional renewal should receive its driving impulse from spiritual renewal; otherwise, reform is doomed to failure.[41]

Although the Catholic Church claims to possess without defect the whole deposit of revealed truth, institutional renewal also regards the doctrinal aspect. Reform in doctrine does not in any way imply making concessions with regard to the truths of the faith. Rather, the Church seeks to better express the truths of faith and find the right balance in presenting the contents of the deposit entrusted to her. As the Second Vatican Council's Dogmatic Constitution on Divine Revelation points out, "this tradition which comes from the Apostles" undergoes a development in the Church "with the help of the Holy Spirit. For there is a growth in the understanding of the realities and the words which have been handed down . . . through the contemplation and study made by believers, who treasure these things in their hearts."[42]

Christian tradition, as Johann Adam Möhler and John Henry Newman so keenly realized, has undergone a legitimate development in doctrine. One example of a successful *doctrinal* renewal would be the revaluation of the common priesthood of the faithful during the last ecumenical council. The ecclesial communities that arose from the Reformation gave great importance to this idea. The same could be said about the increased awareness of the importance of the ministry of the word, which began during the Council of Trent and received new impetus in Vatican II. There are other areas where doctrinal development is still underway, such as pneumatology and the renewal of moral theology.

Among the institutions to be renewed, the office of the bishop of Rome stands out, due to its pivotal importance in ecumenical dialogue. Paradoxically, the Petrine ministry of communion has become the greatest obstacle

39 Cereti, *Ecumenismo*, 53.
40 Cereti, *Ecumenismo*, 48. Our translation.
41 Sandro Spinsanti, *Ecumenismo* (Rome: Istituto di teologia a distanza "Ut unum sint," 1982), 140.
42 Vatican II, *Dei Verbum* (November 18, 1965), 8.

on the path to full communion.[43] John Paul II himself recalled the difficulty which Roman primacy poses for other Christians, and encouraged study aiming to "find a way of exercising the primacy which, while in no way renouncing what is essential to its mission, is nonetheless open to a new situation."[44] This effort is quintessentially ecumenical, implying the distinction between the substantial—"what is essential to its mission"—and that which is accidental and thus susceptible to change—"a way of exercising" which is "open to a new situation."[45] The issues to be resolved at the doctrinal level will be mentioned later.

We must also bear in mind that the Catholic Church has recognized, with honesty, that in the divisions which have arisen in the Church, "often enough, men of both sides were to blame."[46] With regard to the responsibility that the Catholic Church may have had from a doctrinal point of view, one could include situations in which a certain doctrine was not expressed with sufficient catholicity or universal horizon, so that the teaching might be properly understood and accepted in the various cultural settings. Cath-

43 The words of Paul VI before the assembly of the then-Secretariat for the Unity of Christians (April 28, 1967) are famous: "the Pope, we know well, is without a doubt the greatest obstacle on the path of ecumenism." Our translation.

44 John Paul II, *Ut unum sint*, 88; 95. This papal appeal was enthusiastically welcomed in the ecumenical sphere and in the following years there have been various assemblies for the study of this topic. Among the different publications that can be cited are: Congregation for the Doctrine of the Faith, *The Primacy of the Successor of Peter in the Mystery of the Church* (October 31, 1998); James Puglisi, ed., "Il ministero petrino e l'unità della Chiesa: Atti del Simposio (Rome, December 4–6, 1997)," *Studi Ecumenici* 17, no. 1 (1999); Antonio Acerbi, ed., *Il ministero del papa in prospettiva ecuménica: Atti del colloquio Milano, 16–18 aprile 1998* (Milan: Vita e pensiero, 1999); Istituto Theologico Marchigiano, *Atti dell'incontro ecumenico su "Il primato del Papa,"* (Bologna: Dehoniane, 1999); Peter Hünermann, ed., *Papato ed ecumenismo: Il ministero petrino al servizio dell'unità* (Bologna: Dehoniane, 1999); Carl E. Braaten and Robert W. Jenson, eds., *Church Unity and the Papal Office: An Ecumenical Dialogue on John Paul II's Encyclical* Ut Unum Sint *(That All May Be One)* (Grand Rapids, Mich.: Eerdmans, 2001); Walter Kasper, ed., *The Petrine Ministry: Catholics and Orthodox in Dialogue* (New York: Newman Press, 2005); on the topic of the primacy in general, see also Michele Maccarrone, ed., *Il primato del vescovo di Roma nel primo millennio: Ricerche e testimonianze: Atti del Symposium storico-teologico* (Rome: Libreria editrice Vaticana, 1991); Joseph Ratzinger, "The Primacy of the Pope and the Unity of the People of God," *Fundamental Speeches from Five Decades*, trans. Michael J. Miller, J. R. Foster, and Adrian Walker (San Francisco: Ignatius Press, 2012), 13–33; Adriano Garuti, *The Primacy of the Bishop of Rome and the Ecumenical Dialogue*, trans. Michael J. Miller (San Francisco: Ignatius Press, 2004).

45 The study of this topic is too complex to be developed here. For a first look at the problem of the conjunction between the variable historical forms of the primacy and its immutable essential substance, see Congregation for the Doctrine of the Faith, *The Primacy of the Successor of Peter*, and Philip Goyret, "Ermeneutica conciliare ed ecclesiologia contemporanea," *Annales Theologici* 23, no. 2 (2009): 428–39.

46 *Unitatis Redintegratio*, 3.

olicity, not only in the doctrinal realm, thus has a decisive significance as a point of arrival for ecumenism. "It must therefore be concerned with reintegration in the *Una Catholica*, which is one and unique not because of a lack and an exclusion of what belongs to that fullness but precisely by reason of its fullness, the fact that it is the totality and not a part."[47]

THE CATHOLICITY OF THE CHURCH'S MISSION AND THE ECUMENICAL MINDSET

"All men are called to belong to the new people of God. Wherefore this people, while remaining one and only one, is to be spread throughout the whole world and must exist in all ages, so that the decree of God's will may be fulfilled. In the beginning God made human nature one and decreed that all His children, scattered as they were, would finally be gathered together as one."[48] With these words, *Lumen Gentium* introduces its description of the catholicity of the Church, situating this property in the context of God's will for unity. We have had the opportunity to analyze this text earlier, in discussing the council's vision of catholicity and its significance for ecumenism. *Lumen Gentium* number 13 describes catholicity in what we might term an extensive sense, meaning the Church's orientation towards all persons. At the same time, the text also refers to what can we call an intensive sense of catholicity, which regards diversity within the Church herself. As the dogmatic constitution states, expounding upon this intensive aspect: "Not only, then, is the people of God made up of different peoples but in its inner structure also it is composed of various ranks."[49] In the realm of ecumenism, this intensive catholicity has a special importance, legitimizing distinctions within the Church and furthermore affirming the importance of diversity.

This appreciation of the catholicity internal to the Church should not lead to a pejorative view of extensive catholicity. As "the universal sacrament of salvation," the Church is called to offer all persons the means of salvation.[50] As a consequence, there is an essential bond between intensive and extensive catholicity, and one cannot affirm one of these forms of catholicity at the expense of the other.

47 Yves Congar, *Divided Christendom*, 252.
48 *Lumen Gentium*, 13.
49 *Lumen Gentium*, 13.
50 *Lumen Gentium*, 48.

Within this ecclesiological framework, one can situate the previously mentioned relationship between ecumenical activity as such and the reception of individual persons into full communion with the Catholic Church. Distinguishing such reception from ecumenism, without opposing these two realities, has implications for the concept and activity known as *apostolate*. Apostolate refers to the personal initiative of one who, moved by communion with God and with his or her brothers and sisters in the faith, seeks to extend this communion to others so that they might come to full communion in the Church. This action, which takes its name from the twelve apostles, is essential to the Church's mission, as authentic communion always seeks to expand.[51] The vertical dimension of communion with God is always connected to the horizontal dimension of communion with one's fellow men. Thus, a given church should not be blamed for welcoming those who, after mature reflection and following the dictates of conscience, freely decide to enter that same community: "A Church, in fact, cannot preclude the possibility of an individual conversion and cannot reject those who, out of sincere conviction, would desire to join. This would be in contradiction with the universal mission of the Church."[52]

The case of *proselytism*—with the negative connotation that this word has taken on in recent years—is quite different. This term has come to indicate activity lacking in good faith, which is geared at taking groups of faithful from other communities and bringing them to one's own. In contrast with genuine apostolate, proselytism typically implies the use of deception, defamation, coercion, or overly aggressive propaganda for one's own group. According to this sense, proselytism, from whichever source, can never be approved and must be strongly rejected. For example, a definition of the term is offered in a study document from 1970, entitled *Common Witness and Proselytism*, prepared by a Joint Theological Commission from the Catholic Church and the World Council of Churches. The document states:

> [Proselytism means] improper attitudes and behavior in the practice of Christian witness. Proselytism embraces whatever violates the right of the human person, Christian or non-Christian, to be free from external coercion in religious matters, or whatever, in the proclamation of the gospel,

51 Nicola Bux, *Il quinto sigillo: L'unità dei cristiani verso il terzo millennio* (Vatican City: Libreria editrice Vaticana, 1997), 109, 120, 127; and "Il proselitismo religioso," *Civiltà Cattolica* 1, no. 3544 (1998): 319–28.

52 Kasper, "Le radici teologiche del conflitto tra Mosca e Roma," 539 (section: *What does proselytism mean?*). Our translation.

does not conform to the ways God draws free men to himself in response to his calls to serve in spirit and in truth.[53]

The notion of apostolate as a specific aspect of evangelization, in contrast to this present-day understanding of proselytism, is present in the Declaration *Dignitatis Humanae* of the Second Vatican Council. The document affirms, with regard to the obligation of men to adhere and order their lives to the truth: "Men cannot discharge these obligations in a manner in keeping with their own nature unless they enjoy immunity from external coercion as well as psychological freedom."[54] More specifically, "in spreading religious faith and in introducing religious practices everyone ought at all times to refrain from any manner of action which might seem to carry a hint of coercion or of a kind of persuasion that would be dishonorable or unworthy, especially when dealing with poor or uneducated people."[55]

On the other hand, one should not consider the mere fact of the spread of a specific Christian community—through the sending of missionaries, the erection of ecclesiastical circumscriptions for the care of faithful, and so on—as being proselytism within a territory already occupied by another community. If such were the case, the intrinsic catholicity claimed by the various communities—not just by Catholics—would be lacking. This catholicity necessarily implies geographic extension. In this regard, the suggestion contained in the Princeton Proposal for Christian Unity for an ecumenical attitude within missionary activity is relevant: "Missionary strategies should be developed across denominational lines, so that church growth is not accomplished by sheep-stealing but rather by evangelization of the unbaptized and re-evangelization of the lapsed. Protestant missionaries to historically Roman Catholic and Orthodox societies must be able to articulate the ways in which their work builds up the *whole church* in those places."[56] An authentic missionary attitude necessarily seeks to recognize the spiritual goods found in other Christian communities.

It should be noted that the concept of apostolate corresponds to a traditional notion of proselytism with biblical roots.[57] Jesus does not have a neg-

53 Joint Working Group, "Third Official Report," *Centro Pro Unione*, 11, no. 8. www.prounione.it/dialogues/jwg.

54 Vatican Council II, *Dignitatis Humanae* (December 7, 1965), 2.

55 *Dignitatis Humanae*, 4.

56 Braaten and Jenson, *Princeton Proposal*, no. 52.

57 Mt. 23:15; Acts 2:11; 6:5; 13:43; and C. Gancho, "Proseliti," in *Enchiridion Biblicum* 5, nos. 1295–97.

ative attitude toward Jewish proselytism and in fact places the universality of his mission in continuity with the Jewish proselytizing spirit.[58] However, with time a more pejorative meaning of "proselytizing" has gained ground, partly due to the influence of terminology from the political realm.[59] Hence, an ecumenical mindset requires care in distinguishing the original from current sense of this notion, taking into account the possibility of being misunderstood.[60] Ecumenism must always protect the freedom of consciences: "The legitimate hunger for truth must be respected. Man has a grave obligation to seek God, to know him and worship him, but no one on earth is permitted to impose on his neighbor the practice of a faith he lacks; just as no one can claim the right to harm those who have received the faith from God."[61]

THE SHARING OF SPIRITUAL GOODS

It is not surprising that the *communicatio in spiritualibus*, or sharing of spiritual goods, is a recurrent theme in ecumenism.[62] All Christians are called to partake of the same spiritual realities. From a Catholic understanding of ecumenism, as presented by the last council, we can draw principles which regulate the *communicatio in sacris*, or sharing of sacramental goods, among Christians of distinct communities. This type of sharing should reflect a double reality, as noted in the *Ecumenical Directory*: first, the real communion existing among Christians, which can find expression in prayer and liturgical worship; and second, the incomplete character of this communion, due to differences in life, doctrine, or government, which prevents complete sharing in spiritual goods.[63]

58 Fernando Ocáriz, "Evangelización, proselitismo y ecumenismo," *Scripta Theologica* 38, no. 2 (2006): 623.

59 "Il proselitismo religioso," *Civiltà Cattolica*, 320.

60 In his commentary on the Declaration on Religious Freedom *Dignitatis Humanae* of the Second Vatican Council, Cardinal Johannes Willebrands says that "usage has given to this word diverse resonances. One can certainly use it in a positive sense: in this case it signifies every effort to make adherents. But in our contemporary world, the pejorative sense prevails the majority of the time, and in this case the word designates the whole sum of efforts to make adherents at any cost and by all efficacious means, without much regard for the quality of these means." "La liberté religiouse et l'oecuménisme," in *La liberté religieuse: Déclaration "Dignitatis humanae personae": Texte latin et traduction française*, ed. J. Hamer and Yves Congar (Paris: Cerf, 1967), 246. Our translation.

61 Josemaría Escrivá, "Freedom, A Gift from God," *Friends of God* (London: Scepter, 1981), 23, http://www.escrivaworks.org/book/friends_of_god.htm.

62 This is a broader notion than *communicatio in sacris*, which, strictly speaking, only includes the sacraments.

63 Pontifical Council for Promoting Christian Unity, *Directory for the Application of Principles*, 104.

These two dimensions oblige Christians to discern, among the various spiritual goods, those elements which are a spiritual heritage in common, such as prayer. Such discernment also leads to the identification of those spiritual goods which, by the very fact of signifying and requiring the unity of those who partake of these same goods, cannot be shared among all Christians. Some of the goods within this latter category can be shared in exceptional situations, respecting the *salus animarum* or good of souls which is always the dominant criteria.

We have already spoken of joint prayer for Christian unity. The *Ecumenical Directory* also regulates the common participation of different Christian communities in nonsacramental liturgy, such as Liturgy of the Hours, funerals, and the like.[64] With regard to the sacramental life, the Catholic Church needs to distinguish the Orthodox Churches, which possess the episcopate and the Eucharist, from the other Christian communities. In the former case, when a true spiritual necessity arises, it is possible for members of other churches to receive the sacraments of the Eucharist, penance, and the anointing of the sick from a minister of a community distinct from one's own. Such genuine necessity takes place when there is a lack of a minister from one's own church and an urgent need. The faithful must freely ask for the sacraments in this manner, and the sharing of sacramental goods must not be an occasion for proselytism by any of the parties involved.[65]

Outside of the special case of the Orthodox Churches, the Catholic Church has a more restrictive practice with regard to the sharing of sacramental goods with other Christian communities. This praxis is meant affirm the authentic faith with respect to the sacraments in question, as well as to assure the validity of these sacraments. This topic admits of great variability and does not allow for a general rule. The *Ecumenical Directory* describes the general principles in numbers 129 to 136.[66]

It should be noted that the situations of sharing in sacramental goods are to be considered exceptional, and not a means of ecumenical activity. Participation in the sacraments, as already mentioned, requires a prior unity

64 *Ecumenical Directory*, 116–21.

65 Pontifical Council for Promoting Christian Unity, *Directory for the Application of Principles*, 122–28.

66 The discipline that regulates mixed marriages is too extensive to be discussed here. One may consult Pontifical Council for Promoting Christian Unity, *Directory for the Application of Principles*, 143–60. See also the canonical legislation in *Code of Canon Law*, 1124–1129 and *Code of Canons of the Eastern Churches* (October 18, 1990), 813–16.

in faith and doctrine. This is because the sacraments not only confer grace but also *signify* the unity of the Church. Regular shared participation in them by persons of different faith communities would thus contradict a fundamental aspect of what the sacraments mean.

EUCHARISTIC COMMUNION AND ECCLESIAL COMMUNION

The Eucharist is the sacrament of the unity of the Church, and for this reason the Church absolutely prohibits Eucharistic concelebration among ministers of different communities, including those who celebrate the Eucharist in a sacramentally valid way.[67] As John Paul II affirmed towards the end of his pontificate, "the profound relationship between the invisible and the visible elements of ecclesial communion is constitutive of the Church as the sacrament of salvation. Only in this context can there be a legitimate celebration of the Eucharist and true participation in it. Consequently it is an intrinsic requirement of the Eucharist that it should be celebrated in communion, and specifically maintaining the various bonds of that communion intact."[68] Consistent with this assertion, the pontiff reaffirms, with regard to concelebration, that "precisely because the Church's unity . . . absolutely requires full communion in the bonds of the profession of faith, the sacraments and ecclesiastical governance, it is not possible to celebrate together the same Eucharistic liturgy until those bonds are fully re-established."[69]

This emphatic position of the Catholic Church is not simply a disciplinary matter, which could be subject to future change. The Church feels herself bound to a tradition which goes back to the beginnings of Christianity. In Acts 2:42, "the teaching of the apostles" is united with "the breaking of the bread." The earliest account of the institution of the Eucharist, from the First Letter to the Corinthians, states that "anyone who eats and drinks without discerning the body, eats and drinks judgment on himself" (1 Cor 11:29). "Discerning the body" not only implies distinguishing the Eucharist from ordinary bread, but also understanding the ecclesial community as the Lord's body. In other words, access to the Eucharist is conditioned by the acceptance of the community in its unity, as a single body and as the one Church. The lack of unity was in fact the

67 *Code of Canon Law*, 908, and *Code of Canons of the Eastern Churches*, 702.
68 John Paul II, *Ecclesia de Eucharistia*, 35.
69 John Paul II, *Ecclesia de Eucharistia*, 44.

problem for the community of Corinth, as described in the first chapter of Saint Paul's letter.[70]

Subsequent ancient witnesses to Christian life confirmed and consolidated this practice of linking unity in the Eucharistic Body with unity with the Church. The *Didache* warns: "But let no one eat or drink of your Thanksgiving (Eucharist), but they who have been baptized into the name of the Lord; for concerning this also the Lord has said, 'Give not that which is holy to the dogs' [Mt 7.6]."[71] Saint Justin, in his *First Apology*, states: "And this food is called among us Εὐχαριστία [*Eucharistia*], of which no one is allowed to partake but the man who believes that the things which we teach are true, and who has been washed with the washing that is for the remission of sins, and unto regeneration, and who is so living as Christ has enjoined."[72] The conditioning of Eucharistic communion upon ecclesial communion gave rise, in the patristic period, to the practice of letters of communion—*litterae communionis*—in their varying forms such as *litterae communicatoriae, litterae pacis,* and *litterae recomendationis*. By means of these documents, traveling Christians would be recognized as fully belonging to the Church, and thus could be welcomed to Eucharistic communion.[73]

In this context, one can understand how the concept of "excommunication," before acquiring juridical significance, arose from the exclusion from participation at the Eucharistic table. Today's liturgy expresses these ideas in a positive manner, by placing the rite of peace immediately prior to communion. As the *General Instruction of the Roman Missal* states, through the rite of peace "the Church entreats peace and unity for herself and for the whole human family, and the faithful express to each other

70 It is not possible here to get into the whole exegetical debate regarding this verse. However, it is not difficult to appreciate how both interpretations—"body" understood as the person of Christ present in the Eucharist or as the true Church—are legitimate and complementary, even referring to one another. For a specific bibliography, see Philip Goyret, "Cuerpo eucarístico y cuerpo eclesial: la communicatio in sacris en la Enc. *Ecclesia de Eucharistia*," *Annales Theologici* 19, no. 1 (2005): 151–52.

71 *The Didache*, trans. M. B. Riddle, Ante-Nicene Fathers 7 (Buffalo, N.Y.: Christian Literature Publishing, 1886), 9.5, http://www.newadvent.org/fathers/0714.htm.

72 Justin Martyr, *First Apology*, trans. Marcus Dods and George Reith, Ante-Nicene Fathers 1 (Buffalo, N.Y.: Christian Literature Publishing, 1885), 66, http://www.newadvent.org/fathers/0126.htm.

73 Josep Vilella, "Letters of Communion," in *Encyclopedia of Ancient Christianity*, ed. Angelo Di Bernardino (Downers Grove, Ill.: InterVarsity Press Academic, 2014), 557–59. More information is found in Ludwig Hertling, *Communio: Chiesa e papato nell'antichità cristiana* (Rome: Libreria editrice della Pontificia Università Gregoriana, 1961), 16–22.

their ecclesial communion and mutual charity before communicating in the Sacrament."[74]

At the level of theological reflection, the issue of Eucharistic and ecclesial communion has three interrelated aspects which merit mention. In the first place, there is the distinction between imperfect communion, founded on the authentic ecclesial bond coming from baptism, and the full communion in faith, worship, and hierarchy that is necessary for participation in the Eucharist. Although, as the *Ecumenical Directory* states, "baptismal communion tends towards full ecclesial communion," the latter communion is not a necessary corollary of the former.[75] As Congar affirmed, "one understands that, united in Baptism, one may not be so with regard to the Eucharist. Because [the Eucharist] is, in relation to Baptism, consummation and, in relation to the mystery of the Church, fullness."[76]

Secondly, one should keep in mind that the mutual interdependence between Eucharistic communion and ecclesial communion is a consequence of a singular communion in truth. Indeed, there exists "an ontological interdependence between the fullness of the Revelation of the Logos and the fullness of his presence in the Sacrament of the Altar. . . . Therefore, Eucharistic communion and communion in truth cannot be separated."[77]

Finally, although what has been said so far concerns both the faithful and ministers, the exceptions to the general discipline for the former, as mentioned in the previous section, cannot be applied to the latter. This is a consequence of the specific role of the minister in the Eucharistic assembly. *Lumen Gentium* number 10 says, speaking of the ministerial priest, "acting in the person of Christ, he makes present the Eucharistic sacrifice, and offers it to God in the name of all the people." The priest carries out this task acting as "a sacramental representation of Jesus Christ—the head and shepherd."[78] The rest of the faithful do not possess the capacity to act in this manner. In this context, one can appreciate why a hypothetical concelebration between distinct ecclesial communities

74 Congregation for Divine Worship and the Discipline of the Sacraments, *General Instruction of the Roman Missal*, 82.

75 Pontifical Council for Promoting Christian Unity, *Directory for the Application of Principles*, 22.

76 Yves Congar, "Unis dans le baptême, désunis dans l'Eucharistie," in *Essais Oecuméniques* (Paris: Centurion, 1984), 253. Our translation.

77 Pedro Rodríguez, "La Eucaristía y la unidad de la Iglesia," *Scripta Theologica* 7, no. 2 (1975): 592–93. Our translation.

78 John Paul II, Post-Synodal Apostolic Exhortation *Pastores dabo vobis* (March 25, 1992), 15.

would not make sense. Such a concelebration would sacramentally represent a complete unity which in reality would be lacking.

Thus, recourse to intercommunion as a way of promoting Christian unity must be rejected in no uncertain terms.[79] It would be false to affirm that, since the Eucharist "makes the Church" and therefore brings about unity, it would be better to celebrate this sacrament together to increase unity. The patristic phrase "the Eucharist makes the Church" is inseparable from the other patristic affirmation that "The Church makes the Eucharist."[80] In the later dictum, "Church" is to be understood as implying the fullness of the bonds of communion. The Decree *Unitatis Redintegratio* affirms that "baptism, therefore, envisages a complete profession of faith, complete incorporation in the system of salvation such as Christ willed it to be, and finally complete ingrafting in eucharistic communion."[81] The path which leads from baptism "finally" to the Eucharist necessarily passes through the complete profession of faith and full incorporation into the Church. The previously existing reality of the Church, in her unity of faith and communion, is an essential prerequisite for the fruitful celebration of the Eucharist.[82]

THEOLOGICAL DIALOGUE AND ITS RECEPTION

The unity of full communion can only come from unity in faith. Without the latter, churches and ecclesial communities could at most reach a

79 It has been appropriately said that the use of the word "intercommunion" "is in fact contradictory when it intends to signify that in the intercommunion there is a partaking in the sacrament on the part of Christians who, otherwise, are not in communion: *inter* negates what is affirmed as *communion*." Spinsanti, *Ecumenismo*, 143. Our translation. The adherent of an authentic ecclesiology of communion is left bewildered and wounded in the face of the expansion of the lexicon developed in this context: there is talk of intercelebration, intercommunion, hospitality, open communion, mutual open communion, limited open communion, closed communion, and so on. Chris O'Donnell, "Intercommunion," in *Ecclesia: A Theological Encyclopedia of the Church*, ed. Chris O'Donnell (Collegeville, Minn.: Liturgical Press, 1996), 220–22.

80 On the Church-Eucharist relationship in the patristic period and the Middle Ages, see De Lubac, *Corpus Mysticum*.

81 *Unitatis Redintegratio*, 22.

82 Ecumenical dialogue at the doctrinal level has become much more strenuous than predicted at the time of the last council. For some, this has produced a certain discouragement, which has led these persons to propose the abandonment of *doctrinal* dialogue in order to concentrate efforts on the common collaboration in moral and social issues. Cf. Konrad Raiser, "Thirty Years in the Service of the Ecumenical Movement: The Joint Working Group between the Roman Catholic Church and the World Council of Churches," *Centro Pro Unione Bulletin* 48 (Fall 1995): 3–8. However, this does not seem to be an appropriate strategy; something similar had already been attempted at the dawn of the ecumenical movement with the Life and Action movement, with very ephemeral results. This experience was useful precisely for realizing the need for a common faith as a necessary foundation for common action.

closer collaboration on social and moral objectives or other worthy goals. Nevertheless, such efforts would fall short of the ultimate goal of ecumenism, which is full visible communion in the one Church. Hence, the various Christian communities have engaged in a fraternal and sincere theological dialogue on the doctrinal problems and other issues that divide them. As mentioned previously, the Catholic Church participates fully in this dialogue.

The dialogues and their respective documents are of various kinds, and are not always strictly doctrinal. At times, for example, they have involved clarifications regarding the past or agreements for collaboration. These efforts can take place at the local or international level. When all, or nearly all, of the Christian communities are involved, these dialogues typically take place in the Faith and Order Commission of the World Council of Churches.[83] More frequent, however, are bilateral dialogues between two specific communities. One reason for this is that the involvement of only two interlocutors results in less differences on the topics to be dealt with. In Chapter 1, the main documents of bilateral dialogue between the Catholic Church and the other communities were mentioned.[84] We will now reflect, briefly, on the nature of these exchanges.

The dialogues take place among experts officially designated by the respective churches or communities. They seek to overcome denominational differences by returning to the roots of faith, through sincere reflection on Sacred Scripture and on each one's own tradition. In doing so, each community seeks to minimize any unilaterality or partiality which would prevent a harmonious insertion of their own faith tradition into the whole of Tradition. Often this leads primarily to a deeper understanding of one's own faith, and this already is a great good.

On the Catholic side, the *magna carta* for ecumenical dialogue is a document published on August 15, 1970, by the then-Secretariat for Christian Unity, entitled *Reflections and Suggestions concerning Ecumenical Dialogue*. The document describes the nature of this dialogue as follows:

83 The most appreciated fruit of the multilateral dialogue is the so-called Lima Text: World Council of Churches, *Baptism, Eucharist, and Ministry* (Geneva: World Council of Churches, 1982); this was followed by an interesting study document entitled *Confessing One Faith: Towards an Ecumenical Explication of the Apostolic Faith as Expressed in the Nicene-Constantinopolitan Creed (381)*, published in 1987 and intended to be continuously improved with the contribution of all Christian communities.

84 The existence of bilateral dialogues between the different non-Catholic Christian communities should also be kept in mind. This subject, however, goes beyond the scope of this work.

> In general terms, dialogue exists between individuals and groups from the moment when each party begins both to listen and reply, to seek to understand and to be understood, to pose questions and to be questioned in turn, to be freely forthcoming himself and receptive to the other party, concerning a given situation, research project or course of action, with the aim of progressing in unison towards a greater community of life, outlook and accomplishment. Each of the parties to the dialogue is ready to clarify further his ideas and his ways of living and acting, if it appears that truth is leading him in this direction. Thus reciprocity and a mutual commitment are essential elements of dialogue.[85]

These indications should not remain simply at the level of cordiality; they must be accepted within the Christian conception of faith. Such a perspective conceives faith as the fruit of a dialogue between God and man—between the God who calls and the man who answers. Furthermore, the Church herself has an intrinsically dialogical character, rooted in her essential nature as communion. Communication necessarily emerges as a dynamic aspect of this nature. All of this necessarily presupposes religious freedom. In the words of Cardinal Willebrands, "it is not in spite of our ecclesiology that we profess religious freedom, but it is precisely because of our doctrine on the Church."[86]

In this dialogue mutually informed by faith, participants need to be wary of uncritical assimilation to other modes of mediation present in the civil sphere. Ecumenism can never be a question of simple negotiation but needs to be rooted in faith in biblical Revelation. In recent decades, ecumenism has been criticized for forgetting this perspective in the name of cooperation in other areas. The prominent Lutheran ecumenical theologian Harding Meyer has decried what he sees as a shift from unity at the level of faith and sacraments to a merely external unity at the level of political and social action.[87]

Cooperation, however valuable, must never lose sight of the authentic nature of the Church's unity. This unity is essentially distinct from the unity proper to a human organization. The unity of the Church is always a unity willed by the Father, founded upon a mutual faith in Christ, and brought about through the strength of the Holy Spirit.

85 Secretariat for Promoting Christian Unity, *Reflections and Suggestions concerning Ecumenical Dialogue* (August 15, 1970), 6.
86 Johannes Willebrands, "La liberté religiouse et l'oecuménisme," 245. Our translation.
87 Meyer, *That All May Be One*, 151–56; cited with commentary in Daley, "Rebuilding the Structure of Love," 102.

Genuine Catholic ecumenism must seek to distance itself from any form of syncretism adopted in the name of a wrongly understood dialogue. "Dialogue does not produce truth, dialogue discovers the truth which is given to us once and for all in Jesus Christ."[88] A perspective of faith, therefore, is far removed from any kind of "relativistic dialogue," but not from the use of dialogue as an instrument for coming to know the truth.[89] The council's Declaration on Religious Freedom expresses this authentic Catholic sense when it speaks of "dialogue, in the course of which men explain to one another the truth they have discovered, or think they have discovered, in order thus to assist one another in the quest for truth."[90] It must therefore be seen "as one way in which the Church grows in insight into the once and for all revealed truth, and advances towards a fuller understanding of divine truth." Christ, ultimately, "is the fulfillment and the fullness of dialogue, not its end or its suppression."[91]

In a parallel way, Catholic ecumenism should also avoid every "false irenicism, in which the purity of Catholic doctrine suffers loss," and which our separated brethren should also reject.[92] An important non-Catholic theologian, Oscar Cullmann, insightfully comments:

> I consider the tendency to hide that which separates us to be the greatest contemporary danger of ecumenism, above all when we assemble among Christians known as "open to dialogue." . . . There exists, on both sides, the dangerous temptation to consider, as manifestations of a particularly ecumenical spirit, discussions in which the participants adjust, in one way or another, the emphases given in the presentation of their points of view, in such a manner to assimilate one position to the other. In reality, these adjustments (however small they might seem) often distort the truth, engender illusions and by this harm the ecumenical cause since, sooner or later, they lead to a great deception.[93]

The development of various dialogues over the course of the postconciliar period has revealed the need to identify a methodology which can obtain more consistent results. Up until now, for the most part, the efforts at dialogue have aimed at reaching a "differentiated consensus." With the words of Kurt Koch:

88 Kasper, *That They May All Be One*, 38.
89 Kasper, *Harvesting the Fruits*, 6.
90 *Dignitatis Humanae*, 3.
91 Kasper, *That They May All Be One*, 38 and 40.
92 *Unitatis Redintegratio*, 11.
93 Text published in *Documentation catholique*, June 1965, col. 1115. Our translation.

> According to this method, on the one hand the consensus reached in the dialogue on a fundamental content, which would have been the source of polemic in the past, is formulated and articulated jointly; on the other hand, the remaining differences are mentioned in an equally clear way, showing that they do not undermine the consensus reached and are no longer differences that cause a division between the Churches, but must be developed further by future theological dialogue.[94]

This method has been criticized in multiple aspects. Still, Koch himself encourages its use, "especially if it is animated by the 'hermeneutic of mutual trust.'"[95] This method has emerged as a significant means for ecumenical progress.

While recognizing the risks of the differentiated-consensus approach, Hervé Legrand argues that "the method of differentiated consensus has actually enabled more progress in 40 years than in the previous five centuries."[96] A prime example would be the Lutheran-Catholic *Joint Declaration on the Doctrine of Justification* from 1999, which describes "a consensus of basic truths of the doctrine of justification" alongside "differences of language, theological elaboration, and emphasis in the understanding of justification" which are "acceptable."[97] Legrand sees this joint declaration as opening up a new phase in ecumenical dialogue. In this new phase, the Magisterium would seek a greater fidelity to the Word in contrast to a more juridical approach characteristic of the past.[98]

Differentiated consensus seeks to overcome the divisions of the past by situating doctrinal statements "in their linguistic and socio-political context without neglecting the linguistic turn that comes from philosophy."[99] The new perspectives can help to discover an underlying unity, at times obscured by historical, political, and cultural divisions. For example, the doctrinal agreements of the 1970s with the Armenian, Syrian, and Coptic churches have shown an underlying doctrinal unity which exists alongside the rejection of the terminology of the Council of Chalcedon.[100] Such an

94 Koch, "Sviluppi ecumenici e nuove sfide," 192. Our translation.
95 Koch, "Sviluppi ecumenici e nuove sfide," 192. Our translation.
96 Hervé Legrand, "Differentiated Consensus as a Means of Correcting Unilateral Ecclesiological Developments?" *The Ecumenical Review* 71, no. 3 (July 2019): 268, http://dx.doi.org/10.1111/erev.12436.
97 *Joint Declaration on the Doctrine of Justification*, 40.
98 Legrand, "Differentiated Consensus," 273.
99 Legrand, "Differentiated Consensus," 274.
100 Legrand, "Differentiated Consensus," 275.

approach does not necessarily involve falling into cultural and doctrinal relativism. Rather, we can see differentiated consensus as an expansion of the Church's catholicity, through which the Church comes to appreciate the various perspectives from which believers can express the one mystery of faith.

The importance of methodological questions has taken on particular relevance in relation to the phenomenon of the "ecumenism of profiles," which has increased in recent years. This kind of ecumenism consists in the renewed effort to elaborate the identity of one's own community in contrast with other institutions.[101] The process is complicated by the fact that, for many Christian communities arising from the Reformation, the objective of ecumenism no longer consists in visible communion in faith, worship, and hierarchy, but rather in the mutual recognition of other churches as churches. This recognition would not involve actual changes by the parties involved.[102] Karl Lehmann denounced this practice of mutual recognition without conversion as "spiritual heresy."[103] In light of these phenomena, one can understand the discouraged tone of Protestant ecumenist Harding Meyer when he warns of the "danger of ecumenical oblivion," when "everything that has already been accomplished in dialogue becomes uncertain and slips from our grasp once more, and what has been achieved seeps away and evaporates as though it had never existed."[104]

A more recent proposal aims to return to the ecclesiological article of the creed, which professes the Church be one, holy, catholic, and apostolic. The proposed methodology would focus on this affirmation, professed by all the parties involved in ecumenical dialogue. An examination of this article of faith would take place in light of the sacramentality of the Church and of the mutual interrelation which the four properties have with one another.

In the background of this proposal is the text of *Lumen Gentium* number 8, which has received much attention due to the phrase *subsistit in*. However, there has not always been enough attention given to the fact that "many elements of sanctification and of truth," as the same text affirmed,

101 Koch, "Sviluppi ecumenici e nuove sfide," 192–93.
102 Koch, "Sviluppi ecumenici e nuove sfide," 193–94.
103 "Wie viel Hoffnung bringt die Ökumene?" *Katholische Nachrichten Agentur—Ökumenische Information* 20–21 (June 2010): 8. Our translation.
104 "Ökumenische Perspektiven aus evangelischer Sicht," in *Unus fons, unus spiritus, una fides*, ed. Jürgen Krüger and Jens-Martin Kruse (Karlsruhe: Arte Factum, 2010), 234; the English quote is taken from "Developments and Challenges in Ecumenism Today: Address by Kurt Cardinal Koch in Trondheim, Norway, 29 July 2011," *Den Katolske Kirke*, http://www.katolsk.no/tro/tema/ekumenikk/artikler/developments-and-challenges-in-ecumenism-today.

are to be found outside of the Catholic Church's visible structure. The text goes on to say that "these elements, as gifts belonging to the Church of Christ, are forces impelling toward catholic unity." Among these elements are the four traditional properties of the Church. In this proposal, the terms of the dialogue do not situate the position of one community against another, but rather each is called to encounter revealed truth. Each group seeks to realize a greater coherence with its own tradition, and, in this process, they should look to the creed as a guide for their faithfulness.[105]

The work of commissions for ecumenical dialogue can come to fruition in various types of documents such as joint declarations on doctrine, accounts of the work carried out, and final reports. These various statements and their titles often use very measured language to describe the degree of agreement attained. They employ words such as "convergence," "agreed statement," "full agreement," or "substantial agreement." The language of these documents is very nuanced and sometimes intentionally generic, so as to reach an agreement that can be shared by both parties. However, this approach can also run the risk of reducing the substance of what has been agreed upon.

For an adequate understanding of these documents, one must examine not only the aforementioned aspects, but also the degree of reception of the documents in the respective church. Many of these texts are the work of experts in the field, and thus "have intrinsic weight because of the competence and status of their authors." However, in order that these documents might truly lead to the restoration of ecclesial communion, they must be "approved by the appropriate ecclesiastical authorities."[106] This is often a complex matter, which in many respects goes beyond the strictly doctrinal perspective. It may happen that the respective authorities have reservations about what has been agreed upon by a commission for bilateral dialogue, and express these concerns in the form of clarifications, observations, or responses.[107] Or it may be the case, and indeed a desired one, that both parties officially accept the agreement which has been reached. In such

105 Philip Goyret, "Credo Ecclesiam e rilancio ecumenico," *Nicolaus* 37, no. 2 (2010): 251–59.
106 Pontifical Council for Promoting Christian Unity, *Directory for the Application of Principles*, 178.
107 In the Catholic-Anglican dialogue we find several examples, like the Congregation for the Doctrine of the Faith, *Observations on ARCIC II's "Salvation and the Church"* (1989); the *Lambeth Conference Response to the Final Report of the ARCIC* (1988); the *Catholic Church's Response to the Final Report of ARCIC I* (1991); and ARCIC, *Clarifications of Certain Aspects of the Agreed Statements on Eucharist and Ministry* (September, 1993), which is a letter of Cardinal Cassidy to the copresidents of ARCIC II.

instances, the competent authorities would sign the accord, which would in turn become binding for the next phase of dialogue.[108]

The experience up to now indicates that the reception of ecumenical agreements is not an easy or straightforward matter, and in recent years it has emerged as a cause for concern and reflection. Among the various difficulties, a prominent one is the absence of equivalence between the different churches and communities with regard to the level of reception for an agreement and the degree to which an agreement would be binding. While the Catholic Church has a Magisterium that serves as a reference point and implies a clear level of adherence, many of the partners to dialogue do not have a centralized, institutional structure capable of making binding decisions. The denominational bodies which carry out ecumenical dialogue can easily be very distinct from the individual pastors who are the ones with authority in each individual community.[109] As a result, the commitments which follow an agreement between communities remain open to later changes.

Thus, progress in ecumenical dialogue requires a clearer understanding of who the participants to dialogue are. The Princeton Proposal for Christian Unity, while recognizing the value in ecumenical work of worldwide organizations of Protestant churches—such as the World Methodist Council or the Lutheran World Federation—calls upon these same organizations to discern more clearly their identity as agents of unity within their own tradition and also on behalf of the wider Church. In a parallel vein, the same document calls for Roman Catholics, Orthodox, and Anglicans to distinguish "between the divinely appointed functions of oversight and ministry and current juridical, bureaucratic, and institutionalized forms of those functions."[110] Such clarity is necessary for dialogue to effectively function in the service of truth and unity.

A final, salient characteristic of this process of reception is that it is not simply intellectual in nature. Existential, pastoral, and spiritual factors play a significant role:

> The life of faith and the prayer of faith, no less than reflection on the doctrine of faith, enter into this process of reception, by which the whole Church, under the inspiration of the Holy Spirit "who distributes special

108 Examples would be the Christological declarations between the Catholic Church and some ancient Eastern Churches, and the Joint Declaration between the Catholic Church and the Lutheran World Federation of October 31, 1999.
109 Yeago, "Ecclesial Context of Ecumenical Reception," 35–37.
110 Braaten and Jenson, *Princeton Proposal*, nos. 62–63.

> graces among the faithful of every rank" [*Lumen Gentium*, 12] and guides in a special way the ministry of those who teach, makes its own the fruits of a dialogue, in a process of listening, of testing, of judging and of living.[111]

Ecumenical reception requires a process of "death and resurrection," through which the ecclesial subject is reformed amidst divisions.[112]

THE EXPRESSION OF THE DOCTRINE OF FAITH

The path towards the truth, so that it might be shared by all, is not easy. The methodological problems in the elaboration and reception of the documents of dialogue have just been mentioned. In the final analysis, this process is a matter of bringing together, in the formulation of the truth, two qualities that might appear to be opposed to one another, but that must integrate harmoniously: *purity* and *fullness*.[113] When, instead, one privileges a disproportionate and unilateral search for *purity*, or the precision with which a particular truth is expressed, one also risks doing so to the detriment of the fullness of truth. The deposit of faith could thus be reduced exclusively to its central core and lack full development. On the other extreme, a disproportionate search for the *fullness* of truth tends to neglect its purity; there is then the risk of falsely expanding the deposit of faith and going beyond the boundaries of Revelation. We will now describe three guiding principles which facilitate the pursuit of shared truth while respecting this delicate balance.

With respect to the first principle, that of *the difference between expression and content*, the council warns us that "the way and method in which the Catholic faith is expressed should never become an obstacle to dialogue with our brethren."[114] The council thus distinguishes between expression, or the "way and method," on the one hand, and on the other "the Catholic faith," or the content of the deposit of faith. In other words, the expression of faith and the content of this faith are not necessarily one and identifiable. The expression is conditioned by many factors, including language, culture, and time period, which vary and admit of diversity. At the same time, the content of faith itself, to which the supernatural act of faith of the believer is directed, is necessarily one and unique.[115]

111 Pontifical Council for Promoting Christian Unity, *Directory for the Application of Principles*, 180.
112 Yeago, "Ecclesial Context of Ecumenical Reception," 44.
113 Congar, *Chrétiens en dialogue*, 180.
114 *Unitatis Redintegratio*, 11.
115 John Paul II, *Ut unum sint*, 19.

Much ecumenical dialogue at the theological level operates according to this principle. This effort involves seeking expressions of faith that are *apostolic*—corresponding to the faith transmitted by the apostles—as well as *catholic*—that is, sufficiently open to the understanding and acceptance of all. This principle can be seen as a development of the understanding of Tradition. As Vatican II's Dogmatic Constitution *Dei Verbum* points out, the tradition of the apostles develops in the Church by the help of the Holy Spirit: "For as the centuries succeed one another, the Church constantly moves forward toward the fullness of divine truth until the words of God reach their complete fulfillment in her."[116]

In this context, one should understand that, just as within the one Church there must be shared and binding formulations regarding the fundamental truths, such as the creed, so also, within Catholic communion, different formulations of the same faith can exist in respect to less central aspects. The expression of faith depends not only on the doctrinal content but also on the cultural context, the general vision of the cosmos, and the way of understanding the relationship of man with creation and with the Creator. The Christian churches, as we have seen, have also experienced division because of these nondoctrinal reasons. One can think, for example, of the Latin character of Roman Catholicism, the German aspect of Lutheranism, the profoundly British dimension of Anglicanism, and the Eastern nature of Orthodoxy.

Finally, the historical dimension of dogmatic definitions, including those at the origin of the divisions among Christian communities, brings powerfully to light the tension between the permanent value of doctrinal formulas and the hermeneutical process at the root of these same statements. This tension includes the complex relationships between history and truth, between language and its interpretation, and between knowledge and reality. Such questions cannot be ignored in ecumenical dialogue.[117]

The *principle of integrity* is very important for a sincere theological dialogue: "It is, of course, essential that the doctrine should be clearly presented in its entirety. Nothing is so foreign to the spirit of ecumenism as a false irenicism, in which the purity of Catholic doctrine suffers loss and its genuine and certain meaning is clouded."[118] With these words, the council rejects

116 *Dei Verbum*, 8.
117 For a deeper examination of this topic, one can consult the document published in 1990 by the International Theological Commission, entitled *The Interpretation of Dogma*.
118 *Unitatis Redintegratio*, 11.

the false ecumenism which would seek to evade the difficult truths so as to achieve a greater consensus.[119] Nonetheless, the fact remains that theological dialogue begins from areas of agreement. Proceeding otherwise would be absurd. Still, the final goal is always that of integral unity in the faith. As John Paul II pointed out, an authentic vision of unity necessarily "takes account of all the demands of revealed truth."[120] Within this perspective, the precise identification of the elements of agreement, distinguished from those areas where agreement is lacking, is a step forward.

With regard to other Christian communities, the principle of integrity does not simply imply giving voice to those truths which are known to each party. In addition, each party must have the desire to come to that truth which still remains unknown, up to the whole truth. In this sense, the churches engaged in ecumenical dialogue are called to keep alive the conviction that the possibilities for understanding the mystery of faith have not been fully realized. Communities distinct from one's own can offer a fuller insight into this mystery. Such recognition does not necessarily imply a betrayal of one's own confession of faith or the summing up of loose and heterogenous elements between different communities.

The principle of integrity also implies an effort which is directed inward. Each community should seek to delineate, on the one hand, those elements which belong to the substance of their doctrine and are therefore binding, and, on the other hand, those aspects which are circumstantial and hence not essential. The process of integration does not imply assimilating everything in an indiscriminate way. Ecumenism, in fact, is not a simple mixing of elements taken from Luther, Calvin, Saint Thomas Aquinas, Gregory Palamas, and Saint Augustine. Instead, ecumenism is fidelity to one's own tradition, which cannot lead one to ignore Christ's desire for the Church's unity.

Finally, the principle of *the hierarchy of truths* has increasingly become a methodological key for ecumenical dialogue at the theological level.[121] "When comparing doctrines with one another, [Catholic theo-

119 John Paul II, *Ut unum sint*, 18.

120 John Paul II, *Ut unum sint*, 79.

121 Paolo Fontana, "Gerarchia delle verità: Una categoria controversa," in *Lo Spirito Santo Teologo del Popolo di Dio*, ed. Gianfranco Calabrese (Casale Monferrato: Piemme, 1997), 221–34; Carlos Cardona, *La "jerarquía de las verdades" y el orden de lo real: Los movimientos teológicos secularizantes* (Madrid: Biblioteca de Autores Cristianos, 1973), 143–64; Gustave Thils, "Hiérarchie des vérités de la foi et dialogue oecuménique," *Revue Théologique de Louvain* 15, no. 2 (1984): 150–51.

logians] should remember that in Catholic doctrine there exists a 'hierarchy' of truths, since they vary in their relation to the fundamental Christian faith."[122]

The concept of hierarchy, in this context, obviously does not indicate that some truths are truer than others, since truth does not allow for graduality. As the Secretariat for Promoting Christian Unity stated in 1970, "all revealed truths demand the same acceptance of faith, but according to the greater or lesser proximity that they have to the basis of the revealed mystery, they are variously placed with regard to one another and have varying connections among themselves."[123] Some doctrines, such as the Holy Trinity and the Incarnation of the Son of God, are central mysteries of the faith. Other teachings, while equally true and revealed, are not at the foundation of the Church's doctrine and therefore should be understood in light of the central mysteries. An example of such a less central teaching would be the fact that only a priest can administer the sacrament of anointing of the sick.

Hence, one can understand why the postconciliar declaration *Mysterium Ecclesiae* speaks prudentially of something similar to a hierarchy (*veluti hierarchia*) among the dogmas of the faith.[124] The document uses less reserve with the word "order" (*ordo*), which better emphasizes the interrelation between various elements without necessarily negating an equality among them.[125] This order among truths is not simply an intellectual question but comes from the fact that the deposit of faith is a living, organic reality made up of elements harmoniously related to one other. This harmony arises from the internal logic of salvation itself. In other words, the different truths relate to each other according to a certain objective order of importance, because not all of them contain and express the same salvific meaning.[126] All of these truths need to be ultimately seen in their relation

122 *Unitatis Redintegratio*, 11.
123 Secretariat for Promoting Christian Unity, *Reflections and Suggestions concerning Ecumenical Dialogue* (1970), IV.4.b.
124 Issued by the Congregation for the Doctrine of the Faith on June 24, 1973.
125 The study document rightly says "by using the words 'order' or 'hierarchy' the Council intended to affirm the organic nature of faith. Truths are articulated around a centre or foundation; they are not placed side by side." Pontifical Council for Promoting Christian Unity and World Council of Churches, *The Notion of "Hierarchy of Truths": An Ecumenical Interpretation* (1990), 9.
126 Stanislas Nagy, "La jerarquía de los dogmas a la luz del pensamiento teológico contemporáneo," in *El misterio de la Iglesia y la Iglesia como comunión*, ed. Pedro Rodriguez (Madrid: Palabra, 1994), 87–88.

to "the fundamental Christian faith," which primarily refers to a living and vivifying reality, the mystery of the person of Jesus Christ.[127]

Ecumenical dialogue does not aim to identify those truths which would be the so-called fundamental truths of faith, or those supposed to be at the center of the Gospel message, so as to establish a lowest common denominator among the various Christian communities.[128] Such a process would risk reducing the faith to a specific nucleus.[129] The Magisterium has emphasized that "all dogmas, since they are revealed, must be believed with the same divine faith."[130] The principle of hierarchy of truths, therefore, is not to be located in the act of belief itself, or *fides qua*. Rather, the principle is of great relevance in the ambit of the *fides quae*, or the objective content of faith. As *Mysterium Ecclesiae* notes, "some dogmas are founded on other dogmas which are the principal ones, and are illuminated by these latter."[131]

The importance of this theme for ecumenical dialogue lies in the fact that often the disagreement does not refer to the falsity or truth of certain positions but rather "to the different links they establish between the truths and the foundation of faith."[132] Such links can highlight certain aspects not present in another position. Furthermore, the principle of hierarchy of truths also has great methodological importance in theological dialogue for assessing the significance of existing doctrinal differences. Such differences "vary in importance according to their relation to the central mystery of Christ."[133]

ROMAN PRIMACY IN AN ECUMENICAL PERSPECTIVE

At the methodological level, therefore, ecumenical dialogue should seek to establish an order for addressing the various questions, in line with the principle of hierarchy of truths. It would not always be best to simply consider one issue after another. This is because agreement on a particular issue usually depends on certain premises, about which sufficient agreement must

127 *Unitatis Redintegratio*, 11; Pontifical Council for Promoting Christian Unity and World Council of Churches, *"Hierarchy of Truths,"* 20–22.

128 These expressions were strongly criticized during the pontificate of Pius XI. Yves Congar, *Diversity and Communion*, trans. John Bowden (London: SMC Press, 1984), 130.

129 Wacław Hryniewicz, "*Hierarchia veritatum*," in *Swieta tajemnica jednosci*, ed. Piotr Jaskóła and Wacław Hryníewicz (Lublin: Redakcja Wydawnictw KUL, 1988), 38.

130 Congregation for the Doctrine of the Faith, *Mysterium Ecclesiae*, 4.

131 Congregation for the Doctrine of the Faith, *Mysterium Ecclesiae*, 4.

132 Pontifical Council for Promoting Christian Unity and World Council of Churches, *"Hierarchy of Truths,"* 35.

133 Pontifical Council for Promoting Christian Unity and World Council of Churches, *"Hierarchy of Truths,"* 33.

first be found. Ultimately, in the articulation of an order of themes there is a logical architecture. At times, this architecture imposes an order which proceeds step-by-step. At other times, there is a certain circularity, in which various aspects of doctrine might be examined, even when all the essential presuppositions are not fully accepted by all parties in dialogue.

In a more directly ecclesiological context, the most basic issue to face, as noted previously, regards the very concept of the Church and its unity. For the ecclesial communities which exited from full Catholic communion at the time of the Reformation, the central topic seems to be the sacramental nature of the Church, along with the sacramentality of the episcopate and of holy orders in general. Reformed communities tend to see the institutional aspects of the Church, and the Roman pontiff in particular, in juridical and authoritative terms, and thus in opposition to the Word of God.[134] An important goal, in this regard, is to manifest how these institutional elements of the Church are reflections of Christ's will and are at service of the Word of God. Vatican II's Dogmatic Constitution on the Church, *Lumen Gentium*, is an important step in this direction.

In this context, ecumenical dialogue seeks to find agreement with respect to the relationship between the apostolicity of the Church and apostolic succession. Catholic doctrine understands the apostolicity of the Church as the identity of the Church today with the Church of Pentecost, presided over by the apostolic college. In the Catholic perspective, apostolicity is guaranteed by the apostolic succession sacramentally present in the episcopate. Reformed communities accept the concept of apostolic succession, but without necessarily including the episcopate. Apostolic succession is a sign, though not an indispensable one, of the apostolicity of the Church but does not serve as a guarantor of this property. The background of this debate lies in fundamentally different conceptions of both the content and transmission of the apostolic tradition.[135]

For the Orthodox Churches, the problem seems to be at a higher level of the architecture mentioned above. The apostolic succession belongs to their heritage of faith as a sacramental reality. However, the Orthodox concept of succession is situated within an ecclesiology in which the role of the Petrine succession is very reduced, to the point of being incompatible with Catholic doctrine. In favoring the local church too unilaterally with regard

134 For a Protestant perspective on Catholic ecclesiology, see, for example, Whitlock, *Divided We Fall*, 40–41.

135 Goyret, *Dalla Pasqua alla Parusia*, 281–300.

to the broader communion of churches, the apostolic succession comes to be seen more as a succession of churches than as a succession of bishops.[136] This vision lacks a strong sense of episcopal collegiality which would arise from seeing the college of bishops as successor to the apostolic college. Still less is there a recognition of the head of the episcopal college, which the Catholic Church identifies as the successor of Peter.

According to the Orthodox perspective, the pope is not head but only the first among bishops who are fundamentally equal. This role of being *primus inter pares*, the first among equals, corresponds to a primacy of honor but not of jurisdiction. While agreement has not been easy on this point, Catholics and Orthodox continue to work together in dialogue towards a deeper articulation of the truth which they jointly recognize. The Ravenna Document speaks of a common agreement that "Rome, as the Church that 'presides in love' according to the phrase of St Ignatius of Antioch (*Epistle to the Romans,* Prologue), occupied the first place in the *taxis*, and that the bishop of Rome was therefore the *protos* among the patriarchs."[137] Such a perspective still needs to be adequately integrated into Orthodox thinking. Still, in light of the progress in dialogue, Hervé Legrand holds that "a differentiated consensus on the exercise of Roman primacy in the first millennium is no longer out of reach."[138]

The different ecclesiological perspectives can allow us to appreciate why the theme of the Roman primacy has not often been dealt with in a substantial way in the documents of official ecumenical dialogue.[139] Frequently,

136 This is the approach of modern Orthodox ecclesiology, which contrasts with traditional Orthodox theology. On the former point, see José R. Villar, "La teologia ortodoxa de la Iglesia local," in *Eclesiologia 30 años despues de "Lumen Gentium,"* ed. Pedro Rodríguez (Madrid: Rialp, 1994), 237–64; on the latter, Villar, "Il ministero episcopale nella *communio Ecclesiarum*," in *I vescovi e il loro ministero*, ed. Philip Goyret (Vatican City: Libreria editrice Vaticana, 2000), 78. For a general overview of Orthodox theology on this subject, see Goyret, *Dalla Pasqua alla Parusia*, 263–81.

137 Joint International Commission for the Theological Dialogue between the Roman Catholic Church and the Orthodox Church, *Ecclesiological and Canonical Consequences*, no. 41.

138 Legrand, "Differentiated Consensus," 278.

139 This topic was examined in *Ecclesiological and Canonical Consequences of the Sacramental Nature of the Church: Ecclesial Communion, Conciliarity and Authority* of the Joint International Commission for the Theological Dialogue between the Roman Catholic Church and the Orthodox Church (October 13, 2007). This theme is also increasingly present in Anglican-Catholic dialogue: The Agreed Statements on Authority in the Church (I and II): Venice (1976); Windsor (1981); and *The Gift of Authority* (September 3, 1998). However, this theme was never the central subject of an official document in international ecumenical dialogue. At the local level, the topic has been addressed in the Joint Statement *Papal Primacy and the Universal Church* (Minneapolis: Augsburg Publishing House, 1974) of the US Catholic-Lutheran Commission; in the Joint

there has been a lack of sufficient agreement on the premises which would be necessary for a more fruitful dialogue on the subject. Even so, at the level of theological debate the Roman primacy is increasingly at the center of ecumenical talks, above all following the papal appeal, already mentioned, to "seek—together, of course—the forms in which this ministry may accomplish a service of love recognized by all concerned."[140]

Regarding this subject, the most prominent international agreement in recent decades has been *The Gift of Authority*, published by the Anglican-Roman Catholic International Commission on May 12, 1999. This document makes a significant advance in the appreciation of the Roman primacy in the larger context of ecclesial communion, although it has not found full acceptance among the whole Anglican Communion. The document deals with the question of authority, a central issue in Anglican-Roman Catholic dialogue. In 1996, the Archbishop of Canterbury, Dr. George Carey, and Pope John Paul II stated emphatically that without agreement on the question of authority, their respective communities could not reach the full, visible unity to which they are committed.[141]

The Gift of Authority describes primacy within the context of the synodality and communion which have characterized the Church from her beginning, and with the awareness that primacy remains at the service of the wider communion. The commission expresses its "agreement on universal primacy as a gift to be shared," to such an extent as "to propose that such a primacy could be offered and received even before our churches are in full communion." Such a primacy, the text continues, "will even now help to uphold the legitimate diversity of traditions, strengthening and safeguarding them in fidelity to the Gospel. It will encourage the churches in their mission." In light of this, the commission asks "that Anglicans be open to and desire a recovery and re-reception under certain clear conditions of the exercise of universal primacy by the Bishop of Rome." At the same time, Roman Catholics are called to "be open to and desire a re-reception of the

---

Statement *Conciliarity and Primacy in the Church*, 1989 (Brighton) by the Orthodox/Roman Catholic Commission of the United States; and in the Statement *The Roman Primacy in the Communion of Churches* [*La primauté romaine dans la communion des églises*], of the Joint Catholic-Orthodox Committee in France (Paris: Cerf, 1991). For a general perspective on the subject, see Adriano Garuti, *The Primacy of the Bishop of Rome and the Ecumenical Dialogue*, trans. Michael J. Miller (San Francisco: Ignatius Press, 2004).

140 John Paul II, *Ut unum sint*, 95.

141 John Paul II and George Carey, Archbishop of Canterbury, *Common Declaration* (December 5, 1996).

exercise of primacy by the Bishop of Rome and the offering of such a ministry to the whole Church of God."[142]

Such a renewed appreciation of the role of the bishop of Rome is not simply a question of evaluating his own special task but—perhaps most importantly—of a sufficiently far-reaching vision of the universal Church and her mystery. The particular role of the Roman pontiff forms part of the fulfillment of Christ's promise to guide his Church into all truth. At the same time, the whole college of bishops is charged with preserving the Apostolic Tradition. In this process, the faithfulness of the whole people of God, through the baptismal gift of the *sensus fidei*, also has an essential place.[143]

Bringing such a vision of primacy into actual practice between Catholics and Anglicans would certainly not be easy in the light of pastoral realities. Still, one should not undervalue the fact that the Anglican-Roman Catholic International Commission, in a unanimous vote, "is actually calling for Anglican acceptance of papal primacy, perhaps even infallibility, not at some vague time of the future but right now!"[144] Christians of varied confessions, even with their reservations about the papacy, recognize that the bishop of Rome is "the only historically plausible candidate to exercise an effective worldwide ministry of unity." They recognize the importance of the Roman pontiff's exercise of his teaching office, carried out in such a way as to shape the minds of the entire Christian faithful and not simply those in communion with the Catholic Church.[145]

For non-Catholics, prior to the issue of the Petrine succession is that of the personal primacy of Peter himself within the apostolic college. Some understand this primacy not as the primacy of the person of Peter himself with respect to the other apostles, but rather as the primacy of the faith he professed at Caesarea Philippi (Mt 16: 13–18).[146] The question then arises of the transmission of this primacy, which is not explicitly attested to by Scripture, although it is confirmed in the most ancient non-

142 Anglican-Roman Catholic International Commission, *The Gift of Authority*, 60.

143 Anglican-Roman Catholic International Commission, *The Gift of Authority*, 42–43.

144 J. Robert Wright, "The Possible Contribution of Papal Authority to Church Unity: An Anglican/Episcopalian Perspective," in Braaten and Jenson, *Ecumenical Future*, 144.

145 Braaten and Jenson, *Princeton Proposal*, no. 65.

146 Bartholomew I, "Discours du Patriarche Bartholoméos 1er aux évêques de Suisse" (December 1995), in *La Documentation Catholique* 2131 (February 1996): 134–35; on the latter issue, see Joachim Gnilka, "Il ministero petrino: Fondazione nel nuovo testamento e configurazione nella Chiesa primitiva," in Hünermann, *Papato ed ecumenismo*, 9–21.

canonical Christian testimonies.[147] This issue is in turn linked to the problem of the location of the transmission, whether it be in Rome, Constantinople, or elsewhere, and the foundations for such claims.[148] The subject becomes even more difficult when dealing with the meaning of the authority exercised through Petrine primacy, especially the immediate jurisdictional power over all pastors and all the faithful, as well as the infallibility of magisterial teaching when exercised *ex cathedra*.[149] In the background to these questions there is the most basic problem of whether the Roman primacy belongs to the being of the Church, as part of the divine will, or rather is simply a good of the Church, one which is fitting but not intrinsically necessary.

The complexity of this subject is evident and should not be surprising, since we are at the very top of the architecture mentioned above. The primacy is, in the words of Johann Adam Möhler, the "keystone of the whole."[150] In spite of the difficulties, ecumenical dialogue must seek to address this issue. Such efforts should not hope for a solution independent of the necessary premises. Still, a circular methodology of debate can look beyond these premises so as to appreciate the underlying problems and then address attention to subsequent difficulties.

EPILOGUE

At the end of this introduction to ecumenical theology, the need for a great love of unity in diversity should be clear. The Church needs to identify that which is fundamental to her being, and which therefore cannot be changed and needs to be accepted by all. At the same, the Church needs to also determine that which admits of plurality in the manner of expressing the faith, in discipline, in rites, in spirituality, and so on. We must be convinced that both dimensions—unity and plurality—are necessary, even within the Catholic Church. With regard to freedom in temporal matters—and this also concerns many aspects of the Church—a twentieth-century saint affirmed: "We cannot forget that the existence among Catholics of a true diversity of criterion and opinion in matters which God has left to the free discussion of men is in no way opposed to the hierarchical structure or the unity of

147 Gnilka, "Il ministero petrino," 19.
148 Olivier Clément, *L'Église Orthodoxe* (Paris: Presses Universitaires de France, 1961), 68.
149 Vatican Council I, *Pastor Aeternus* (July 18, 1870), in Denzinger, *Enchiridion symbolorum*, 3050–75.
150 Johann Adam Möhler, *Unity in the Church*, 255.

the people of God. On the contrary, it strengthens them and defends them against possible impurities."[151] Living this authentically catholic mindset, and trusting in the power of the Cross of Christ, the Church is called to advance along the ecumenical path laid out for her by the Lord. She does so, praying with boldness and risking herself in "new forms of ecumenical endeavor," so that she can clearly and persuasively witness to Christ in today's world.[152]

151 Josemaría Escrivá, *Conversations with Monsignor Escrivá de Balaguer* (Sydney: Little Hills and Scepter, 1993), 12, https://www.escrivaworks.org/book/conversations-chapter-1.htm.
152 Braaten and Jenson, *Princeton Proposal*, no. 56.

Bibliography

Abraham, William J. "Ecumenism and the Rocky Road to Renewal." In *The Ecumenical Future*, edited by Braaten and Jenson, 176–87.

Acerbi, Antonio, ed. *Il ministero del papa in prospettiva ecuménica: Atti del colloquio Milano, 16–18 aprile 1998*. Milan: Vita e pensiero, 1999.

Alexander VIII. *Decree of the Holy Office*. December 7, 1690.

Algermissen, Konrad. *Konfessionskunde: Ein Handbuch der christlichen Kirchen und Sektenkunde der Gegenwort*. 6th ed. Hanover: Giesel, 1950. First published 1930. Translated by Joseph W. Grundner as *Christian Denominations*. St. Louis, Mo.: B. Herder, 1948.

Álvarez, Elena. *Procede del Padre y del Hijo: Estudio de la "Clarificación Romana" de 1995 y de sus fuentes patrísticas*. Bern: Lang, 2011.

Antinucci, Lucia. *Ecumenismo*. Casale Monferrato: Piemme, 1991.

Antón, Ángel. *El misterio de la Iglesia*. Madrid: Biblioteca de Autores Cristianos, 1986.

Anglican-Roman Catholic International Commission I. *The Malta Report*. February 2, 1968.

______. *The Final Report*. September 3, 1981.

Anglican-Roman Catholic International Commission II. *Salvation and the Church*. September 4, 1986.

______. *The Gift of Authority*. November 3, 1998.

Arinze, Francis. "La sfida delle sette o nuovi movimenti religiosi: Un approccio pastorale. Relazione generale al Concistoro Straordinario del 1991." In *La questione della nuova religiosità*, edited by Massimo Introvigne, 59–93. Piacenza: Cristianità, 1993.

Augustine. *De Baptismo*. In *Polemica contro i Donatisti*, edited by Agostino Trapè, 243–607. Opere di sant'Agostino, vol. 15, no. 1. Rome: Citta Nuova, 1998.

______. *Epistula* 185. In *Le lettere*, edited by Agostino Trapè, 72–75. Opere di sant'Agostino 23. Rome: Citta Nuova, 1974.

______. *De Trinitate*. Edited by John E. Rotelle, OSA. Translated by Edmund Hill, OP. The Works of Saint Augustine: A Translation for the 21st Century, part 1, vol. 5. Hyde Park, N.Y.: New City Press, 1991.

Asimakis, Ioannis. "Alcune considerazioni sull'ecclesiologia ecuménica." *Studi ecumenici* 29, no. 2 (2011): 207–26.

"The Athanasian Creed." In *Creeds and Confessions of Faith in the Christian Tradition*, vol. 1, edited by Jaroslav Pelikan and Valerie Hotchkiss, 673–78. New Haven, Conn.: Yale University Press, 2003.

Balabanski, Vicky, and Geraldine Hawkes. "Introduction." In *Receptive Ecumenism: Listening, Learning and Loving in the Way of Christ*, edited by Vicky Balabanski and Hawkes Geraldine, vii-xiv. Adelaide: ATF, 2018. http://www.jstor.org/stable/j.ctvjdzcmh.3.

Baptist-Roman Catholic International Conversations. *Summons to Witness to Christ in Today's World.* Falls Church, Va.: Baptist World Alliance, 1988.

Barbaglio, Giuseppe and Severino Dianich, eds. *Nuovo dizionario di teologia.* Cinisello Balsamo: Edizioni San Paolo, 2000.

Barbaglio, Giuseppe, Giampero Boff, and Severino Dianich, eds. *Teologia.* Cinisello Balsamo: San Paolo, 2002.

Barreto, Raimundo C., Jr. "Introduction: World Christianity as Public Religion." In *World Christianity as Public Religion*, edited by Barreto, Ronaldo Cavalcante, and Wanderley P. Da Rosa, 1–14. Minneapolis: Fortress Press, 2017.

Bartholomew I. "Discours du Patriarche Bartholoméos 1er aux évêques de Suisse." *La Documentation Catholique* 2131 (February 1996): 134–35.

Bellarmine, Robert. *De controversiis christianae fidei adversus huius temporis haereticos*, Seconda Controversia Generalis, Liber 3, *De Ecclesia militante.* Naples, Italy: J. Giuliano, 1857.

Benedict XV. *Dei providentis.* Motu proprio. May 1, 1917.

Benedict XVI. "Address to the Roman Curia." December 22, 2005.

______. *Anglicanorum coetibus.* Apostolic Constitution. November 4, 2009.

______. "Homily at the Mass with the Beatification of Venerable Cardinal John Henry Newman." September 19, 2010.

Betti, Umberto. "Chiesa di Cristo e Chiesa Cattolica: A proposito di una espressione della '*Lumen Gentium*.'" *Antonianum* 61 (1986): 726–45.

Bosch, Juan. *Para comprender el ecumenismo.* Estella: Verbo Divino, 1991.

Bouchard, Giorgio. *Chiese e movimenti evangelici del nostro tempo.* 3rd ed. Turin: Claudiana, 2006.

Bouyer, Louis. *The Church of God: Body of Christ, and Temple of the Spirit.* Translated by Charles Underhill Quinn. Chicago: Mayer, 1982. Originally published as *L'Eglise de Dieu, corps du Christ et temple de l'Esprit.* Paris: Cerf, 1970.

Braaten, Carl E. and Robert W. Jenson, eds. *Church Unity and the Papal Office: An Ecumenical Dialogue on John Paul II's Encyclical* Ut Unum Sint (*That All May Be One).* Grand Rapids, Mich.: Eerdmans, 2001.

______. *In One Body through the Cross: The Princeton Proposal for Christian Unity: A Call to the Churches from an Ecumenical Study Group.* Grand Rapids, Mich.: Eerdmans, 2003.

______. *The Ecumenical Future: Background Papers for* In One Body through the Cross: The Princeton Proposal for Christian Unity. Grand Rapids, Mich.: Eerdmans, 2004.

Browne, John. *History of Congregationalism and Memorials of the Churches in Norfolk and Suffolk.* London: Jarrold and Sons, 1877.

Burggraf, Jutta. *Conocerse y comprenderse: Una introducción al ecumenismo.* 2nd ed. Madrid: Rialp, 2003.

Bux, Nicola. *Il quinto sigillo: L'unità dei cristiani verso il terzo millennio*. Vatican City: Libreria editrice Vaticana, 1997.

Buzzi, Franco. *Breve storia del pensiero protestante: Da Lutero a Pannenberg*. Milan: Ancora, 2007.

Cacciatore, Fortunato M. *Protestantesimo e filosofia in Hegel*. Soveria Mannelli: Rubettino, 2003.

Calabrese, Gianfranco, Philip Goyret, and Orazio Piazza, eds. *Dizionario di ecclesiologia*. Rome: Città Nuova, 2010.

Calvin, John. *Institution de la religion chrétienne*. Geneva: Labor et Fides, 1958. Translated by Henry Beveridge as *Institutes of the Christian Religion*. London: James Clarke, 1949.

Canobbio, Giacomo. *Nessuna salvezza fuori della Chiesa? Storia e senso di un controverso principio teologico*. Brescia: Queriniana, 2009.

______. "*Extra Ecclesiam nulla salus*: Interpretazioni e prospettive." *Annales Theologici* 25 (2011): 391–420.

Cardona, Carlos. *La "jerarquía de las verdades" y el orden de lo real: Los movimientos teológicos secularizantes*. Madrid: Biblioteca de Autores Cristianos, 1973.

Capelle, Bernard. "Alcuin et l'histoire du symbolo de la Messe." In *Travaux liturgiques de doctrine et d'histoire*, edited by Bernard Capelle, 211–21. Louvain: Volz, 1962.

Charles, Prince of Wales. "John Henry Newman: The Harmony of Difference." *L'Osservatore Romano*. October 12, 2019.

Cereti, Giovanni. *Ecumenismo: Corso di metodologia ecumenica*. Rome: Istituto di Teologia a Distanza, 1991.

______. *Molte Chiese cristiane, un'unica Chiesa di Cristo: Corso di ecumenismo*. Brescia: Queriniana, 1992.

Cioffari, Gerardo. "Il vero uniatismo in un sincero dialogo ecumenico." *Studi Ecumenici* 11, no. 2 (1993): 177–202.

Civiltà Cattolica Editorial Board. "Il proselitismo religioso." *Civiltà Cattolica* 1, no. 3544 (1998): 319–28.

Clément, Olivier. *L'Église Orthodoxe*. Paris: Presses Universitaires de France, 1961.

Community of Protestant Churches in Europe. *Leuenberg Agreement*. In *Creeds and Confessions of Faith*, edited by Pelikan and Hotchkiss, 3:744–752.

Congar, Yves. *Chrétiens désunis: Principes d'un "oecuménisme" catholique*. Paris: Cerf, 1937. Translated by Maud A. Bousfield as *Divided Christendom: A Catholic Study of the Problem of Reunion*. London: Centenary, 1939.

______. *Esquisses du Mystère de L'Église*. Paris: Cerf, 1941. Translated by A. V. Littledale as *The Mystery of the Church*. Baltimore, Md.: Helicon, 1965.

______. "Note sur les mots confession, Église et communion." *Irénikon* 23 (1950): 14–20.

______. *True and False Reform in the Church.* Translated by Paul Philibert. Collegeville, Minn.: Liturgical Press, 2011. Originally published as *Vrai e fausse réforme dans l'Eglise.* Paris: Cerf, 1950.

______. *Jalons pour une Théologie du Laïcat.* Paris: Cerf, 1953.

______. "Hors de l'Église, pas de salut." In vol. 5 of *Catholicisme Hier Aujourd'hui Demain,* edited by Gabriel Jacquemet. Paris: Letouzey et Ané, 1962.

______. *Dialogue between Christians: Catholic Contributions to Ecumenism.* Translated by Philip Loretz. Westminster, Md.: Newman Press, 1966. First published as *Chretiens en dialogue: Contributions catholiques a l'oecumenisme.* Paris: Cerf, 1964.

______. "Proprietà essenziali della Chiesa." In *L'evento salvifico nella comunità di Gesù Cristo,* edited by Johannes Feiner and Magnus Löhrer, 440–714, 3rd ed. Vol. 7 of *Mysterium Salutis.* Brescia: Queriniana, 1981. First published in 1973.

______. *Diversity and Communion.* Translated by John Bowden. London: SCM Press, 1984. First published as *Diversités et communion: Dossier historique et conclusion théologique.* Paris: Cerf, 1982.

______. "Unis dans le baptême, désunis dans l'Eucharistie." In *Essais Oecuméniques: Le mouvement, le hommes, les problèmes,* 242–54. Paris: Centurion, 1984.

Congar, Yves and Jérôme Hamer. *La liberté religieuse: Déclaration "Dignitatis humanae personae": Texte latin et traduction française.* Paris: Cerf, 1967.

Congregation for the Doctrine of the Faith. *Mysterium Ecclesiae.* Declaration. June 24, 1973.

______. *Notification on the Book "Church: Charism and Power" by Father Leonardo Boff O.F.M.* March 11, 1985.

______. *Observations on ARCIC II's "Salvation and the Church."* November 18, 1988.

______. *Communionis notio.* Letter. May 28, 1992.

______. *The Primacy of the Successor of Peter in the Mystery of the Church.* October 31, 1998.

______. *Dominus Iesus.* June 16, 2000.

______. *Note on the Expression "Sister Churches."* June 30, 2000.

______. *Responses to Some Questions Regarding Certain Aspects of the Doctrine on the Church.* June 29, 2007.

______. "Presentation to the Vatican *Sala Stampa* of His Eminence Edward Idris Cardinal Cassidy." June 25, 1998.

______. *Justification and Sacramentality: The Christian Community as an Agent for Justice.* 2015.

Council of Chalcedon. *Acts.* In *The Seven Ecumenical Councils,* translated by Henry Percival, 243–92. Nicene and Post-Nicene Fathers, Second Series, edited by Philip Schaff and Henry Wace, 14. Edinburgh: T and T Clark, 1899.

Council of Florence. *Laetentur Caeli.* Bull. 1439. In Tanner, *Decrees of the Ecumenical Councils.* https://www.papalencyclicals.net/councils/ecum17.htm.

______. *Cantate Domino*. Bull. 1442. In Tanner, *Decrees of the Ecumenical Councils*. https://www.papalencyclicals.net/councils/ecum17.htm.

Couturier, Paul. "Prayer and Christian Unity," translated by Geoffrey Curtis. In Geoffrey Curtis, *Paul Couturier and Unity in Christ*, 329–51. Westminster, Mass.: J. William Eckenrode, 1964.

Cross, Frank L. and Elizabeth Livingstone, eds. *The Oxford Dictionary of the Christian Church*. 3rd ed. Oxford: Oxford University Press, 1997.

Curtis, W. R. The Lambeth Conferences: The Solution for Pan-Anglican Organization. New York: Columbia University Press, 1942.

Cyprian. *Epistulae*. Edited by G. F. Diercks. Corpus Christianorum Series Latina 3B–3C. Turnhout: Brepols, 1994–96.

______. *De Oratione Dominica*. In *S. Cypriani Tomus Unicus*, edited by Jacques-Paul Migne, 519–45. Patrologiae cursus completus: Series Latina 4. Paris: J. P. Migne, 1844.

Cyril of Alexandria. *Thesaurus*. In *S. Cyrili Tomus Octavus*, edited by Jacques-Paul Migne, 9–1075. Patrologiae cursus completus: Series Graeca 75. Paris: J. P. Migne, 1863.

Cyril of Jerusalem. *Catechetical Lectures*. Translated by Edwin Hamilton Gifford. In *S. Cyril of Jerusalem, S. Gregory Nazianzen*. Nicene and Post-Nicene Fathers, Second Series 7. Buffalo, N.Y.: Christian Literature Publishing, 1894. https://www.newadvent.org/fathers/3101.htm.

Dal Ferro, Giuseppe. "L'anglicanesimo, presenza cristiana di comunione." *Studi Ecumenici* 39, no. 2 (2011): 62–264.

Daley, Brian E., SJ. "Rebuilding the Structure of Love: The Quest for Visible Unity among the Churches." In *Ecumenical Future*, edited by Braaten and Jenson, 73–105.

De Lubac, Henri. *Corpus Mysticum: L'Eucharistie et l'Église au moyen age: Étude historique*. 2nd ed. Paris: Aubier Montaigne, 1949.

De Rosa, Michele. *Teologia protestante: Momenti e figure*. Salerno: Elea Press, 1990.

De Salis, Miguel. "*Extra Ecclesiam nulla salus*: Prospettiva conciliare." *Annales Theologici* 25 (2011): 353–75.

Decrees of the Ecumenical Councils. Edited by Norman P. Tanner. 2 vols. Washington, D.C: Georgetown University Press, 1990.

Denzinger, Heinrich and Adolfus Schönmetzer, eds. *Enchiridion symbolorum: Definitionum et declarationum de rebus fidei et morum*, 36th ed. Barcelona: Herder, 1976.

The Didache. In *Lactantius, Venantius, Asterius, Victorinus, Dionysius, Apostolic Teaching and Constitutions, Homily, and Liturgies*, translated by Matthew B. Riddle, 369–82. The Ante-Nicene Fathers: Translations of the Writings of the Fathers down to A.D. 325, edited by Alexander Roberts, James Donaldson, and A. Cleveland Coxe, vol. 7. Buffalo, N.Y.: Christian Literature Publishing, 1886. http://www.newadvent.org/fathers/0714.htm.

Dumont, Christophe Jean, OP. *Les voies de l'unité chrétienne: Doctrine et spiritualité*. Paris: Cerf, 1954.

Dulles, Avery. *The Catholicity of the Church*. Oxford: Clarendon Press, 1985.

Erickson, John H. "The One True Church: Thoughts concerning an Ecumenical Conundrum." In *Ecumenical Future*, edited by Braaten and Jenson, 145–61.

Ernst, Harold E. "The 'Hierarchy of Truths' in the Thought of John Henry Newman." *Irish Theological Quarterly* 70, no. 4 (2005): 307–30.

Escrivá, Josemaría. "Freedom, A Gift from God." *Friends of God*, 23–38. London: Scepter, 1981. http://www.escrivaworks.org/book/friends_of_god.htm.

______. "The Supernatural Aim of the Church." *In Love with the Church*, 17–33. London: Scepter, 1989. http://www.escrivaworks.org/book/in_love_with_the_church.htm.

______. *Conversations with Monsignor Escrivá de Balaguer*. Sydney: Little Hills and Scepter, 1993. https://www.escrivaworks.org/book/conversations-chapter-1.htm.

"Evangelicals and Catholics Together: The Christian Mission in the Third Millennium." *First Things*, May 1994. https://www.firstthings.com/article/1994/05/evangelicals-catholics-together-the-christian-mission-in-the-third-millennium.

Faynel, Paul. *L'Église*. Paris: Desclée, 1970.

Fortino, Eleuterio. "El diálogo teológico entre la Iglesia Católica y la Iglesia Ortodoxa: III. La cuestión del '*uniatismo*' y su solución." In *Las iglesias orientales*, edited by González Montes, 565–92.

Fontana, Paolo. "Gerarchia delle verità: Una categoria controversa." In *Lo Spirito Santo Teologo del Popolo di Dio*, edited by Gianfranco Calabrese, 221–34. Casale Monferrato: Piemme, 1997.

Francis. *Laudato si'*. Encyclical Letter. May 24, 2015.

______. "Common Ecumenical Prayer at the Lutheran Cathedral of Lund." October 31, 2016.

______. "Address to Participants at the Plenary of the Pontifical Council for Promoting Christian Unity." September 28, 2018.

______. "Press Conference during the Return Flight from Apostolic Trip to Bulgaria." June 2, 2019.

______. "General Audience." June 5, 2019.

______. "Greeting at Opening of Synod of Bishops for the Pan-Amazon Region." October 7, 2019.

______. "General Audience." October 23, 2019.

______. "Homily at Celebration of 2nd Vespers for the Feast of the Conversion of St. Paul." January 25, 2020.

Francis, Pope and Patriarch Kirill. "Joint Declaration." February 12, 2016.

Franklin, R. William, ed. *Anglican Orders: Essays on the Centenary of Apostolicae Curae 1896–1996*. London: Mowbray, 1996.

Fulgentius of Ruspe. *De fide ad Petrum*. In *Fulgentius: Selected Works*, translated by Robert B. Eno, 57–108. Fathers of the Church 95. Washington, D.C.: The Catholic University of America Press, 2002.

Garuti, Adriano. *Saggi di ecumenismo*. Rome: Pontificium Athenaeum Antonianum, 2003.

______. *The Primacy of the Bishop of Rome and the Ecumenical Dialogue*. Translated by Michael J. Miller. San Francisco: Ignatius Press, 2004.

Gefaell, Pablo. "Las Iglesias Orientales Antiguas Ortodoxas y Católicas." In *Las iglesias orientales*, edited by González Montes, 595–644.

Gesy, Lawrence J. and Carol Giambalvo, eds. *Today's Destructive Cults and Movements*. Huntington, Ind.: Our Sunday Visitor, 1993.

Gil Hellín, Francisco. *Constitutio dogmatica de ecclesia* Lumen Gentium. *Concilii Vaticani II synopsis* 2. Vatican City: Libreria editrice Vaticana, 1995.

______.*Decretum de oecumenismo* Unitatis redintegratio. Concilii Vaticani II synopsis 6. Vatican City: Libreria editrice Vaticana, 2005.

Gil Sousa, José Antonio. "Ordenados a la Iglesia." *Aurensia* 5 (2002): 61–99.

Gnilka, Joachim. "Il ministero petrino: Fondazione nel nuovo testamento e configurazione nella Chiesa primitiva." In *Papato ed ecumenismo*, edited by Hünermann, 9–21.

González Montes, Adolfo, ed. *Las iglesias orientales*. Madrid: Biblioteca de Autores Cristianos, 2000.

Goosen, Gideon. *Bringing Churches Together: A Popular Introduction to Ecumenism*. Geneva: World Council of Churches, 1993.

Goyret, Philip. *El obispo, Pastor de la Iglesia: Estudio teológico del munus regendi en* Lumen gentium *27*. Pamplona: Ediciones Universidad de Navarra, 1998.

______. "Cuerpo eucarístico y cuerpo eclesial: La communicatio in sacris en la Enc. *Ecclesia de Eucharistia*." *Annales Theologici* 19, no. 1 (2005): 135–70.

______. *Dalla Pasqua alla Parusia: La successione apostolica nel "tempus Ecclesiae"*. Rome: Edusc, 2007.

______. "Ermeneutica conciliare ed ecclesiologia contemporanea." *Annales Theologici* 23, no. 2 (2009): 405–40.

______. "*Credo Ecclesiam* e rilancio ecumenico." *Nicolaus* 37, no. 2 (2010): 251–59.

Gregory of Nyssa. *Against Eunomius*. In *Gregorii Nysseni Tomus Secundus*, edited by Migne, 245–1122. Patrologiae Graeca 45. 1858.

Gros, Jeffrey, Harding Meyer, William G. Rusch, and Lukas Vischer, eds. *Growth in Agreement: Reports and Agreed Statements of Ecumenical Conversations on a World Level*. New York: Paulist Press, 1984.

______. *Growth in Agreement II: Reports and Agreed Statements of Ecumenical Conversations on a World Level*. Geneva: World Council of Churches, 2000.

Guroian, Vigen. "The Crisis of Orthodox Ecclesiology." In *Ecumenical Future*, edited by Braaten and Jenson, 162–75.

Guitton, Jean. *La philosophie de Newman: Essai sur l'idée de développement*. Paris: Bovin et Cie, 1933.

Halecki, Oscar. *From Florence to Brest (1439–1596)*. Rome: Sacrum Poloniae Millennium, 1958.

Hertling, Ludwig. *Communio: Chiesa e papato nell'antichità cristiana*. Rome: Libreria editrice della Pontificia Università Gregoriana, 1961.

Hill, Christopher and Edward Yarnold, eds. *Anglican Orders: The Documents in the Debate*. Norwich: Canterbury Press, 1997.

Hofmann, Georgius. "Notae historicae de terminologia theologica Concilii Florentini." *Gregorianum* 20, no. 2 (1939): 257–63.

Holy Office. *Letter to the Archbishop of Boston*. August 8, 1949. https://www.ewtn.com/catholicism/library/letter-to-the-archbishop-of-boston-2076

______. Instruction *Ecclesia Catholica*. December 20, 1949. Also known as *On the "Ecumenical Movement."* In *Acta Apostolicae Sedis* 42 (1950): 142–47.

Hryniewicz, Wacław. "Hierarchia veritatum." In *Swieta tajemnica jednosci*, edited by Piotr Jaskóła and Wacław Hryniewicz, 37–64. Lublin: Redakcja Wydawnictw KUL, 1988.

Hünermann, Peter, ed. *Papato ed ecumenismo: Il ministero petrino al servizio dell'unità*. Bologna: Dehoniane, 1999.

International Theological Commission. *The Interpretation of Dogma*. Document. 1990.

______. *Memory and Reconciliation: The Church and the Faults of the Past*. Document. March 7, 2000.

Introvigne, Massimo. "Le 'nuove religiosità' e la religione." In *La verità della religione*, edited by Giovanni Tanzella-Nitti and Giulio Maspero, 139–54. Rome: Cantagalli, 2007.

Irenaeus of Lyons. *Adversus haereses*. Translated by Alexander Roberts and William Rambaut. In *The Apostolic Fathers with Justin Martyr and Irenaeus*, 309–567. Ante-Nicene Fathers 1. 1885. Reprint, Peabody, Mass.: Hendrickson Publishers, 1994. Citations refer to the Hendrickson edition.

Iserloh, Erwin, Joseph Glazik, and Hubert Jedin. *Reformation and Counter-Reformation*. Vol. 5 of *Handbook of Church History*, edited by Hubert Jedin and John Patrick Dolan. New York: Crossroad, 1967.

Istituto Theologico Marchigiano. *Atti dell'incontro ecumenico su "Il primato del Papa."* Bologna: Dehoniane, 1999.

Jaeger, Lorenz. *Il decreto conciliare sull'ecumenismo: Storia, contenuto e significato*. Brescia: Morcelliana, 1965.

Jenson, Robert. *Unbaptized God: The Basic Flaw in Ecumenical Theology*. Minneapolis: Fortress Press, 1992.

Johann Adam Möhler Institut. *Le chiese cristiane nel Duemila*. Brescia: Queriniana, 1998.

John XXIII. "Address at the Solemn Opening of the Second Vatican Council." October 11, 1962.

John Paul II. *Slavorum Apostoli*. Encyclical Letter. June 2, 1985.

______. "Address to the Bishops of the United States of America." September 16, 1987.

______. *Redemptoris missio*. Encyclical Letter. December 7, 1990.

______. "Speech to the Roman Curia." December 20, 1990.

______. *Pastores dabo vobis*. Post-Synodal Apostolic Exhortation. March 25, 1992.

______. *Tertio millennio adveniente*. Apostolic Letter. November 10, 1994.

______. *Ut unum sint*. Encyclical Letter. May 25, 1995.

______. "Homily on the Day of Pardon." March 12, 2000.

______. *Ecclesia de Eucharistia*. Encyclical Letter. April 17, 2003.

John Paul II and George Carey, Archbishop of Canterbury. *Common Declaration*. December 5, 1996.

Joint Catholic-Orthodox Committee. *La primauté romaine dans la communion des églises*. Paris: Cerf, 1991.

Joint Commission of the Anglican Communion and the Old Catholic Churches. *Joint Declaration*. July 2, 1931.

Joint International Commission for the Theological Dialogue between the Roman Catholic Church and the Orthodox Church. *The Mystery of the Church and of the Eucharist in the Light of the Mystery of the Holy Trinity*. Munich. July 6, 1982.

______. *Faith, Sacraments and the Unity of the Church*. Bari. June 16, 1987.

______. *The Sacrament of Order in the Sacramental Structure of the Church, with Particular Reference to the Importance of the Apostolic Succession for the Sanctification and Unity of the People of God*. Valamo. June 26, 1988.

______. *Uniatism: Method of Union of the Past, and Present Search for Full Communion*. Balamand. June 23, 1993.

______. *Ecclesiological and Canonical Consequences of the Sacramental Nature of the Church: Ecclesial Communion, Conciliarity and Authority*. Ravenna. October 13, 2007.

______. *Synodality and Primacy during the First Millennium: Towards a Common Understanding in Service to the Unity of the Church*. Chieti. September 21, 2016.

Joint International Commission for Dialogue between the World Methodist Council and the Roman Catholic Church. *The Call to Holiness: From Glory to Glory*. 2016.

Joint Working Group of the Theological Commission from the Catholic Church and the World Council of Churches. "Third Official Report." *Centro Pro Unione* 11, no. 8. www.prounione.it/dialogues/jwg.

Jubilee Bishops' Council of the Russian Orthodox Church. "Basic Principles of the Attitude of the Russian Orthodox Church toward the Other Christian Confessions, 08-14-2000." *One in Christ* 41, no. 2 (April 2006): 88–100.

Jugie, Martin. *Theologiae Dogmaticae Graeco-Russorum*. Vol. 1 of *Theologia dogmatica christianorum orientalium*. Paris: Letouzey et Ané, 1926.

Justin Martyr. *First Apology*. Translated by Marcus Dods and George Reith. In *The Apostolic Fathers with Justin Martyr and Irenaeus*, 159–187. Ante-Nicene Fathers 1. 1885. http://www.newadvent.org/fathers/0126.htm.

Kasper, Walter. "La successione apostolica nel ministero episcopale come problema ecumenico," Salesianum 59, no. 3 (1997): 397–408.

______. "Una pietra miliare nel cammino dell'ecumene." In *Dossier sulla giustificazione*, edited by Angelo Maffeis, 305–9. Brescia: Queriniana, 2000.

______, ed. *Lexikon für Theologie und Kirche*, 3rd ed. 10 vols. Freiburg: Herder, 1993–2001.

______. "Le radici teologiche del conflitto tra Mosca e Roma." *La Civiltà Cattolica* 3642, no. 1 (2002): 531–41.

______. *That They May All Be One: The Call to Unity*. New York: Burns and Oates, 2004.

______. *The Petrine Ministry: Catholics and Orthodox in Dialogue*. New York: Newman Press, 2005.

______. *L'ecumenismo spirituale: Linee-guida per la sua attuazione*. Rome: Città Nuova, 2006. Translated as *A Handbook of Spiritual Ecumenism*. Hyde Park, N.Y.: New City Press, 2007.

______. *Harvesting the Fruits: Aspects of Christian Faith in Ecumenical Dialogue*. London: Continuum, 2009.

Ker, Ian. *John Henry Newman: A Biography*. New York: Oxford University Press, 1990.

Khomych, Taras. "Eastern Catholic Churches and the Question of 'Uniatism': Problems of the Past, Challenges of the Present and Hopes for the Future." *Louvain Studies* 31, no. 3–4 (2006): 214–37.

Kittel, Gerhard and Gerhard Friedrich, eds. *Grande lessico del nuovo testamento*. 15 vols. Brescia: Paideia, 1965–92.

Knittel, Reinhard. "Il '*Subsistit* in' di *Lumen Gentium* 8 e la permanenza indeffettibile della Chiesa pellegrinante." *Divinitas* 44, no. 3 (2001): 253–71.

Krikorian, Mesrob K. "Calcedonia: Storia, conflitti cristologici e riconciliazione." In *Il Concilio di Calcedonia 1550 anni dopo*, edited by Antonio Ducay, 114–37. Vatican City: Libreria editrice Vaticana, 2003.

Koch, Kurt. "Sviluppi ecumenici e nuove sfide." *Studi Ecumenici* 29, no. 2 (2011): 181–206.

Küng, Hans. *Structures of the Church*. London: Burns and Oates, 1965.

Lacoste, Jean-Yves, ed. *Storia della teologia*. Brescia: Queriniana, 2011.

Lacoste, Jean-Yves, Gilles Berceville, Patrick Descourtieux, Pierre Gibert, and Marc Ozilou. *Histoire de la théologie*. Paris: Seiul, 2009.

Latourelle, René and Rino Fisichella, eds. Dictionary of Fundamental Theology. New York: Crossroad, 1994.

Legrand, Hervé. "Differentiated Consensus as a Means of Correcting Unilateral Ecclesiological Developments?" *The Ecumenical Review* 71, no. 3 (July 2019): 267–79. http://dx.doi.org/10.1111/erev.12436.

Le Guillou, Marie-Joseph. "Des controverses au dialogue oecuménique." *Istina* 5, no. 1 (1958): 65–112.

Leo IX. *Congratulamur vehementer*. Letter. April 13, 1053.

Leo XIII. *Orientalium dignitas*. Encyclical Letter. November 30, 1894.

______. *Apostolicae curae*. Bull. September 13, 1896.

Lehmann, Karl. "Wie viel Hoffnung bringt die Ökumene?" *Katholische Nachrichten Agentur—Ökumenische Information* 20–21 (June 2010): 5–16.

Loisy, Alfred. *The Gospel and the Church*. Translated by Christopher Home. New York: Charles Scribner's Sons, 1912.

Lopes, Stephen. "Unity in Diversity: Towards a New Ecumenical Springtime." Lecture, Aquinas Institute for Catholic Life, Princeton University, Princeton, N.J., March 7, 2019.

Lossky, Nicolas, ed. *Dictionary of the Ecumenical Movement*. Grand Rapids, Mich.: Eerdmans, 1991.

Luther, Martin. *The Babylonian Captivity of the Church*. Translated by Albert T. W. Steinhaeuser. In *Works of Martin Luther*, vol. 2, 170–293. Philadelphia: The Castle Press, 1915.

______. *Genesisvorlesung (cap. 1–17)*. D. Martin Luthers Werke: Kritische Gesammtausgabe 42. Weimar: Böhlau, 1911.

______. "Preface to the First Volume of Latin Writings." Translated by Lewis W. Spitz. In *Career of the Reformer IV*. Vol. 34 of *Luther's Works*, edited by Helmut T. Lehmann , 323–38. Philadelphia: Muhlenberg Press, 1960.

______. *The Augsburg Confession*. In *Creeds and Confessions of Faith*, edited by Pelikan and Hotchkiss, 2:49–118.

Lutheran-Roman Catholic Commission for Unity. *Facing Unity: Models, Forms and Phases of Catholic-Lutheran Church Fellowship*. March 3, 1984.

______. *Church and Justification: Understanding the Church in the Light of the Doctrine of Justification*. Geneva: Lutheran World Federation, 1993.

______. "The Apostolicity of the Church." *Service d'Information* 128, no. 2 (2008): 59–133.

Lutheran World Federation and Anglican Consultative Council. "The Porvoo Common Statement, Järvenpää 1992." In *Anglican-Lutheran Agreements: Regional and International Agreements 1972–2002*, edited by Sven Oppegaard and Gregory Cameron, 145–76. Geneva: Lutheran World Federation, 2004. This agreement was formally joined by, within the Anglican Communion, the Churches of England and Ireland, the Church in Wales and the Episcopal Church of Scotland, together with the Churches of Denmark, Norway and Sweden; and the Evangelical-Lutheran Churches of Estonia, Finland, Iceland, Latvia and Lithuania.

Lutheran World Federation and the Roman Catholic Church. *Joint Declaration on the Doctrine of Justification*. October 31, 1999.

Maccarrone, Michele, ed. *Il primato del vescovo di Roma nel primo millennio: Ricerche e testimonianze: Atti del Symposium storico-teologico*. Rome: Libreria editrice Vaticana, 1991.

Maffeis, Angelo, ed. *Dossier sulla giustificazione*. Brescia: Queriniana, 2000.

Malcolm, Lois. "'It Has Seemed Good to the Holy Spirit and to Us': Mission and Ecumenism in the Power of the Holy Spirit." In *Ecumenical Future*, edited by Braaten and Jenson, 218–35.

Maspero, Giulio and Giuseppe Tanzella-Nitti. *La verità della religione: La specificità cristiana in contesto*. Siena: Cantagalli, 2007.

Maximus the Confessor. *Epistula ad Marinum*. In *Maximi Confessoris Opera Omnia Tomus Secundus*, edited by Migne, 287–353. Patrologiae Graeca 91. 1863.

Mazzolini, Sandra. "*Extra Ecclesiam nulla salus*: Prospettiva patristica." *Annales Theologici* 25 (2011): 321–37.

McDonnell, Kilian. "The Ratzinger/Kasper Debate: The Universal Church and Local Churches." *Theological Studies* 63, no. 2 (2002): 227–50.

Medawar, Pierre K. "On Safeguarding the Rights of the Oriental Church." In *The Unity of the Churches of God*, translated by Polycarp Sherwood, 11–33. Baltimore, Md.: Helicon, 1963.

Meeking, Basil and John Stott, eds. *The Evangelical-Roman Catholic Dialogue on Mission, 1977–1984: A Report*. Grand Rapids, Mich.: Eerdmans, 1986. http://www.christianunity.va/content/unitacristiani/en/dialoghi/sezione-occidentale/evangelici/dialogo/documenti-di-dialogo/en.html

Melanchthon, Philip. "The Apology: The Apology of the Augsburg Confession with Key Historical Documents." In *The Augsburg Confession and the Apology of the Augsburg Confession with Key Historical Documents: The Concordia Reader's Edition*, edited by Paul T. McCain, 55–240. St. Louis, Mo.: Concordia, 2020.

Meyer, Harding. "La Chiesa Popolo di Dio, Corpo di Cristo, Tempio dello Spirito Santo, nel dialogo tra la Chiesa cattolica romana e le confessioni protestanti: Una prospettiva luterana." In *L'ecclesiologia trent'anni dopo la "Lumen gentium,"* edited by Pedro Rodríguez, 225–37. Armando: Rome 1995.

______. *That All May Be One. Perceptions and Models of Ecumenicity*. Grand Rapids, Mich.: Eerdmans, 1999.

______. "Ökumenische Perspektiven aus evangelischer Sicht." In *Unus fons, unus spiritus, una fides*, edited by Jürgen Krüger and Jens-Martin Kruse, 214–34. Karlsruhe: Arte Factum, 2010.

Moda, Aldo. *Strutture della fede: Un dialogo con Karl Barth*. Padua: Edizioni Messaggero, 1990.

Möhler, Johann Adam. *Unity in the Church or the Principle of Catholicism: Presented in the Spirit of the Church Fathers of the First Three Centuries*. Translated by Peter C. Erb. Washington, D.C.: The Catholic University of America Press, 1996.

Molac, Philippe. "La réception du '*subsistit in*': Une premièrè étape: Du concile Vatican II à l'encyclique *Ut unum sint*." *Bulletin de Litterature Ecclesiastique* 107, no. 1 (2006): 23–50.

Mondin, Battista. *L'ecumenismo nella Chiesa Cattolica prima, durante e dopo il concilio*. Rome: Herder, 1966.

Montanari, Franco. *The Brill Dictionary of Ancient Greek*. English edition edited by Madeleine Goh and Chad Schroeder. Leiden: Brill, 2015.

Morerod, Charles. "Réflexions sur l'Accord de Porvoo entre Anglicans et Luthériens." *Nova et Vetera* 72, no. 3 (1997): 71–103.

Müller, Gerhard Ludwig. *Katholische Dogmatik: Für Studium und Praxis der Theologie*. Freibug: Herder, 1995. Translated as *Dogmática cattolica: Per lo studio e la prassi della teología*. Cinisello Balsamo: San Paolo, 1999. The first portion of this text has been translated as *Catholic Dogmatics: For the Study and Practice of Theology*, vol. 1: *Doctrine of Creation, Eschatology*. Translated by William Hadfield-Burkardt. New York: Crossroad, 2017.

Murray, Paul. "Receptive Ecumenism and Catholic Learning—Establishing the Agenda." In *Receptive Ecumenism and the Call to Catholic Learning: Exploring a Way for Contemporary Ecumenism*, edited by Paul Murray, 5–19. Oxford: Oxford University Press, 2008. http://dx.doi.org/10.1093/acprof:oso/9780199216451.003.0002.

Nagy, Stanislas. "La jerarquía de los dogmas a la luz del pensamiento teológico contemporáneo." In *El misterio de la Iglesia y la Iglesia como comunión*, 3rd ed., edited by Pedro Rodriguez, 77–97. Madrid: Palabra, 1994.

Newbigin, Lesslie. *The Household of God: Lectures on the Nature of the Church*. New York: Friendship Press, 1954.

Nichols, Aidan. *Rome and the Eastern Churches: A Study in Schism*. New York: T and T Clark, 1992.

———. *The Panther and the Hind: A Theological History of Anglicanism*. Edinburgh: T and T Clark, 1994.

———. *Light from the East: Authors and Themes in Orthodox Theology*. London: Sheed and Ward, 1995.

Noll, Mark A. "Defining Evangelicalism." In *Global Evangelicalism: Theology, History and Culture in Regional Perspective*, edited by Donald M. Lewis and Richard V. Pierard, 17–37. Downers Grove, Ill.: InterVarsity Press, 2014.

Ocáriz, Fernando. "Evangelización, proselitismo y ecumenismo." *Scripta Theologica* 38, no. 2 (2006): 617–36.

O'Donnell, Chris. "Intercommunion." In *Ecclesia: A Theological Encyclopedia of the Church*, edited by Chris O'Donnell, 220–22. Collegeville, Minn.: Liturgical Press, 1996.

Origen. *Homilies on Joshua*. Translated by Barbara J. Bruce. Fathers of the Church 105. Washington, D.C.: The Catholic University of America Press, 2002.

Orlandis, José. *La Iglesia en la España visigótica y medieval*. Pamplona: Ediciones Universidad de Navarra, 1976.

Orthodox/Roman Catholic Commission of the United States. *An Agreed Statement on Conciliarity and Primacy in the Church*. Brighton. 1989.

Pacomio, Luciano and Giuseppe Occhipinti, eds. *Lexicon: Dizionario dei teologi*. Casale Monferrato: Piemme, 1998.

Pascal, Blaise. *The Thoughts of Blaise Pascal*. Translated by Charles Kegan Paul. London: George Bell and Sons, 1901.

Pattaro, Germano. *Corso di teologia dell'ecumenismo*. Brescia: Queriniana, 1985.

Paul VI. "Speech at the Inauguration of the Third Session of the Second Vatican Council." September 14, 1964. Available on vatican.va in Italian, Latin, Portuguese, and Spanish.

______. "Speech at the Conclusion of the Third Session of the Second Vatican Council." November 21, 1964. Available on vatican.va in Italian, Latin, Portuguese, and Spanish.

Pelikan, Jaroslav and Valerie Hotchkiss, eds. *Creeds and Confessions of Faith in the Christian Tradition*. 4 vols. New Haven, Conn.: Yale University Press, 2003.

Peri, Vittorio. "Considerazioni sull'uniatismo." In *Lo scambio fraterno tra le Chiese*, 365–94. Vatican City: Libreria editrice Vaticana, 1993.

Philips, Gérard, *L'Église et son Mystère au II Concile du Vatican*. Paris: Desclée, 1967.

Pius IX. *Quanto conficiamur moerore*. Encyclical Letter. August 10, 1863. https://www.papalencyclicals.net/pius09/p9quanto.htm.

Pius XI. "Speech." January 10, 1927.

Pius XII. *Mystici Corporis*. Encyclical Letter. June 29, 1943.

______. *Humani generis*. Encyclical Letter. August 12, 1950.

Pontifical Council for Promoting Christian Unity. *The Denver Report*. 1971.

______. *The Dublin Report*. 1976.

______. *The Honolulu Report*. January 31, 1981.

______. *Final Report of the Dialogue between the Secretariat for Promoting Christian Unity of the Roman Catholic Church and Leaders of Some Pentecostal Churches and Participants in the Charismatic Movement within Protestant and Anglican Churches 1972–1976*. 1976.

______. *Final Report of the Dialogue between the Secretariat for Promoting Christian Unity of the Roman Catholic Church and Some Classical Pentecostals 1977–82*. May 9, 1984.

______. *Towards a Statement on the Church*. Nairobi. 1986.

______. *Perspectives on* Koinonia. 1989.

______. "The Greek and Latin Traditions about the Procession of the Holy Spirit." *L'Osservatore Romano: Weekly Edition in English*. September 20, 1995.

______. *The Catholic Church's Response to the Final Report of ARCIC I*. 1991.

______. *The Apostolic Tradition*. Singapore. 1991.

______. *Directory for the Application of Principles and Norms on Ecumenism*. March 25, 1993.

______. *The Word of Life*. Rio de Janeiro. 1996.

______. *The Ecumenical Dimension in the Formation of Those Engaged in Pastoral Work*. 1997.

______. *Speaking the Truth in Love*. Brighton. 2001.

______. *The Grace Given You in Christ*. Seoul. 2006.

______. *Unità dei cristiani: Dovere e speranza*. Vatican City: Libreria editrice Vaticana, 2010.

______. *The Bishop and Christian Unity: An Ecumenical Vademecum*. 2020.

Porro, Carlo. "Dichiarazione congiunta sulla giustificazione: Orientamenti per la lettura." *Rassegna di Teologia* 41, no. 6 (2000): 889–99.

Puglisi, James, ed. *Continuità apostolica della Chiesa e successione apostolica: Corso breve di ecumenismo*. Rome: Centro pro Unione, 1996.

______, ed. "Il ministero petrino e l'unità della Chiesa: Atti del Simposio (Rome, December 4–6, 1997)." *Studi Ecumenici* 17, no. 1 (1999).

Raiser, Konrad. "Thirty Years in the Service of the Ecumenical Movement: The Joint Working Group between the Roman Catholic Church and the World Council of Churches." *Centro Pro Unione Bulletin* 48 (Fall 1995): 3–8.

Rambaldi, Giuseppe. *Ordinazioni anglicane e sacramento dell'ordine nella Chiesa: Aspetti storici e teologici a cento anni della bolla Apostolicae curae di Leone XIII*. Rome: Editrice Pontificia Università Gregoriana, 1995.

Ratzinger, Joseph. *Das neue Volk Gottes: Entwürfe zur Ekklesioloigie*. Düsseldorf: Patmos-Verlag, 1972.

______. *Theologische Prinzipienlehre: Bausteine zur Fundamentaltheologie*. Munich: Wewel, 1982. Translated by Mary Frances McCarthy, SND as *Principles of Catholic Theology: Building Stones for a Fundamental Theology*. San Francisco: Ignatius Press, 1987.

______. "On the Progress of Ecumenism." *Church, Ecumenism and Politics*, translated by Michael J. Miller et al., 133–42. San Francisco: Ignatius Press, 2008. Originally published as *Kirche, Ökumene und Politik*. Einsiedeln: Johannes, 1987.

______. "Problems and Prospects of the Anglican–Catholic Dialogue." *Church, Ecumenism and Politics*, 69–99.

______. "*Deus locutus est nobis in Filio*: Some Reflections on Subjectivity, Christology, and the Church." In *Proclaiming the Truth of Jesus Christ: Papers from the Vallombrosa Meeting*, edited by the Congregation for the Doctrine of the Faith. Washington, D.C.: United States Catholic Conference, 2000.

______. "L'ecclesiologia della *Lumen gentium*." *La comunione nella Chiesa*, 129–61. Cinisello Balsamo: San Paolo, 2004.

______. "The Primacy of the Pope and the Unity of the People of God." *Fundamental Speeches from Five Decades*, translated by Michael J. Miller, J. R. Foster, and Adrian Walker, 13–33. San Francisco: Ignatius Press, 2012.

Reno, R. R. "The Debilitation of the Churches." In *Ecumenical Future*, edited by Braaten and Jenson, 46–72.

Rodríguez, Pedro. "Ordenación e incorporación a la Iglesia. Síntesis doctrinal." *Teología Espiritual* 17 (1972): 353–66.

______. "La Eucaristía y la unidad de la Iglesia." *Scripta Theologica* 7, no. 2 (1975): 563–617.

______. *Iglesia y ecumenismo*. Madrid: Rialp, 1979.

Rodríguez, Pedro and José R. Villar. "Las Iglesias y comunidades eclesiales separadas de la Sede Apostólica Romana." *Diálogo Ecuménico* 39 (2004): 537–623.

Root, Michael. "Essential Unity and Lived Communion: The Interrelation of the Unity We Have and the Unity We Seek." In *Ecumenical Future*, edited by Braaten and Jenson, 106–25.

______. "Normal Ecumenism: Ecumenism for the Long Haul." *Pro Ecclesia: A Journal of Catholic and Evangelical Theology* 28, no. 1 (February 2019): 60–77.

Rosenthal, George D. "The Unity of the Church." In Anglo-Catholic Congress. *Report of the Anglo-Catholic Congress 1930*, 22–29. London: Catholic Literature Association, 1930.

Rossano, Pietro, Gianfranco Ravasi, and Antonio Girlanda, ed. *Nuovo Dizionario de Teologia Bíblica*. Cinisello Balsamo: San Paolo, 1988.

Rouse, Ruth. "The World Christian Lay Movements." In *Ecumenical Movement*, edited by Rouse and Neill, 599–612.

______. "Voluntary Movements in the Second Half-Century." In *Ecumenical Movement*, edited by Rouse and Neill, 324–32.

______. "World Denominational Fellowships." In *Ecumenical Movement*, edited by Rouse and Neill, 613–19.

Rouse, Ruth and Stephen Neill, eds. *A History of the Ecumenical Movement, 1517–1948*. 2nd ed. Vol. 1 of *A History of the Ecumenical Movement*. Philadelphia: Westminster Press, 1967.

Rusch, William G. "A Survey of Ecumenical Reflection about Unity." In *Ecumenical Future*, edited by Braaten and Jenson, 1–10.

Sartori, Luigi. *Teologia ecumenica*. Padua: Libreria Gregoriana Editrice, 1987.

Schlier, Heinrich. "Kurze Rechenschaft." In *Bekenntnis zur katholischen Kirche*, edited by Karl Hardt, SJ, 167–93 (Würzburg: Echter-Verlag, 1956).

Schönborn, Christoph. "Are There Sects in the Catholic Church?" *L'Osservatore Romano: Weekly Edition in English* 13, no. 20 (August 13, 1997): 3.

Schultze, Bernardo. "Riflessione teologica sul significato di 'Chiesa Orientale' e 'Ortodossia.'" *Gregorianum* 42, no. 3 (1961): 444–62.

Secretariat for Promoting Christian Unity. *Reflections and Suggestions concerning Ecumenical Dialogue*. August 15, 1970.

Semeraro, Marcello. *Mistero, comunione e missione: Manuale di ecclesiologia*. 2nd ed. Bologna: Dehoniane, 1998.

Sesboüé, Bernard. *"Hors de l'Église, pas de salut." Histoire d'une formule et problèmes d'interprétation*. Paris: Desclée de Brouwer, 2004.

Siniscalco, Paolo, ed. *Le antiche Chiese orientali*. Rome: Città Nuova, 2005.

Spener, Philipp Jacob. *Pia desideria oder Herzliches Verlangen nach gottgefälliger Besserung der wahren evangelischen Kirche*. London: Wentworth Press, 2018.

Spinsanti, Sandro. *Ecumenismo*. Rome: Istituto di teologia a distanza "Ut unum sint," 1982.

Spiteris, Yannis. *Ecclesiologia ortodossa: Temi a confronto tra Oriente e Occidente*. Bologna: Dehoniane, 2003.

Stirnemann, Alfred and Gerhard Wilfinger, eds. *Von heilegen Geist: Der gemeinsame trinitarische Glaube und das Problem des Filioque*. Innsbruck: Tyrolia, 1998.

Thils, Gustave. *Histoire doctrinale du movement œcuménique*. Louvain: E. Warny, 1962.

______. *Le décret sur l'œcuménisme*. Tournai: Casterman, 1966.

______. "Hiérarchie des vérités de la foi et dialogue oecuménique." *Revue Théologique de Louvain* 15, no. 2 (1984): 147–59.

Thomas, Joseph. "The Catholicity of the Church in the Second Vatican Council: The Theological Background, Conciliar Elaboration and Dogmatic Content of Lumen Gentium 13." Dissertationes Series Theologica XXXVII. Rome: Pontifical University of the Holy Cross, 2011.

Tillard, Jean-Marie-Roger. *Church of Churches: The Ecclesiology of Communion*. Collegeville, Minn.: Liturgical Press, 1992.

Torabi, Maryamossadat and Seyed Masoud Noori. "Religious Leaders and the Environmental Crisis: Using Knowledge and Social Influence to Counteract Climate Change." *The Ecumenical Review* 71, no. 3 (July 2019): 344–55. http://dx.doi.org/10.1111/erev.12434.

Tourn, Giorgio, ed. *La confessione augustana del 1530*. Turin: Claudiana, 1980.

United Methodist Church and United States Conference of Catholic Bishops. *Catholics and United Methodists Together: We Believe, We Pray, We Act*. 2021.

US Catholic-Lutheran Commission. *Papal Primacy and the Universal Church*. Minneapolis: Augsburg Publishing House, 1974.

Vatican Council II. *Sacrosanctum Concilium*. December 4, 1963.

______. *Relatio super Schema Emendatum Decreti de Oecumenismo*. Vatican City: Tipografia Vaticana, 1964.

______. *Lumen Gentium*. November 21, 1964.

______. *Orientalium Ecclesiarum*. November 21, 1964.

______. *Unitatis Redintegratio*. November 21, 1964.

______. *Dei Verbum*. November 18, 1965.

______. *Ad Gentes*. December 7, 1965.

______. *Dignitatis Humanae*. December 7, 1965.

______. *Gaudium et Spes*. December 7, 1965.

______. *Presbyterorum Ordinis*. December 7, 1965.

______. *Acta Synodalia Sacrosancti Concilii Oecumenici Vaticani II*. Vatican City: Typis Polyglottis Vaticanis, 1970–1978.

Vercruysse, Jos. *Introduzione alla teologia ecumenica*. Casale Monferrato: Piemme, 1992.

Vilella, J. "Letters of Communion." In *Encyclopedia of Ancient Christianity*, edited by Angelo Di Bernardino, 557–59. Downers Grove, Ill.: InterVarsity Press Academic, 2014.

Villar, José R. "La teologia ortodoxa de la Iglesia local" in *Eclesiologia 30 años despues de "Lumen Gentium"*. Edited by Pedro Rodríguez. Madrid: Rialp, 1994.

______. *Eclesiología y ecumenismo: Comunión, Iglesia local, Pedro*. Pamplona: Ediciones Universidad de Navarra, 1999.

______. "Il ministero episcopale nella *communio Ecclesiarum*." In *I vescovi e il loro ministero*, edited by Philip Goyret, 75–84. Vatican City: Libreria editrice Vaticana, 2000.

______. "La declaración común luterano-católica sobre la doctrina de la justificación." *Scripta Theologica* 32, no. 1 (2000): 101–29.

Villain, Maurice. *Introducción al ecumenismo*. Bilbao: Desclée de Brouwer, 1962.

Visser 't Hooft, Willem A. "The Word 'Ecumenical': Its History and Use." In Rouse and Neill, *Ecumenical Movement*, 735–40.

Wainwright, Geoffrey. "The Global Structures of Ecumenism." In *Ecumenical Future*, edited by Braaten and Jenson, 11–28.

Wesley, John. "Methodist Articles of Religion." In *The Evangelical Protestant Creeds*, 4th revised and enlarged edition, edited by Philip Schaff, 807–13. Vol. 3 of *Bibliotheca Symbolica Ecclesiae Universalis: The Creeds of Christendom, with a History and Critical Notes*. Grand Rapids, Mich.: Baker, 1977. First published 1877 by Harper (New York).

Whitlock, Luder G., Jr. *Divided We Fall: Overcoming a History of Christian Disunity*. Phillipsburg, N.J.: P and R Publishing Company, 2017.

Willebrands, Johannes. "La libertà religiosa e l'ecumenismo." In *La liberté religieuse. Déclaration "Dignitatis humanae personae": Texte latin et traduction française*, edited by Jérome Hamer and Yves Congar, 237–51. Paris: Cerf, 1967.

______. "The Future of Ecumenism." *One in Christ* 11 (1975): 310–23.

———. "Chiesa, Corpo di Cristo, comunione nel Concilio Vaticano II." In *Una sfida ecumenica: la nuova Europa (discorsi)*, 83–98. Verucchio: Pazzini Editore, 1995.

Wood, Susan K. "Issues and Perspectives in Roman Catholic Ecclesiology Today." In *Ecumenical Future*, edited by Braaten and Jenson, 126–37.

Work, Telford. "Speaking for the Spirit in the Time of Division." In *Ecumenical Future*, edited by Braaten and Jenson, 198–217.

World Council of Churches. "World Council Diary." *The Ecumenical Review* 2 (Spring 1950): 295–99.

———. *New Delhi Statement on Unity*. December 31, 1961. https://www.oikoumene.org/en/resources/documents/assembly/1961-new-delhi/new-delhi-statement-on-unity.

———. *The Holy Spirit and the Catholicity of the Church*. In *Official Report of the Fourth Assembly of the World Council of Churches: Uppsala, July 4–20, 1968*. Edited by Norman Goodall. Geneva: World Council of Churches, 1968. https://archive.org/stream/wcca14/wcca14_djvu.txt.

———. *Breaking Barriers, Nairobi 1975: Official Report, Fifth Assembly, World Council of Churches*. Edited by David M. Paton. In *The Ecumenical Movement: An Anthology of Key Texts and Voices*, edited by Michael Kinnamon and Brian E. Cope, 110–14. Grand Rapids, Mich.: Eerdmans, 1997.

———. *Baptism, Eucharist, and Ministry*. Geneva: World Council of Churches, 1982.

———. *Confessing One Faith: Towards an Ecumenical Explication of the Apostolic Faith as Expressed in the Nicene-Constantinopolitan Creed (381)*. Geneva: World Council of Churches, 1991.

World Council of Churches and Pontifical Council for Promoting Christian Unity. *The Notion of "Hierarchy of Truths": An Ecumenical Interpretation*. Geneva: World Council of Churches, 1990.

Wright, J. Robert. "The Possible Contribution of Papal Authority to Church Unity: An Anglican/Episcopalian Perspective." In *Ecumenical Future*, edited by Braaten and Jenson, 138–44.

Yeago, David S. "The Ecclesial Context of Ecumenical Reception: A Case Study." In *Ecumenical Future*, edited by Braaten and Jenson, 29–45.

Yoder, John Howard. *The Priestly Kingdom: Social Ethics as Gospel*. Notre Dame, Ind.: University of Notre Dame Press, 1984.

Scriptural Index

Index